Here's What People Are Saying about Virtus' 3-D Creation Products

"This is why Virtus WalkThrough Pro 2.0 has a place in this world. If I render in Stratavision it looks good. But let's say I do an animation of the rendering. On my Quadra 950 it takes 1/2 hour to do one frame. So a 100 frame animation takes about 48 hours. But if I need, say 1000 frames, it takes 20 days to render—not counting modeling time and set up. If that weren't bad enough, I need to run it at 20 frames per second to get a nice quality, smooth-running animation. So my 20 days has boiled down to a 50 second animation! With Virtus WalkThrough Pro I can model a similar environment in a few hours and then move through that environment freely, recording as I go. That's why Virtus WalkThrough Pro 2.0 is so valuable. It draws fast and it lets me go anywhere within that model quickly."

—Dwight Morejohn, Davis, CA

"In the old days, we would spend a lot of time moving cameras and placing people to come up with the right shots. Now, I can explore these camera angles and placements on my computer before the actual filming begins. This saves a lot of time and money…. It's really been a godsend."

—Brian De Palma

"Virtus' acclaimed interface, rich functionality, and cross-platform capabilities will make it a powerful world creation tool for the Web."

—Mark Pesce

"WalkThrough Pro is an excellent tool for helping a director communicate ideas to the rest of the people involved in the production. You can tell a gaffer where to put the lights, but if you can show him [or her], you are communicating much more effectively. Having these explorable 3-D models also encourages more collaboration on the set because the crew can easily try out their ideas in virtual reality and quickly tell if it will work or not."

—Gilbert Hammer, President of Imageworks

"I have been working in the graphics industry for several years from animation, creating images in 3-D, and creating Web sites on the Internet. I recently bought Virtus WalkThrough Pro with the intention of using that program for the World Wide Web. My interest was to be able to create downloadables for my clients; for example, someone could download a model of a house from an architect's page and look at that house and actually visit it and move around inside it. And my second interest was to have a downloadable of Cybertown as a step toward VRML. Virtus WalkThrough Pro is definitely serving my needs! I was amazed at the program when I got it, I actually had no idea that the program was so elaborate! After a day, I was able to create a house and when someone was entering the house there was actually music and video on the screen of a TV I placed in one of the rooms! My next surprise was how small the file sizes of the models I was creating were. You can actually place most of your models on a floppy disk, which makes it easy to share with others, either by mail or by sending it through the Internet or other on-line services. I've been working with several other 3-D programs but Virtus WalkThrough Pro is a brand new category. For the first time I can create something as an artist and have other people actually walk through my creation. I was also amazed by the fact that it was very easy to learn, most programs take days to study before you can actually do something that you would consider good enough. With this program, I was able to do it in a matter of hours. One of the best features was the fact that I was able to build something and actually see it in 3-D as I was building it. That has saved me a lot of time as I could see what was good and what needed corrections right away. My next step is VRML (Virtual Reality for the World Wide Web), and I have complete confidence that Virtus will play a major role in making the World Wide Web exciting and entertaining and a place where artists, designers, architects, people in the movie industry, and others can share their imagination with millions of others."

—Pascal Boudar, art director MultiMedia Magic

If you can draw in MacDraw, you can draw in 3-D with Virtus. Anybody can draw in 3-D with Virtus from the moment they open the box, if they understand the different views. The only creative restrictions you have in Virtus is the memory in your machine, the speed of your processor, and your imagination. If you can sketch it, describe it, or draw plans of it, you can make a 3-D interactive model of it with Virtus.

—Jaque Davison, Davison Productions

Hayden
Books

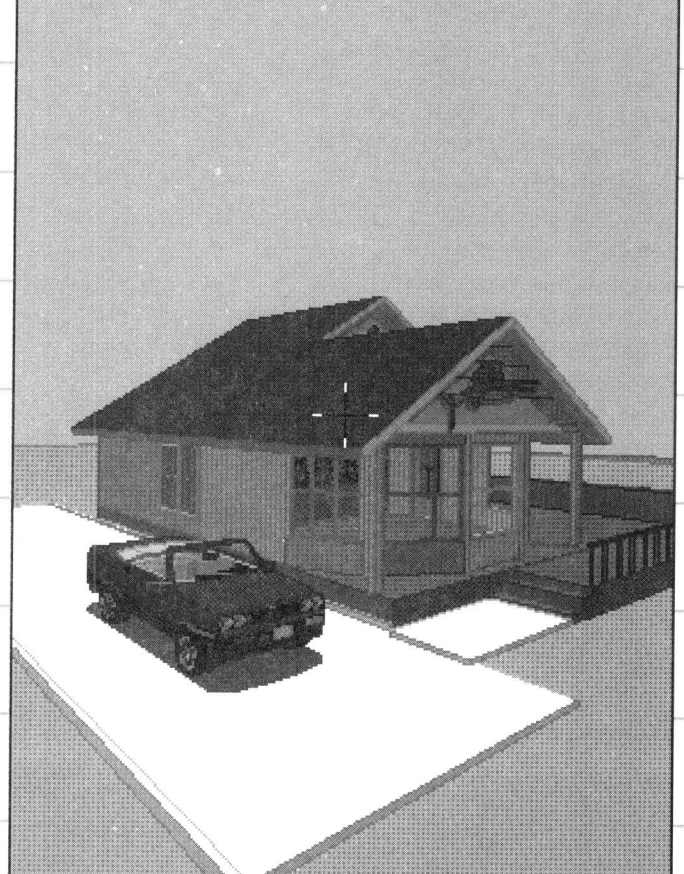

Virtus® VRML Toolkit

David Smith
Richard Boyd
Alan Scott

Publisher
Don Fowley

Publishing Manager
Laurie Petrycki

Acquisitions Editor
Stacy Kaplan

Development Editor
Kezia Endsley

Interior Designer
Sandra Schroeder

Cover Designer
Karen Ruggles

Manufacturing Coordinator
Paul Gilchrist

Production Manager
Kelly Dobbs

Production Team Supervisor
Laurie Casey

Production Team
Heather Butler
Angela Calvert
Dan Caparo
Kim Cofer
Mike Deitch
Rob Falco
Tricia Flodder
Aleata Howard
Erika Millen
Beth Rago
Erich J. Richter
Jennifer Shoemake
Tim Tayler
Christine Tyner
Karen Walsh
Robert Wolf

Indexer
Jeanne Clark

Composed in
Cheltenham
MCP digital

Virtus VRML® Toolkit

©1995 Hayden Books, a division of Macmillan Computer Publishing

Library of Congress Catalog Number: 95-80298
ISBN: 1-56830-247-9

97   96   95   4   3   2   1

Interpretation of the printing code: the rightmost double-digit number is the year of the book's printing; the rightmost single-digit number is the number of the book's printing. For example, a printing code of 95-1 shows that the first printing of the book occurred in 1995.

Trademark Acknowledgments

All products mentioned in this book are either trademarks of the companies referenced in this book, registered trademarks of the companies referenced in this book, or neither. We strongly advise that you investigate a particular product's name thoroughly before you use the name as your own.

Dedication

We dedicate this book to our family and friends, who we think still love us even though they don't get to see us for weeks at a time....

About the Authors

David Smith is the CEO and founder of Virtus Corporation. He is also the creator of the award-winning computer game, *The Colony*. In 1986, he joined Lord Corporation in Cary, NC, where he performed research in human-computer interfaces for robotics. This research led to the development system and prototype for Virtus Walkthrough Pro, which Lord Corporation granted to Virtus in 1989.

Richard Boyd is Vice President and General Manager of Virtus Works and a graduate of the University of North Carolina at Chapel Hill. He has been active on the speaking circuit at several industry conferences including MACWORLD Boston and MACWORLD Canada. His previous positions at Virtus also include International Sales Manager and Director of Sales and Marketing. The Virtus Works division is responsible for developing and marketing Virtus' 3-D multimedia tools. Richard is an avid fitness buff and enjoys cooking and reminiscing about all the famous people he's met since college.

Alan Scott is a product manager (and diehard Mac head) at Virtus Corporation and has been working in the computer and related design publishing industry for 10+ years. A textile design major from NCSU, his love for contemporary design and graphics led him to the world of 3-D graphics and modeling. He is a visiting instructor at The American Film Institute in Los Angeles and at UCLA teaching pre-visualization for the film industry. He enjoys training others to use their computers, personal fitness, cooking. and telling everyone else how to run their lives.

Acknowledgments

There are many people without whom this book would not have been possible. Special thanks to those at Hayden Books, especially Kezia and Stacy for their patience, humor (though they didn't always get it...), and criticisms. As well, thanks to a great development and testing team at Virtus including Steve Chall, Brian Upton, Drew Davidson, Byran "Quality" Nelson, Peter "Tech" Zenge, Paul "MWC" Wirth, John Alspaugh, Bill Gibson, Wendy "New Girl" Berkenbush and, of course, thanks to our fearless leader DAS who didn't help one bit, but says he supported us just the same.

Contents at a Glance

Part IV: Appendixes 257

Table of Contents

Foreword

VRML is an important step in the evolution of the Internet. The Internet currently has the potential to become the first mass medium to emerge since broadcast television in the late 1940s. But in the mid-1990s, the Net as a mass communication medium is still in its infancy. But even in the early stages, the Net seems to have the potential for replacing the current personal computer as the foremost technology in our new information society. The vast amount of information that is now available through the Net has created the need for a richer human/computer interface paradigm. And while the current popularity of icon-based window interfaces is appropriate for application-based computing, it is completely inadequate for accessing the Net. There is simply too much information flooding into the Net everyday. Filtering mechanisms, such as intelligent software agents, may help to search this universe of data, but agents don't address the problem of navigation of the Net on a macro level.

Virtual Reality Modeling Language, or VRML, addresses this problem directly. VRML addresses the problem by introducing the concept of space into the cyberspace of the Net. What we're really looking at with a window-type interface is more akin to a whiteboard covered with little icons. In the real world, windows allow us to look out into a 3-D space, and now VRML makes this possible on our computer screens. But how do we architect these synthetic spaces?

It would be foolish to just create a cybersprawl of 3-D information. We need to look at how humans best use conventional space and then create a design grammar for cyberspace. Just creating cybermalls filled with thousands of shopping avatars would be an appalling mistake. The answer to this fundamental design issue may lie in reinventing and expanding our conception of spatial design. While it is possible to recreate the physical world in cyberspace, the potential is there for creating something far more compelling: an annotated space, or hyperspace. A hyperspatial object would appear three-dimensional like its real world equivalent, but unlike the real world object, the hyperspatial object could be linked to another object or piece of information. It is the spatial equivalent of hypertext. A hyperspatial object could represent a real world space such as the Louvre Museum. The space could represent the dimensions of the actual building. The artwork could be displayed as it is in the museum. Hyperspatial links could be incorporated so that information could be accessed at each piece of art or within a specific room, or these spatial and information links could be designed to assist in navigating the collection by theme or other forms of context. Spatial representation of information helps us view that information in context, and without context, information is essentially useless. Organization alone, whether spatial or not, does not provide context. While VRML is a powerful tool, it is up to the designers who use it to provide meaningful context to the information which is being represented and shaped in three dimensions.

One of the most common errors in the design of 3-D interfaces is falling into the trap of trying to re-create the world inside a computer. Despite theological arguments to the contrary, much of the real world has no overall sense of plan or design. There is no reason why cyberspace should suffer the same fate. By bringing intention and context to our conception of cyberspace, we create more than just a place, we create a repository of information that can be usefully accessed by others. Current CD-ROM-based reference works are an excellent example of how to misuse computer technology in the delivery of information.

Most CD-ROMs are designed to just deliver a vast amount of information, with a crude search engine and a feeble interface tacked on to mask the deficiencies of that engine. These "electronic books" are pale imitations of real books—they are the low-resolution, often poorly organized, and context-free stepchildren of real books. What we've effectively done is use technology to take a step backward in our ability to deliver information. And because CD-ROM is about to go the way of the apatosaurus, isn't it time to coolly assess where we've gone wrong, before we repeat this mistake on the Net? Humans have developed an aesthetic of spatial organization over thousands of years. We need to examine this aesthetic: the aesthetics of architecture, of information delivery, of urban design, and begin to cast a harsh critical gaze on what we're willing to accept as good human-machine interface design. Look at seminal works on spatial design such as *A Pattern Language* by Christopher Alexander, and then look at work that shows how good 2-D information design is accomplished, such as *Envisioning Information* by Edward Tufte, and then figure out how these two disciplines can be combined.

Our collective intuition tells us that there is something new to be discovered in cyberspace and that the task ahead may lie in mapping information into three dimensions. We need to think of information as a spatial matrix, and then go beyond just trying to mate hypertext and architecture, because cyberspace deserves something much bolder. VRML is a step toward a rich world of useful information and communication, and I hope you'll use it as such to create the real cyberspace, not the weaker stuff of science fiction. So get going. Finish this book and build cyberspace, before they just put up a mall in its place.

—Michael Backes
Hollywood Technical and Entertainment Consultant

Introduction

Any worthwhile technological accomplishment in the scope of human endeavor begins with a dream. The ability to dream is the ability to visualize the future. And for many endeavors, dreams serve as the sustaining food during long years, even decades of toil toward a distant goal.

Ten years ago novelists like William Gibson and Neal Stephenson were just beginning to dream of three-dimensional computer interfaces. William Gibson's 1984 cyberpunk thriller *Neuromancer* was the origin of the term "cyberspace" and is largely responsible for the proliferation of the idea of shared 3-D computer-generated realities. The term virtual reality also surfaced only ten years ago on the lips of Jaron Lanier, founder of VPL Research and one of the growing number of folk heroes spun off by the maelstrom of the computer industry.

And here we are on the eve of realizing a goal only dreamed of a short ten years ago. If our dreams from so short a time ago are coming true now, what can we dream of for the future? Most importantly, what lies between what we can dream now and the realization of that dream?

What This Book Does

This book takes you on a journey. The chapters are a metaphor for the steps we take to realize dreams, whether they are technological or not. We first begin to dream and to visualize the goals we seek. We review some of the dreams that visualized the present and then we will turn to penetrate the mists of the future. The people who are interested in this book are those who are interested in dreaming and shaping the future.

It is important when dreaming to put no restraints on the imagination and to not think of the future in the context of the present or the past. For the future we have before us is impenetrable and we can be certain of only one thing: that our future will bear little resemblance to past or present.

A thousand years ago people could be assured that the tools used by their grandchildren would resemble those they used. With the current accelerating pace of technological advancement, this is no longer true. In their youth, my grandparents never dreamed of a worldwide network of machines that place people into artificial 3-D realities where they shop, play, work, and communicate. My children will one day listen in awe while I describe the primitive tools at my disposal to create this book. And they will hug their knees to their chests suppressing giggles while I tell the story of the beginning of networked 3-D cyberspace; the same way I did when my father talked about radio and black and white television.

So we dream big expansive dreams of the future in Part 1. After we have clarified our dreams through fictional visualizations, we then explore the ideas behind them. For before we embark on years of endeavor toward our mighty goal, we should make sure that the premise of our dream is sound. Part I begins with short stories I call visualizations that help define the dream, and then it examines the technologies and ideas that make our dream possible.

After exploring these ideas, we roll up our sleeves in Part II and get busy creating the cyberworlds of the future. This book is accompanied by a CD-ROM containing Virtus VRML, a toolkit for creating 3-D cyberspaces for the Internet, your home computer, or whatever medium comes next. The software is very easy to use. Its 3-D drag-and-drop interface will have you up and running and creating virtual worlds in less than an hour.

When you have conquered the mechanics around creating these worlds, we take a look at how people are making practical use of these worlds today for fun and profit in Part III. We also take a look at some imminent technologies that speed us on the road to the future. Part IV contains appendixes on using the CD and on common terms you need to know.

In short, everything you need to make your cyberworld dreams come true is contained within the covers of this tome. We provide some possible visualizations, a background on the terms and technologies at play in the field of networked 3-D space, some philosophical ramblings on the repercussions of this technology, the tools to make it happen, and directions to resources for further exploration. The rest is up to your imagination.

Who's This Book For?

This book is for anyone interested in the emerging 3-D world of VRML. A good understanding of the Internet is key to understanding the concepts of VRML. A healthy dose of curiosity is encouraged.

What's on the CD

The CD for this book contains the complete version of Virtus VRML and the Virtus Voyager browser (you can download updated versions at http://www.virtus.com). Also included with your program are numerous galleries of 2-D surface features and textures, and 3-D objects that can be added to your Virtus VRML worlds. Also, two additional galleries, the Archaeology Gallery (just like it sounds) and the Home Remodeling Gallery (a collection of lots of home stuff) and pre-built "scenes" that illustrate the program's modeling, texture mapping and real-time "walk through" capabilities are provided on the CD.

Book Conventions

In order to use this book properly, it helps to know how we have set up the conventions and graphical elements. The following graphical elements are used to differentiate information in this book.

Note   A note provides you with special information on the topic at hand that you might not catch otherwise.

Tip   Tips give you helpful shortcuts, hints, and tricks so that you can master the art of drag-and-drop VRML quicker and easier.

Now that you know what's waiting for you on the following pages, all you have to do is embark on your journey. Please boot both your computer and your imagination now!

A **definition box** defines a VRML term used within the current chapter so that you can master the terminology and refer easily to terms within the chapter.

What's In a Sidebar?

Sidebars provide information on the VRML culture, opinions and ideas of the authors, suggested additional reading, and other theories on VRML that aren't necessarily essential to the text, but provide stimulating and interesting reading for you.

Cyber Dreams

Part I

1

Visualizing Our Online Future

Because this part is entitled "Cyber Dreams," we are obligated to explore some of the dreams that may be fulfilled with the next few technological leaps. Instead of a dry treatise on the actual lines of software code and hardware configurations that will be required to make our dreams come true, we will have a little fun. You deserve it since you are about to toil laboriously through the tutorial part of this book. We will again use fictional visualizations to see exactly what these new technologies may do for us.

In this chapter you will be exposed to the following visualizations:

■ Net World: A day in 3-D cyberspace

■ Distributed Simulation: A View from the Future

■ Education

■ ICE: an Interactive Collaborative Environment

■ Premonition and Definition: The worlds created by authors Neal Stephenson and William Gibson

A thousand years ago humans could be fairly assured that their grandchildren would live lives similar to theirs. We can make no such assumptions anymore. In their youth my grandparents never dreamed that people separated by thousands of miles would communicate, shop, and play in shared 3-D virtual spaces. I know that my children will listen to my description of writing this book on my Macintosh Powerbook and wonder how I ever accomplished anything with so primitive a tool.

This is a very useful exercise for those of us who optimistically believe that whatever humans can dream can be achieved. What is most intriguing about this exercise is that it is almost certain that whatever our imaginations conjure today will only be a shadow of what our future will bring. At the current rate of progress, we can be assured that our future will be very unlike what we can even imagine today. Dream on....

An Increasingly Plausible Visualization of our Online Future

Robin moved briskly down the crowded avenue, barely acknowledging the thousands of other visitors who stopped to attempt to engage her in "chat." Some were more adept at movement and attempted to follow while most, demonstrating their inadequate connection or lack of experience, stumbled awkwardly past her as she flowed right through them. The built-in L.O.D. (level of detail) filter converted all but the closest entities to ghostly apparitions, but in the interest of speed she switched to fast mode anyway, rendering only the 10 closest avatars.

She thought about changing to invisible mode as well to avoid the entourage that was building behind her, but decided to stay in "full rez" so David could find her once she reached the gallery.

She moved easily from one portal to the next, browsing the many worlds she had added to her personalized space. She passed through the L.L. Bean outdoor space. Today it featured breathtaking scenery from the Swiss Alps along with relaxing forest sounds designed to slow her pace and lure her closer to the displayed merchandise. AI (artificial intelligence) agents moved briskly toward her as their programming, no doubt, recognized her and her generous spending history. She toggled her "just looking" mode option to inform them that she didn't need any product information at this time.

As she passed the travel agent space she used frequently she was reminded to send her own agent to collect information on real world travel to Thailand, as she and David were discussing vacation plans. She knew the agent would assemble information on the packages that best matched her interests and budget and would deposit them on her hard drive for later reference.

"People Like you" was one of the services she and David had started after they formed their "virtual corporation" (a term that had become recursive in meaning). This service provided personal AI agents who learned someone's likes and dislikes both by asking a set of questions and monitoring their purchasing decisions. It then proceeded to select music, books, movies, games, and clothing, among other things, that best matched the "trainer's" tastes and budget. That was their first home run venture.

She could have zipped immediately to her destination, but she always enjoyed window shopping through the custom shopping, education, and entertainment spaces she chose for her own cyberspace.

The quality of her photorealistic avatar and the grace and celerity with which she navigated the familiar landscape made her stand out in the teeming mass of low rez, often grayscale, avatars like a beacon. This was, after all, what attracted David to begin with. There was certainly a different aesthetic in cyberspace. One that could be adorned only with the best equipment, connections, and experience. People valued these attributes the way they once valued someone's beauty, possessions, and social skills. The value system had certainly changed once the information age hit full swing.

She met David while in game mode one afternoon. She had advanced several levels in the latest Tom Clancy adventure series only to run into a dead end with three samurai robots poised to take her head and the valuable game points she had amassed in that level. David materialized out of nowhere in knight's armor and together they had defeated the last of the samurai opponents and had rescued the Empress from the evil warlord. They found that they made a terrific team, she was adept at problem solving and distractions while he mastered the weapons and armor.

In chat mode they discovered they had many things in common and enjoyed shopping and traveling the virtual geography of the Net together. It didn't matter that he was wheelchair bound. They had enjoyed their cyber-relationship to the fullest, finally meeting in person and getting married. They were now discussing renewing their marriage vows online. Some "early adopters" were actually performing their real marriage rights online, an increasingly frequent phenomenon that was being considered by the church for ordination. People were beginning to grow accustomed to the merging reality of real world and online personae.

At last she reached the WorldGallery where they had gone on their first real date. Like most users, they had both added this popular model to their personalized virtual worlds. The gallery included 24-bit images of paintings and 3-D objects d'art from every museum in the real world. The halls were divided into their real-world museum counterparts and each museum received a 25 cent donation from each visitor who entered its portal. The number of avatars who entered here every day ensured a flow of funds to every museum. Like most of the nonprofit ventures, the World-Gallery had still not recognized game credits as currency.

Turning to her right she saw a line of white avatars proceeding from the Prado exhibition to the portal for the National Gallery of London. Their uniform avatars revealed them to be students under the age of 18. Those projecting that avatar received free access to all educational and edutainment spaces, but were prohibited from any "adult" entertainment spaces. The penalty for allowing minors to don adult avatars was severe.

In her HUD she saw that David was already 10 minutes late. He was probably absorbed in one of his Dungeon games, but she decided to send him an online page anyway. She pulled down her address list and selected David's nom de online from the list, selected record, and spoke into her mike, "Khan, are you out there?"

She turned down her stereo with another control as she waited for his response. After a few minutes she was rewarded with "Coming Dear." She could almost feel him rushing over the coaxial cable and fiber network to her impatient avatar.

"Where are you?"

"I'm at the WorldGallery, near the Prado," she replied.

Then he materialized some distance away and turned toward her. Today he had chosen the knight's armor again and was wearing live video feed for his face. "Who was he trying to impress?" she thought. He had upgraded to color after their business venture received its funding. Together they made quite a sight. They both stood outside the Prado entrance, conscious of the envious stares they were receiving from the bandwidth-challenged gray avatars. The full-motion video feeds for their faces and the stunning photorealistic bodies that represented them in cyberspace were more luxury than necessity, but when you were in business as the hottest Net navigation guides online, it paid to be flashy. David's back actually had a running advertisement for the game guide service they had started together. He was a shameless self-promoter, but then every successful small businessperson on the Net was.

As if to illustrate this thought, an enterprising avatar walked by hawking some of the game credits he had amassed. His colorful avatar, draped in armor and objects won from completing the levels of several popular games, betrayed him as a proficient gamer. She thought about trying to recruit him, but turned to David instead.

"Where have you been, I was worried sick," she taunted playfully.

"Oh Robin, you have to see the new release from DreamWorks. This is one of the most engaging worlds I've visited so far, the new high water mark for simulations. It's Jurassic Park times 10. I was almost eaten alive by a T-Rex!"

"Oh, today was the private tour from Spielberg, Geffen, and Katzenberg wasn't it?" she said half enviously, "How is it that you always get those glamorous gigs while I end up doing the accounting?"

"Hey, we're a team, remember? Can I help it if my talent is in networking and you're the numbers person? Besides, schmoozing those Hollywood types is not all fun and games. It's an art. These guys have been pitched by the best. It takes real skill to make them believe you're sincere." He smiled at his own audacity and Robin chuckled despite herself. How can you stay mad at a smiling man in a tin can suit? She wondered briefly about speculating on the increase in value of DreamWorks game credits but was distracted by movement at the entrance to the museum.

A samurai robot character from their previous adventures was moving smoothly and purposefully toward them. Strange, she thought, an artificial intelligence agent taking an interest in art? They rarely ever come out of the game worlds. Unless…"Uh, David, you wouldn't happen to still be in game mode would you?"

"Oh…, " he looked down, "Yeah, I guess I am. I didn't have time to switch when you paged me. I know better than to keep my princess waiting." He paused as he read her televised expression. Then said, "Why do you ask?"

"Oh, no reason," she smiled and backed up from him before adding, "Good-bye sweetie. I hope you didn't have too many uncashed credits."

The shock of recognition on his face was memorable as he turned while trying to toggle off his game mode controls. The samurai robot was already in mid-swing and lopped his immaculately rendered head neatly from the armored body. As David's avatar snowed out, the samurai robot turned to look almost longingly at Robin. "Sorry pal, I'm not in game mode. You know the rules," she said with more apprehension than she intended. And with that he disappeared.

Before turning to enter the shopping area and sending David another teasing page, she made a brief note for her next 'zine article. She would entitle it, "Autonomous agents who bear grudges." Game characters pursuing players outside the game worlds was an increasingly frequent phenomonon since game designers had learned to merge game code with the open file format of the *infolandscape*. No one complained, because it added an extra element of entertainment to everyday events like shopping. Just for safety, she checked her credits and game mode toggle before getting on with another day in cyberspace.

3-D at Work

ICE: Interactive Collaborative Environments

Nothing had gone right all week. Michelle swam forlornly through the 3-D landscape representing the output from different sectors of the gas turbine factory, hoping that being there would yield some new information that would solve the problem that threatened to ruin her career. She hadn't worked 60-hour weeks for three years with the leading power plant producer in the world to have it all end because of some elusive design flaw. Besides her fear of damage to her reputation, her pride motivated her to not allow this to happen. She clung to her confidence in the 3-D virtual factory database while her peers pointed fingers and sidestepped the issue. She would solve this problem.

After being promoted to the head of her division output and efficiency had increased exponentially thanks to the new monitoring system that displayed all of the division's operations in a navigable 3-D database. With this database, she and her managers could monitor all of the activities of the plant by flying over and through the data, seeing everything at once and how different operations fit together, or by zooming in close to inspect a part recently manufactured with the computer-aided manufacturing system. The database was criticized at first by workers who claimed that the system would be spying on them, and by mid-level managers who felt that it would impose a layer of abstraction from the real workings of the plant rendering them incapable of interfacing with the workers.

Michelle pushed for the database despite the protests and had quickly proven its effectiveness. Engineers and managers both were encouraged to navigate the database at the end of the day as it played back the daily operations to see whether they could spot anything that could be improved. Michelle turned it into a contest that awarded sports tickets and mini-vacations to those who spotted inefficiencies or were able to make suggestions for improvements.

The database showed her new perspectives on the functions of the different groups that allowed her to combine some of the work crews to streamline operations. Profits had soared along with her paycheck, not to mention plant morale. The stock for the company rose 25 percent in the last quarter.

The database also helped with sales. Overseas clients were able to see how the final gas turbines were assembled and how they worked. Theoretical stress tests were performed and CAD models of the clients' power plants were created that showed where and how the gas turbines would be mounted. It was especially important to have the virtual environment for assembly because

1. Many of the parts were created in different plants and,

2. Some of the parts for the new model were not created yet.

Based on the simulations alone, they had received orders that would keep the plants humming for the next 18 months.

Then the first complaint came in. A power plant in South Africa had two turbines malfunction at once. Then came calls from all over the globe. Something was seriously amiss. She had to wait only 10 minutes after the first complaint before the inevitable call from the executive level. Then the finger pointing started.

More of a technical than a political animal, Michelle ignored the evasive maneuvering of the other plant managers and concentrated on solving the problem. After two sleepless days she came to the conclusion that the problem did not reside in the plasma coating of the turbine blades or in the other parts her team manufactured. Her plant operated on six sigma quality standards and the blades were machined on the micron level. The only possible answer had to be in assembly. She called an ICE conference for that afternoon. ICE was the interactive collaborative environment that connected the databases of the four plants that manufactured the turbine parts.

When she logged into ICE the executive team was already there buzzing about impatiently like bees. Each one was represented by a flying television set with live video feeds on the screen and helicopter blades on top. Despite herself she giggled like she always did when first viewing the "someone please take me seriously" MBA faces mapped to the flying TVs. The strange juxtapositions in cyberspace always amused her.

In the middle of the environment were an assembled and a disassembled turbine. She exchanged pleasantries with the other plant managers as they appeared while the "suits" kept to themselves at the other end of the grid. This "body language" was important along with facial expressions when gauging moods and responses; and a vast improvement over the disembodied voice conference calls from the early 90s.

When Paul, her counterpart and head of the Durham-based turbine assembly plant, zapped into view she whisked over to him.

"Find anything?" she asked hopefully.

"Nothing," he replied sheepishly, "how about you?"

"No luck either. I was in the database playing back production runs all weekend. I went through the plasma coating machines so many times I feel like I have a coating or two myself." Paul grinned back at her from his screen. She returned his grin and added, "Did you go through your assembly lines?"

"We didn't get around to hooking up the 3-D database until this morning. But I am confident in the reports from my plant floor managers that nothing is out of order." Michelle scrutinized his face but he remained expressionless.

"But you're hooked up now right?" she asked quickly.

"Yeah, I think so." he replied.

Michelle leaned away from the video camera and called her MIS manager on intercom. Covering her mike she said quickly, "Chuck, do you think you can patch the Durham plant database into ICE in the next 15 minutes?"

"Child's play," came his welcome and dry-witted response. "I'll have it in five. I'll just make a few promises, call in a few favors, and take care of it."

"You're my hero," Michelle replied in the normal bantering tone established between them, but with real gratitude, and added, "Why can't all men be as dependable as you?"

"I'm one in a million." he said in his best Dennis Miller voice. "Chuck is on the job."

She turned back to her monitor to see everyone assembled and staring expectantly in her direction. She realized she would have to kill some time so she dragged and dropped a 3-D whiteboard into the shared 3-D space and dropped a globe in next to it. She covered the manufacturing and assembly process and pointed out the locations of the customers with faulty equipment on the globe. She paused to give everyone time to drag and drop the items to their computers if they chose. She then ran the assembled model of the turbine through stress tests again to show there were no problems with the design. She ended by saying that the 3-D production simulator had found no problems in her area or the other plants connected to the simulator.

"We are all amused by your faith in technology, Michelle, but it looks like your system is failing us in this real-world crisis." It was Dan, the Vice President of sales and marketing who had borne the brunt of the customer backlash. "We are going to have to recall those units. The shipping costs alone could ruin our fourth quarter." Dan dropped in a second whiteboard on which he placed a graph with a downward sloping hockey stick line. "For those of you who are interested in the ugly numbers, a spreadsheet is included with this chart."

Michelle dragged and dropped the chart and spreadsheet to her desktop and glanced at the red numbers they brandished at her accusingly. At that moment she heard Chuck's voice over the intercom. "Papa bear to Goldilocks. Come in Goldilocks."

"Yes, Chuck," she responded tersely, not really in the mood for his playfulness just then. He sharpened his voice on the edge in hers and replied in his southern soldier voice.

"You're locked and loaded. Fire when ready. Papa Bear out." Before she could say thanks he was gone.

It was now or never. No time for beta testing the idea. "Ladies and gentlemen, the production simulator found no flaws in any of the information at its disposal. But the information was not complete. The assembly plant was not on the simulator until yesterday. That has to be the source of the problem."

She heard a stifled exclamation she assumed came from Paul. Without pausing she forged ahead. "We have the Durham simulator online. Let's see how that compares to the design simulation." Using the information from the assembly plant the simulator began to assemble the pieces of the disassembled unit. Before it was finished several of the pieces began to flash red. Michelle paused the simulation.

"If you will all step closer you will see that the fasteners used to attach the blades, or "buckets" as we call them, to the rotors are different from the spec. The simulation compared the actual fasteners being used in the Durham plant and compared them to the design. If they are different they flash red."

As everyone moved in and around the flashing pieces Michelle magnified them and displayed the data tag attached to them. "These fasteners withstand up to 2000 degree heat. The spec calls for 5000."

The TVS all rotated away from the simulation until they faced Paul squarely. "These were cheaper." he said weakly. "I was under pressure from Dan to come in under budget. My engineers said that the turbines rarely got over 2000. B-b-but we can replace them with the more expensive ones within a week. No problem." The last word hung in the air.

"Ladies and gentleman." It was the CEO who had been quiet during the entire conference. "If you'll excuse us I'd like some quality time with Dan and Paul." The TV sets began to wink out of existence with little wooshing sounds as everyone was quick to leave the tense atmosphere. The word "ICE" was suddenly all too appropriate an acronym for the environment.

"Good job, Michelle. You just saved us a bundle. Can you get a team of people to replace those fasteners onsite?"

"Yes sir. I'll get right on it." she said.

"Oh, and I would like you to run the Durham plant remotely from your location until further notice." He turned away to face Dan and Paul.

"Yes sir," Michelle replied and logged off with relief. She was very tired all of a sudden, but remembered that she had to find Chuck and apologize for being gruff. She reached for the intercom but decided this should be done in person. Just then he appeared in her doorway.

"Chuck, I was just coming to look for you."

"Let me guess, you want to wallow at my feet in gratitude for saving your career. Hmmm…tempting, but I'll settle for sushi. You drive."

Before she could say anything else his bobbing pony tail disappeared out the door. She smiled to herself. He must have been eavesdropping on the whole conference. She would have to talk to him about that. But not to-day. No, not today.

3-D at Play

Distributed Simulation: A View from the Future

by Steve Seidensticker[1]

The battle date is August 17, 1943. I am the ball turret gunner of Luscious Lady, a brand new B-17F of the 427th squadron, 303rd Bombardment Group, of the Eighth Air Force. Our takeoff from Molesworth was without incident. But as soon as we were off the ground the pilot asked me to check the wheels. He had an indication that the left main gear had not retracted fully. I hopped into the ball, spun it until I had a good view of the wheel. It looked OK. We chalked it up to a bad indicator in the cock-pit. Although the ball with its twin 50s is primarily intended to protect a B-17 from enemy fighters approaching from below, the view from beneath the aircraft comes in handy for other chores.

We climb out and begin a long lazy circle. I keep tabs on and report other squadron aircraft as they join our formation. We are on our second mis-sion and our first over Germany. Our first mission was to bomb a Luft-waffe airfield near Paris. The target was partly obscured by weather. Opposition was light. A few Me-109s came up to meet us. They were not particularly aggressive or well-coordinated. Nevertheless we lost one of our squadron. I saw Old Ironsides get most of its rudder shot off. The pilot was obviously losing control and chose to abandon ship. I saw 10 good chutes. The debriefing team called the mission a "milk run."

The missions would become much tougher as we gained more experience. We were happy to get this far. My pilot and copilot are in Milwaukee. The navigator/bombardier is in Montreal. Other crew members are in Seattle, San Jose, Denver, and Green Bay. We cannot see or touch each other, but we communicate via what appears to be a B-17's standard intercom. In fact we are part of a wide-area high-speed data network that connects all crew stations of all aircraft, both friendly and hostile. I don't know the total number of nodes on this network, but it must be in the thousands. The number of spectators that can tap into the net are in the millions. In addition to our voices, this network carries all the data that our individual crew station simulators need to show other aircraft, the terrain over which we fly, the weather, and other elements of our environment.

To participate in these missions, each of us simply dials into the network at the time scheduled for the mission, gets the standard crew briefing on our screens, and waits for our turn to take off. The pilots, bombardiers, and navigators get a detailed briefing on the target and expected weather. The rest of the crew gets briefed on expected opposition. The briefings are, of course, the same as (or as close as possible to) the original briefings given to the original crews. Like in the original briefings, we can ask questions and get answers.

Not all the crew stations on Luscious Lady are run by humans. The waist gunners and the radio operator are computer-generated entities. They do their jobs reasonably well. They even respond to us when we talk to them over the intercom. However, if the conversation strays from simple orders or reports they quickly become confused and start spouting gibberish. Some of other friendly aircraft on the mission and some of the opposing Luftwaffe fighters have no human crews at all. But it's getting harder to tell who is human and who is computer-generated, because the programmers keep tweaking their behavior algorithms. But my personal feeling is that they will never get to the point where these simulations are totally indistinguishable from real people. I hope they don't.

Over the Channel, the pilot gives us the order to test our guns. This is a ritual that ensures that the guns are working and marks the real beginning of the mission for us gunners. From here we are in harm's way. I cock both guns, point to a clear area, and let loose with a short burst. The tracers arc away gracefully. I have managed not to hit anyone else in the formation. To do so is considered very bad form. It also requires the hapless shooter to buy dinner for the shootee's crew at our next annual convention. Of course, the computers that run this whole operation keep track of everything, so there is no arguing or hiding.

The target today is the Me-109 plant in Regensburg. We know that the Luftwaffe was out in force that day. The Eighth Air Force lost 24 B-17s out of a force of 147. Shortly after we cross the French coast the nose gunner shouts, "Four 109s at 12 o'clock low." The control yoke feels comfortable in my hands as I spin the turret forward. They are coming at our formation four abreast from dead ahead. The winking lights on the leading edge of their wings show that they are firing. I mash the right pedal hard to tell the lead computing gun sight to use maximum range. The left pedal goes to the third notch to input the wing span of an Me-109. I line the sight's pipper on the number two plane and fire short bursts, trying to adjust the range as they close. My shots appear low. Just about everyone in our formation is firing. A puff of smoke bursts from the number three fighter. It continues to smoke as their formation passes right through ours.

This line abreast head-on attack was developed by the Luftwaffe in early '43. It took a lot of courage and discipline on the part of the German pilots, but it was very effective. The idea was not only to get the best shots possible, but to intimidate the bomber pilots and break up the formation. It was probably the greatest game of chicken ever and it frequently ended in collision. The right waist gunner reports another formation at four o'clock level. But they are out of our range and overtaking us on a parallel course, no doubt moving up for another head-on pass through the bomber stream. I can see their yellow cowlings and know that they belong to JG 26, the "Abbeville Kids," one of the best Luftwaffe fighter wings.

The attacks continue sporadically until we are about 30 miles from the target. At that point we start seeing the dreaded flak. The small black clouds bloom innocently in the distance, but we know that as the ground gunners adjust the aim of their 88s, the bursts will be right around us. There is little evasive action that a formation of B-17s can take. We are near the IP (initial point) that the pilot must fly over if we are to get our bombs anywhere near the target. At that point, the bombardier takes over and actually flies the plane to the bomb release point using autopilot controls on the famous Norden bomb sight, probably one of the most famous, but overrated technical developments of WWII. The flak rounds get closer.

The concussion from one of them is louder than the fifties going off next to my ears. The pilot reports that number four engine is starting to vibrate and the manifold pressure is dropping. Bad news. If it fails, we will have to drop out of the formation. Like the weak separated from the herd, we will be on our own. We may have to fight packs of fighters as we try for the coast and the protection of friendly Spitfires. Most who have been through this say that it can be the most exciting part of an afternoon of simulation, but the B-17 seldom survives. Those that do get an award at the next convention and, of course, their battles with the fighters are replayed on the large screen.

We finally reach the target, the bombardier hits the pickle switch, and I watch the bombs fall away. I lose sight of them after a few seconds, but shortly thereafter see a string of explosions on the ground. The bombs land in a rail yard just east of the target complex. But that's closer than the original crew came in '43.

The flight back was challenging. For two hours we endured more flak and almost constant fighter harassment. Our pilot managed to coax enough power out of the number four engine to maintain position in the formation. The rest of the formation was not so lucky. Stric Nine took an 88mm round in the right wing root and the whole wing came off. There were no chutes. Wallaroo lost an engine and had to drop back, but we were close to the coast and a flight of P-47s escorted her back. Once we got over the Channel, I turned over my role to an automatic ball turret simulation and had a quick dinner in the kitchen with my wife. I doubt that the rest of my crew even noticed that I was gone. I rejoined the simulation for the debrief. The colonel told us that we had done reasonably well for a second mission crew.

My ball turret is a medium priced model from RealSim Inc, one of the rising companies in this field. It provides a lot of fidelity for the price, has a lot of update options, and I'm very happy with it. The ball spins and rotates vertically much the way the original did and takes up less than half of my garage. The visual scenes are presented on panels built right into the ball. Sound and vibration are provided by some large, but ordinary speakers. RealSim sells the basic turret dirt cheap, but knows how sim-heads get hooked on fidelity, and they offer a large range of add-ons that can become very expensive. Some of my colleagues have mounted their units on electrically driven motion platforms. I don't know if that is worth the extra cost. Maybe next year. Many other simulated crew stations are built around VR goggles. Those are a lot less expensive but work quite well. One enthusiastic crew has built a whole B-17 fuselage in a warehouse.

As in most simulations, visual scenes provide the dominant cues. The simulation industry has long ago reached its holy grail of creating visual images that are indistinguishable from the real thing. The processing power needed to create them is so cheap that the image generators are no longer a cost factor in most simulators. Databases that represent the terrain of any portion of the earth are readily available at any resolution desired. Specialty "period" databases (Dunkirk or Waterloo for instance) for groundpounders are becoming available but are very expensive.

The key factor that made this kind of group simulation possible was the development of the DIS (Distributed Interactive Simulation) standards about 25 years ago. Once these standards were in place, the designers and builders of simulator components didn't have to spend any more time thinking about linking them together than does the designer of a railroad car need to worry about how to couple a car to a train. The DIS standards allowed the simulation industry to concentrate on functionality, performance, and cost reduction.

My wife used to ask me why I spend so much time and money on this. There are a number of reasons. I, like many middle-aged guys, have often fantasized about going into battle to test my wits and skill with a comparably equipped enemy. In this fantasy I support my comrades and in turn depend on their support. I yearn to experience the heat of battle, victory over my adversary, or a narrow escape from the reach of his weapons. However, I have no desire to shed any of my blood.

I also love history, great battles in particular. I know of no greater battle than that between the U.S. Eighth Air Force and the German Luftwaffe in 1943 and '44. The leaders of the American forces felt that they could win the war with heavy bombing of German military and industrial targets. To be accurate this had to be done in daylight. Escort fighters of the day did not have sufficient range to cover the bombers. The bombers had to depend on their own defensive weapons. Participation in these recreated battles is available at a number of levels. I started as a spectator. The magic carpet mode of my computer let me observe operations from any point in space. It also let me attach myself to any aircraft in the battle and listen to the radio and intercom traffic for that aircraft. Running commentary is available from experts. Previews and schedules of upcoming battles are carried by the major sports pages. Reports of completed battles are also carried. These tend to dwell on the personalities involved and the shoot-em-up aspects. How close the reenactment came to the original battle seems to be getting lost.

After watching several of the major raids, I was hooked and wanted to play an active role. My first desire was to be a Luftwaffe pilot, but the requirement for fluency in German eliminated that. Rumors are that an English-speaking Luftwaffe wing is forming. My second choice was to sit in the cockpit of a B-17. But, like the original aircrews, I needed training. The training course for all pilot positions is long and demanding. I opted for the less ambitious role of gunner. Fortunately, the simulator technology that I own trains me more efficiently and quickly than did similar training programs in 1943. After a few intense weekends, I passed the qualification tests and was assigned to my present crew. We are not the most proficient crew on today's raid, but neither were the new crews in 1943.

As I become more serious in this avocation, I wonder where it is going. Some social commentators are starting to decry the "glorification of war." Others counter with statements about "harmless outlets of male aggression," despite the fact that at last year's convention, the Best B-17 Crew Award went to an all-female crew. Some critics are worried that the super-realistic simulation available today is going to replace drugs as the national addiction. Who knows! The raid on the ball bearing factories in Schweinfurt is scheduled for next week. It was the bloodiest for the Eighth Air Force. I think my crew and I are good enough and lucky enough to survive. I can hardly wait to find out.

3-D at School

by Frank Boosman

Date: 13 Oct 2012 10:21:49 -0800 (EDT)

MIME-Version: 7.0

To: jim-wagner@iridium.co.us

From: skip-wagner@unc.edu.nc.us

Subject: Hi, Dad!

Dad:

I need the writing practice, so instead of sending you a video message as usual, I thought I'd write out my mail to you this week. Besides, it's nice to be able to compose my thoughts this way, taking my time and editing them until they're just right. Where are you this week? I think you're headed for the South Atlantic on the fiber-laying mission. Isn't that for the Chile-South Africa link? How's the Iridium card working down there? Are you able to get a full video stream with no problems?

I'm having a lot of fun in History class. We're studying medieval Europe; today I'm playing with a simulation of the battle of Agincourt. Remember when the English used the longbow and wiped out the French, including their cavalry? Well, in the simulation, I can walk around the site of the battle looking at anything of interest. I can start or stop the battle at any time. The cool part is trying out different strategies. What if the English hadn't had the longbow? What if they had used it differently? What if the French had adjusted their strategy instead of sticking with their original game plan? I can change just about anything and see a simulation of what would have happened.

Well, not really—I can see a representation of what the simulation algorithms predict would have happened. My professor is constantly warning us to be careful about this. "Remember, simulations are just that and nothing more," she says. She's right, but I still can't imagine learning History without being able to experience and change it. Didn't you once tell me that History class used to be boring? Why was that?

Physics is pretty fun this semester as well. We're learning about orbital mechanics this week, and so the professor gave us a solar system simulator. Like the History simulator, it runs on all our computers, so I can take it with me and run simulations over lunch in the cafeteria, or just sit down under a tree someplace. (I wish the batteries in my portable would last longer, though. Think you could spring for a couple of extras?)

The solar system simulator lets me fly through any solar system. I can use the real data for Sol or Alpha Centauri, the hypothetical data for some of the other close systems, or make up a solar system of my own. Remember when you used to order old Star Trek reruns for us to watch late at night? Do you remember the super-powerful being? I think his name was "Q." Anyway, using this simulation is kind of like being Q; I can push around planets, alter their masses or rotational periods, or even change the gravitational constant. I was playing around with velocities and orbital periods this morning, and then the simulation agent popped up and said, "You are now looking at an excellent demonstration of Kepler's Law." I clicked the "Explain" button, and it was right—I was looking at Kepler's Law. In fact, after using the simulation for the last few days, I already knew the law—I just didn't know its name. Well, I should get going; I have to get to my French class (I'll tell you about that simulation next time).

Let me know if you see any penguins!

Love,

—SkipCommunication

Premonition and Definition

Cyberspace is an environment of both correct and incorrect electronic information that is connected to the physical world via one way (televisions) and two way (computers and phones) portals and umbilical cords of copper, coaxial and fiber optic cable, and magnetic waves.

These scenarios are almost certainly some temporal distance away, but the vision of navigating information in a shared three-dimensional computer-generated environment is one to which many continue to aspire. Not only does it capture the imagination, but upon closer inspection seems ultimately a logical step in our continued effort to visualize the burgeoning tide of information at our disposal.

A somewhat more humorous, yet still pessimistic, view of our informational future is portrayed by Neal Stephenson in *Snow Crash*. In this popular novel, Stephenson created the vision of the Black Sun "Metaverse," a 3-D virtual reality environment accessible from any computer that allows people to move through it with *avatars*—3-D graphical representations of themselves that others can see. The sophistication of each avatar depends upon the capability of the user. The title refers to a virus that crashes computers leaving the user staring at a screen of snow.

The metaverse was essentially a never-ending game supplemented by each user. This combination of entertainment and information navigation

---

What Is Cyberspace?

The term cyberspace was coined by the author William Gibson in his dark science fiction premonition of a networked information source called *Neuromancer*, in which users "jack into" computer-generated landscapes of information using virtual reality head-mounted displays. Information in this world, called "The Matrix," is the most precious commodity next to various techno-gadgets embedded by elective surgery into one's flesh.

"**Cyberspace:** A consensual hallucination experienced daily by billions of legitimate operators…A graphical representation of data abstracted from the banks of every computer in the human system. Unthinkable complexity. Lines of light ranged in the non-space of the mind, clusters and constellations of data. Like city lights, receding."

—William Gibson, *Neuromancer*, New York: Berkeley Publications group, 1984.

and retrieval seems like the most plausible culmination of our search for better ways to visualize and explore the staggering amount of information available on the Internet.

Where We Are Going

Today we have made the long journey from UNIX line commands to GUI front ends for the World Wide Web like Mosaic and Netscape Navigator. As processor speed and bandwidth continue to increase, we grow ever nearer the next step—3-D information navigation.

> An **information landscape** is a three-dimensional environment where information is represented by 3-D and 2-D multimedia and through which we will explore n whatever direction our quest for information, education, and entertainment takes us.

Chapters 3 and 4 explain in detail the benefits of 3-D over 2-D, such as the capability to see more information at once and to see relationships among information. 3-D spaces also offer a more natural means for representing information about location and for interacting with other people in cyberspace.

The most frequently used term to describe the communication between large databases of information over phone or other data lines is the information highway. But this label breaks down in a non-linear hypertext environment like the World Wide Web, and will certainly break down once that environment becomes 3-D. I prefer *information landscape*. This term describes a three-dimensional environment where information is represented by 3-D and 2-D multimedia and through which we will explore in whatever direction our quest for information, education, and entertainment takes us.

Summary

The phenomenon that will make the "consensual hallucination" of shared 3-D information landscapes possible is the dynamic growth of the Internet. The next chapter traces the history of this phenomenal growth and suggests how 3-D worlds will evolve as the medium of choice for us to explore information, interpersonal communication, and entertainment.

[1]Seidensticker, Steve, from 8/28/95 email: "Some VRML/DIS Light Reading." Reprinted with permission.

2

The Exponential Growth of the Internet

The Information Highway, the National Information Infrastructure, or whatever your label for the teeming mass of information provided by networked computer databases, continues to grow, seemingly of its own accord. As this book is written the Internet is connected to 2.2 million host computers in 135 countries and is growing at a rate of 100 percent per year.

As Nicholas Negroponte points out in his book, *Being Digital,* at this rate the subscriber base will surpass the population of the Earth by the year 2000. Clearly this is physically impossible, but it does give us reason to believe that a substantial portion of the population of Earth will have access to the Internet in a few years. The Internet may not be the final form that the Information Superhighway assumes, but it is a safe bet that it will play an important role.

Figure 2.1 illustrates the incredible growth of the Internet.

Figure 2.1:

Growth of the Internet.

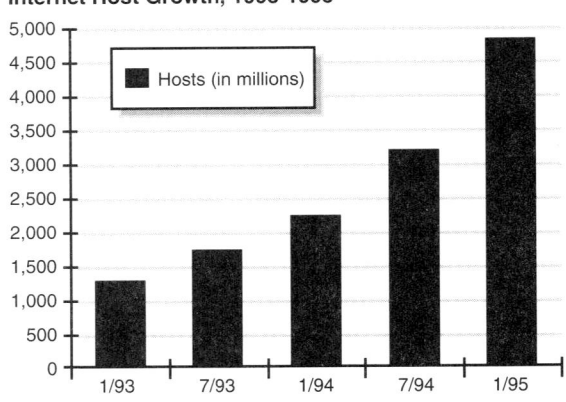

Internet Host Growth, 1993-1995

Source: Network Wizards, http://www.nw.com/.

The Internet traces its lineage back to an idea that grew out of a Rand Corporation desire to create a communication, command, and control network that could survive nuclear attack. The solution to this problem was a network with no central control.[1] As soon as the wealth of information available in the many linked databases was recognized, the network quickly outgrew its original intended use—people began to connect first for education and later for commercial purposes.

Future Now

Just as processor power is increasing rapidly, so is bandwidth. (Bandwidth issues are covered in Chapter 4.) 14,400 baud per second modems will be replaced by 512,000 baud bi-directional connections over existing cable lines by 1997. Because we will upload information at greater speeds, we will have true interactivity and everyone will be a potential publisher. What will we do with this capability?

Current thinking has it that interactive television and video phones will be the media of choice for most bandwidth consumers. The prevalent description of "the Information Highway" as merely a source for hundreds of passive channels patterned after the current television model is the least optimistic description of its potential. Video phones and shared interactive 3-D worlds of information or "information landscapes" where everyone contributes to content are the most likely use of these powerful connections.

Easy-to-use authoring tools like the *Virtus VRML Toolkit* will become more prevalent and remove the barriers that have kept most of us from even dreaming about publishing for the education and entertainment of the World's population. We are just beginning to grasp the importance of the fact that the Internet, and whatever forms it takes in the future, puts us in fairly intimate and direct connection with the population of 135 other countries. Direct democracy has never been closer.

It's All About Communication

The driving reason for the dramatic change we have seen in this century is the increasing capacity for communication. Increased communication means that more people have access to information. In the case of the erstwhile Soviet Union, information about the lifestyle enjoyed by many Americans that reached the ears and hearts of the impoverished Soviet populace undoubtedly contributed to the dissolution of the U.S.S.R. Information is power. When a few people control the volume and content of information, they control the power. When everyone has access to information and can make decisions based on that for themselves, the result is true democracy.

In the Soviet Union, something as seemingly innocuous as a copy machine was deemed a major threat to the control of this information flow. The copy machine empowered those with alternative views to disseminate information themselves. Essentially, anyone with access to a copy machine is a potential publisher. Eventually, technology overran any attempts at stemming that flow.

We are not immune to this information control in the United States. We need only look at our television industry to see the same restrictive communication at work. The paradigm of the television industry is that of a few groups deciding the content for all of us. This is due more to the financial requirements of running a national network than to any insidious plot to control information. But the result is still restrictive.

As George Gilder points out in his book *Life After Television,* people have a wide variety of interests and prefer to interact with information rather than view it passively. The reason most of us are disenchanted with current television fare is because the nature of its distribution method requires those selecting the content to cater to the lowest common denominator. We are all different in our specific interests (there are over 55,000 vertical magazines) and we are all alike in our prurient interests. Thus, television producers select content with the broadest appeal: sex and violence. The myriad publishers for the Internet have a much better chance of catering to our disparate interests.

A Democratic Paradigm

The Internet promises to offer more elevating experiences; experiences that we will each select for ourselves. We are moving from the paradigm of the few publishing for the many to the many publishing for the many. This is a true democratic method for information flow. Everyone is a publisher.

With this empowerment comes the capacity for both good and evil. This is the dichotomy we must live with and even embrace in a free democracy. The fact that everyone has the ability to publish means that we will see the full spectrum of content being supplied. Hitler once said that if he could speak English he could conquer England in a month. When Stalin was transported across Germany, he was confined to one rail car to prevent him the opportunity to influence even one person with his powerful persuasive rhetoric. Information is neither good nor evil, but our use of it makes it so. As Howard Rheingold said, "What we make, makes us." The Internet has attained its current celebrity and usefulness under the guidance of a collective worldwide consciousness, with little or no government intervention. Perhaps that same collective effort is capable of continuing to mold it for the common good. If we don't continue with this noble experiment, we face the prospect of dooming the Internet to the fate of television.

Our television and print media are doing us a disservice by concentrating on only one or two bands in the spectrum. It is true that we will see pornography generated on the Internet for the demand that has been and always will be there. (Pornography is frequently cited as one of the dominant influences in the proliferation of VCRs in the '80s.) But there are also elevating experiences on the Net. I believe we are just beginning to see the full power of the wide dissemination of information made possible by this medium.

The most intriguing aspect of the information on the Internet is its distributed nature. Hypertext allows users to follow threads of information on any given subject from page to page all over the world. This allows us to see a subject from many different points of view. VRML adds another dimension to that information navigation that will give us even more perspectives on information.

Accelerated Development

The paradigm of the industrial age was few-to-many information dispersal. The belief was that only a limited number of elite thinkers in any society had the capacity to evaluate information and act upon it for the good of society. The paradigm for the information age is many-to-many distributed processing of information. When many people have access to information from many perspectives the result is an exponential difference in the time it takes to develop ideas to their fruition. Everything accelerates; just as parallel and distributed processing computers are much faster than monolithic supercomputers.

Nanotechnology: Accelerated Development

Please forgive this digression, but as an eternal optimist, I am completely enamored of Eric Drexler's theory of Nanotechnology[2], the science of creating molecular-sized machines that will use the building blocks of nature to assemble jet engines, eliminate food shortages, and cure cancer. I believe along with Drexler and a growing number of people, that it is inevitable that we will begin to manipulate atoms to do our bidding. We have already seen IBM spelled out in Xenon atoms, the first atomic sized gears and motors, and we've seen a page of the Encyclopedia Britannica written on the head of a pin. Dr. Fred Brooks, the author of *The Mythical Man Month* and head of the graphics lab at the University of North Carolina at Chapel Hill, has a team working with a nanomanipulator. This is a robot arm with force feedback attached to a scanning tunneling microscope that allows users to feel a molecule. The question is how long will Drexler's vision take to be fulfilled?

Distributed communication provided by the Internet and future distributed wide area networks will accelerate the progress of this and other technologies. One promise of this technology is molecular computers that will operate at speeds that dwarf current massively parallel systems. This too will accelerate the achievements of mankind. If today we are manipulating atoms, when only 20 years ago we did not fully believe in their existence, where will we be 20 years from now? If we can travel to the moon with current technology, where will we go with technologies to come?

People will even be able to work on problems around the clock in different time zones. If someone makes a discovery, it can be in the heads and hands of others attending the same problem almost immediately. As one scientist in Peoria logs her work for the day and goes to sleep, her colleague in Japan will wake up to continue where his American colleague left off. Note that the acceleration in technological advancement parallels advances in communication. No one need develop anything in a vacuum anymore. With many minds working on problems or pieces of problems from many perspectives around the clock, we can expect this phenomenon to accelerate further.

Threats to Information Freedom

Of course, this enhanced communication is made possible by unrestricted flow of information. The Internet has grown at breakneck speed precisely because it is a frontier with very little restriction except that imposed by the users on themselves. The idea that the very thing which we are all in some measure betting our futures on is growing of its own accord with little direction frightens many people, especially the U.S. government. And security is an issue that must be addressed if the Internet is to become a successful medium for commerce and communication. But we have to exercise caution when applying restrictions lest we snuff out the freedom that has brought us this far.

The Capstone Chip Debate

The most hotly debated issue in this arena is the proposed capstone chip. This is the 1989 National Security Agency (NSA) encryption system that will allow government agencies to have a decoding key that gives them access to all encoded messages on the Internet. This chip is based on the same algorithm (SKIPJACK) as the clipper chip.[3] The clipper chip, while mentioned frequently when discussing the Internet, is actually designed for communications devices such as telephones and fax machines, whereas the capstone chip is designed for computers.

Under this proposal, every computer will have one of these chips. The chip will scramble a message that can be read only by the person at the intended destination, or by using another hardware key. These keys will be held in escrow by the NIST or the Treasury department and can be obtained by any law enforcement agency with a court order. Little else is known about the actual functioning of the keys because it is classified as a military secret.

Opponents to this scheme argue that it violates the Fourth (right to free speech) and Fifth (unlawful search and seizure) Amendments to the U.S. Constitution. They also fear that government agencies like the CIA, FBI, and NSA have built-in backdoors that allow them to intercept and read coded messages even without the keys or court orders.

A commercial reason for opposing the proposal is that the government intends to forbid export of any cryptography method except the "clipper chip" technology. This will effectively reduce the competitiveness of U.S. software and hardware companies because no foreign government will use an encryption scheme to which the U.S. government holds the keys.

The commercial implications of this restriction are now painfully obvious to the nice folks at Netscape Communications whose Netscape Navigator's Secure Courier protocol was broken by a French computer whiz. The exported version of the encryption is less robust to accommodate U.S. government export restrictions. This effectively makes Netscape less competitive in the world market.

The U.S. version of Secure Courier protocol was also cracked in September of 1995 just prior to the printing of this book.

Right now the proposal is voluntary, but opponents like the Electronic Frontier Foundation fear that the government will have to make it mandatory in order to implement it. The result of such a measure will be a steep decline in the growth of the Internet as people seek other avenues of expression away from the prying eyes of Big Brother.

Censorship

Rather than covering the elevating results of enhanced communication and access to information, the media—in their never-ending quest for readers and ratings—have decided to titillate and scare us with the dark side of online content. Stories of online stalking, pedophilia, and pornography abound, whereas stories about scientists across the planet collaborating to find cures for disease are sparse. The culmination of this alarmist propaganda came in the form of the proposed Communications Decency Act (CDA).

CDA, bill number S314, was introduced by Senators Exon (D-NE) and Gorton (R-WA) on February 1st, 1995, and called for several restrictive measures on the content of email to create an "Internet fit only for children." Organizations such as the Electronic Frontier Foundation mobilized quickly to oppose the bill. Despite their efforts, the bill passed in the Senate as an attachment to the Telecommunications reform bill (S652) by a vote of 84-16.

They were able to encourage House representatives Chris Cox (R-CA), and Ron Wyden (D-OR) with the support of Newt Gingrich to introduce an amendment that came to be known as the Cox/Wyden amendment. Prior to the vote in the House of Representatives, an email that spread across the country like wildfire was sent to encourage people to call their representative in Congress. The following section shows an excerpt of that message.

The Cox/Wyden Amendment

The House of Representatives will vote late Thursday or early Friday (Aug 3 or 4) on whether to add the Cox/Wyden Internet Freedom and Family Empowerment Act as an amendment to the House Telecommunications Reform Bill (HR1555). The Cox/Wyden amendment is a direct attack on the Exon/Coats Communications Decency Act (CDA). House passage of the Cox/Wyden amendment is the last chance we have to defeat the Exon/Coats CDA. If the House fails to pass Cox/Wyden, the Exon bill will likely become law.

We must act now to head off this possibility. Please take a moment to contact your member of Congress and urge them to support the Cox/Wyden legislation (described in the alert that follows).

The attached alert is from a coalition organized by the Voters Telecommunications Watch (VTW) which includes CDT, EFF, EPIC, and other online advocacy organizations. This may be your last chance to make your voice heard on this critical issue, so please call before Friday, August 4.

CAMPAIGN TO STOP THE EXON/COATS COMMUNICATIONS DECENCY ACT

House vows to vote on Telecomm bill (which includes the CDA) this week before recess! The vision of a cyberspace only fit for children will become reality. The Communications Decency Act will be offered by supporters of conservative pro-censorship groups *this week*. They will try and amend HR1555 to include the Communications Decency Act and remove any other net-friendly language such as the Leahy/Klink study.

We discuss the Cox/Wyden amendment in this book because the same issues of freedom of expression and government intervention will affect our dream of realizing a three-dimensional cyberspace. As always, those of us on the cutting and sometimes bleeding edge of technological advancement must work tirelessly in order to mold the democratic future we all envision. Information will be the center of the age that is just now dawning. Remain vigilant, reader. For more information on how you can help, please contact one of the organizations in the list at the end of this chapter.

Summary

The dream of accessing information in a shared three-dimensional environment is well on its way to becoming reality with the rapid growth of the Internet. It is important to remember that the Internet itself is only one step. Information is all around us and is struggling at the tethers of our current media to reach us in new and more visual ways. The final form it will take is still unclear, but 3-D seems a logical step in that evolution. The next chapter looks more closely at the benefits of adding additional dimensions to our exploration of cyberspace.

For More Information...

For more information on how you can help, see the following sites.

Web Sites:

- http://www.panix.com/vtw/exon/

- http://epic.org/

- http://www.eff.org/pub/Alerts/

- http://www.cdt.org/cda.html

- http://outpost.callnet.com/outpost.html

FTP Archives:

- ftp://ftp.cdt.org/pub/cdt/policy/freespeech/00-INDEX.FREESPEECH
- ftp://ftp.eff.org/pub/Alerts/

Gopher Archives:

- gopher://gopher.panix.com/11/vtw/exon
- gopher://gopher.eff.org/11/Alerts

Email:

- vtw@vtw.org (put "send alert" in the subject line for the latest alert, or "send cdafaq" for the CDA FAQ)
- cda-info@cdt.org (General CDA information)
- cda-stat@cdt.org (Current status of the CDA)

[1]*Virtual Communities*, Howard Rheingold, pg. 7, Addison-Wesley Publishing, 1993.

[2]*Engines of Creation*, K. Eric Drexler, Doubleday, 1986.

[3]Baran, Nicholas, *Inside the Information Highway Revolution*, pg. 176, Coriolis Press, 1995.

3

Escaping Flatland[1]
(Why 3-D?)

In the beginning there was DOS. Okay, that really wasn't the beginning. In the beginning there was a person scratching in the dirt with a stick; then came the abacus; then punch cards; and so on. I just don't care to go back that far. The point is that we once communicated with the silicon in our machines via one-dimensional command lines. Xerox PARC, and then the Macintosh, delivered a 2-D plane windowing interface which could show more information at once.

Also, clicking and dragging with a mouse on icons represented commands that we once typed in along with the requisite directory paths with excruciating attention to syntax. The greatest advantage to adding another dimension to our interface with the ghost in the machine was that more information could be shown at once. It logically follows that adding additional dimensions should yield greater access to more information. In the bargain we may just get additional perspective and intimacy with that information as well.

In this chapter, we investigate the following subjects:

- The difference between real-time 3-D and photo-realistic 3-D rendering

- 3-D as an interface

■ Communicating in 3-D

■ Density of information in 3-D

The Ultimate User Interface

One of the things I like about my Macintosh interface is that I can group related files, even those from different applications, into folders. That way I can organize my hard drive so that data is easily accessible and I can see how different kinds of data are interrelated.

But sometimes I have two (or more) folders that relate to each other and they in turn contain folders which may be related to files in other folders. At this point the interface breaks down a bit because once I have one folder open, it overlaps and hides the remaining folders. I have effectively run into a limitation to viewing the data on my hard drive.

It is impossible (especially on the 9.5-inch screen of my PowerBook 165c) for me to see all of the data at once and witness how everything is related. But if I could view it in—you guessed it—3-D, I could view information from every perspective and create more complex matrices of relationships.

Iconification by Distance

In a 3-D space that can be navigated in real-time (okay, it's 4-D), distance is meaningless. You can browse information by moving over or through it or just double-click somewhere and go directly to an object. Related files represented by labeled cubes are located together in space and color-coded. A given topic appears as a solid 3-D object from afar and may be as small as a pixel, but once you draw near or zap yourself there it comes apart into its component files. (See Figure 3.1, yin and yang, for an example.)

You can have as many of these clusters of information as you have pixels on-screen. The closer you get to any given set of files, the more relationship detail you will see; all the way down to the files themselves. Those of you familiar with fractals may be experiencing a sense of deja vu at this point. Okay, so it's not a new idea, but isn't it about time someone applied it to information navigation?

Figure 3.1:
3-D contains 2-D.

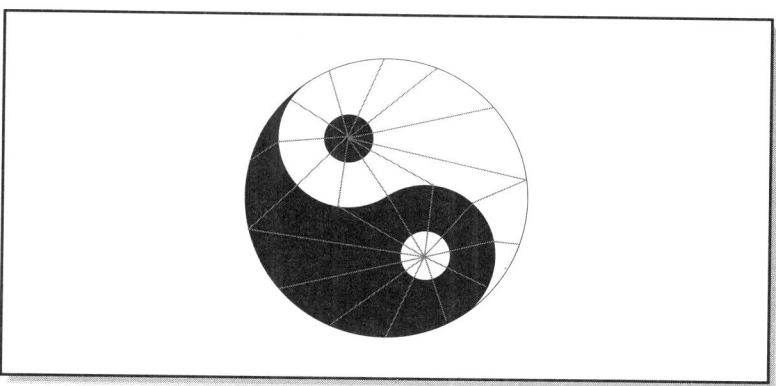

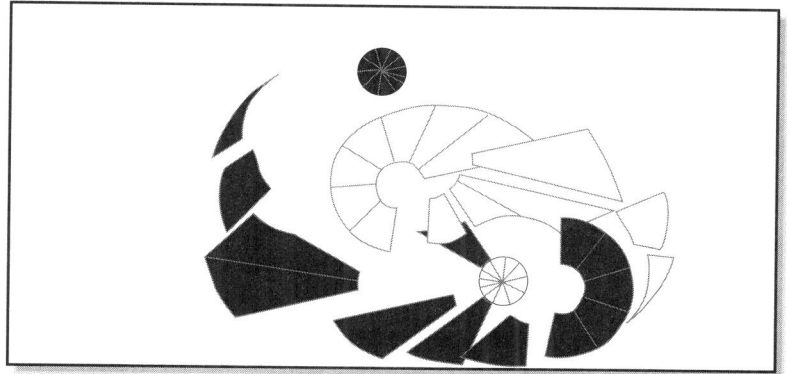

Another intrinsically helpful quality of 3-D space is that it contains 2-D as a subset. Thus, we are not giving up anything. Anything that is expressed in 2-D such as a page of text, a picture, a graphic, a chart or even video footage can be applied to a surface in a 3-D space. Therefore, each 3-D cube representing a file can have informative labels about it mapped without and within it. Because a given 3-D space, whatever its shape, can have a limitless variety of 2-D data types mapped within it, the result is a density of information that is immeasurably helpful in conveying complex ideas. I call these spaces *information landscapes*. Can you say that? I knew you could.

Information Landscapes

With the advent of small component architecture like OpenDoc and OLE (these are explained in Chapter 17), 3-D worlds will be able to be embedded in 2-D documents. A child can be reading about Stonehenge and find a small window in the middle of the document; when the child clicks that window, she or he can actually explore a 3-D model of Stonehenge and see first-hand how the sun lines up with the stones for the vernal equinox.

Stay up late one Sunday night and wait for the get rich quick and twelve step program infomercials on cable access channels. If you're lucky, there will be some guy from Tucson demonstrating his extraordinary memory. As a hundred people file by him into a room, he greets each one and then can recall all of their names as well as some details of their conversation a half hour later. One trick he and others use is the age-old method of envisioning themselves walking down a street with different colored houses and labeling each house they walk by with information about each person. By recalling this visual path, they can see the details they mapped to the buildings. It is simply a matter of engaging as many senses as possible when recording the information. This may be the answer to educating the MTV/Nintendo generation.

We are already able to embed 2-D documents in 3-D spaces. Texture maps of pictures and movies can be placed on surfaces today. With OLE and OpenDoc, entire functional documents are placed on surfaces awaiting the click of a mouse to access. Cyber navigators will be able to stroll through a museum viewing paintings and be able to click those paintings to receive a full multimedia description of the artist and the painting.

3-D worlds will also have peer-to-peer connections with live real-time data such as the stock market or satellite views of the Earth from space that can be represented for efficient viewing and comprehension in 3-D.

Communicating 3-D Information

If I want to convey to you the concept of a house I am building for you, I can send you blueprints of my design. This 2-D schematic has a certain amount of information about my design of your future home. But I still have not conveyed all of the information you need to make decisions. I can take the next step and send you a list of materials and their costs and perhaps even some 2-D renderings from various outside and inside vantage points of the design.

With 3-D, I can send you the space. You can then walk around freely in that space and get a feel for the form and function of my design. Perhaps you will walk into one room where the blueprints are posted on the wall along with the list of materials and several rendered views showing different paint color schemes. I have now conveyed more information to you all in one document. This is the promise of 3-D on the Internet: complete communication.

Real-Time 3-D Is the Key

Another method for conveying 3-D ideas is to do a detailed rendering in a computer program like 3D Studio or Stratavision 3-D and then record a movie of a walk path by moving a camera through the model and rendering each frame in succession. This has been a widely accepted method for conveying the sense of place needed for someone to understand the form and function of a 3-D space, but it has its drawbacks.

Ray-traced rendering is the process of calculating the path of every ray of light through a 3-D scene—tracing the paths—and generating from this a realistic view of the 3-D scene.

The advantage these programs and those like them have over current real-time 3-D programs is that they convey realism through **ray-traced rendering**. They rely on creating realistic lighting effects to show depth, whereas real-time renderers rely on motion parallax, the effect of changing perspectives as one moves through space, to create the 3-D effect. These tend to be less realistic. Although walk-throughs created in ray-tracing programs are very attractive, they are time-consuming to create and require tremendous bandwidth and/or disk space to convey the images to someone else. There are times to use photo-realistic ray traces and times when the rate of information transfer requires using real-time 3-D. This is the strength of Virtus VRML.

Real-time worlds have to be small. Most are less than 200K. Walk-throughs like those rendered in a ray-tracing program can take many megabytes of disk space, and the result is an animation that can only be viewed passively by pressing a Play button. Real-time worlds allow the reader to wander freely and unhindered through a three-dimensional environment deciding with each step where to go. VRML worlds also allow interactivity with embedded URLs, or universal resource locators, which allow readers to jump between 3-D landscapes and 2-D pages or other 3-D landscapes and back again.

Real-time 3-D worlds also conform to Edward Tufte's belief in the importance of keeping a group of related items within the eyespan. This is not accomplished with movies or slides. With these sequentially linear modes of information transfer, a piece of information is available to the eye for a fleeting finite amount of time and then is gone. If we want to see how a slide or image from five minutes ago relates to something we are currently viewing, we have to rewind to that slide or point in time in the movie. With real-time 3-D spaces, we can turn around and see where we have been and see how that information relates to where we are going. Everything is within the eyespan and can be viewed from multiple perspectives. See the following sidebar entitled "Real-Time 3-D, Real Benefits."

Real-Time 3-D, Real Benefits

"This is why Virtus WalkThrough Pro 2.5 has a place in this world. If I render in Stratavision it looks good; it has nice radiosity and mapping and reflection and all that rendering stuff. But let's say I do an animation of the rendering. On my Quadra 950 it takes 1/2 hour to do one frame. So a 100 frame animation takes about 48 hours. But if I really want something useful I need, say 1000 frames. That means it takes 20 days to render my 1000 frame animation—not counting modeling time and set up. If that weren't bad enough, I need to run it at 20 frames per second to get a nice quality, smooth-running animation. So my 20 days has boiled down to a 50 second animation! Most people can't wait that long. That's why Virtus Walk-Through Pro 2.5 is so valuable. It draws FAST! "

—Dwight Morejohn, Capturing Concepts, Davis, CA

Portability

One major advantage of real-time 3-D worlds is their portability. In order for a 3-D space to be navigated in real-time (20-30 frames per second) on a desktop computer it must be compact in size. This means that worlds like those you will create with the *Virtus VRML Toolkit* are small enough to send over the Internet attached to an email or put on a disk and placed in a pocket.

Remember that a 3-D animation consists of a succession of rendered frames that double the size of the file with each frame. An environment designed for real-time navigation includes one copy of the space and allows the navigator to determine a path through that space. Therefore a great deal more information can be contained in a given amount of bytes. This high level of information content per byte is worth the tradeoff in realism in most cases. Figure 3.2 expresses this advantage.

Figure 3.2:
Portability of 3-D worlds.

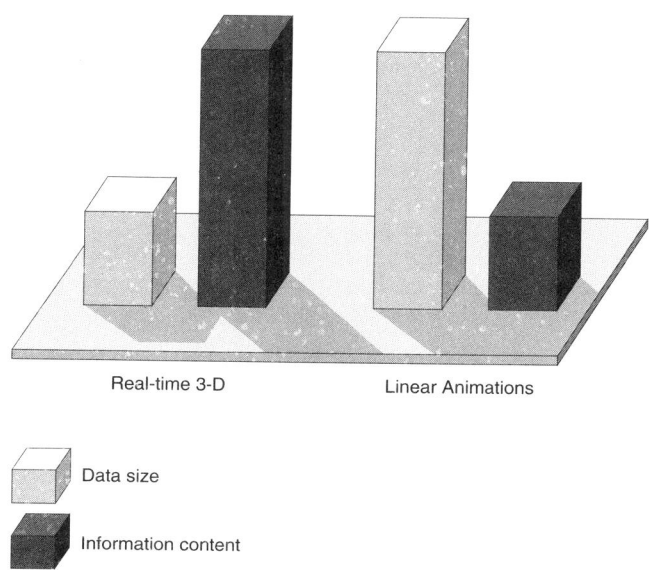

Summary

Intuitively, most of us understand that 3-D, by definition, contains more content than 2-D. That extra dimension adds new perspectives on relationships between pieces of information, and anything expressed in 2-D can be placed in a 3-D environment as a subset. Having said that, I must admit that sometimes information that contains multi-dimensional relationships can be expressed with astonishing elegance in 2-D form.

In *Envisioning Information* and *The Visual Display of Quantitative Information*, Edward Tufte has collected some of the greatest gems of 2-D information transfer in human history. The advantage of such a compact expression, according to Tufte, is that the information can be quickly taken in with one sweep of the eyes. One does not need to peer around corners or move through rooms in order to see the information in its entirety.

Because I am a self-proclaimed evangelist for the cause of 3-D information navigation, this pains more than a few of my senses. If everything I say in this chapter is true, and I believe it is, this information should be able to be improved upon when expressed in a navigable 3-D environment.

Perhaps an extra dimension could be added that displays more cause and effect or makes the cause and effect reveal itself quicker. The cause and effect of the destruction of Napolean's army in the Winter invasion of Russia in 1812 is apparent only after careful scrutiny. Still, this is a graphic that has stood the test of time and is revered by Tufte as perhaps the greatest statistical graph of all time. Can modern technology improve upon it? Can you?

[1]This concept comes from Edward Tufte's book, *Envisioning Information* (Graphics Press, Cheshire, Connecticut 1983), and was originally expressed by Edwin A. Abbott in *Flatland: A Romance of Many Dimensions,* (London, 1884).

[2]Regis, Ed. Nano: *The Emerging Science of Nanotechnology*, (Little, Brown and Co.), pg. 69.

[3]Tufte, Edward. *The Visual Display of Quantitative Information*, (Graphics Press, Cheshire, Connecticut, 1983), pg. 40-41.

4

Barriers and Bandwidth

We have established that 3-D information navigation is desirable and inevitable, but there are clearly some considerable hurdles to cross before it becomes a commonplace reality. The most frequently cited barrier is bandwidth, but other factors such as latency and processor speed will also intervene between our current analog systems of 1-D and 2-D communication and the promise of 3-D digital information landscapes. In this chapter, you learn what all of these terms mean, how they play a role in the development of your 3-D cyberspace worlds, and how you can overcome current limitations.

You learn:

■ What frequency, bandwidth, and latency mean.

■ The difference between digital and analog signals.

■ Delivery systems: cable vs. fiber optics.

■ All about Motorola's CableComm.

Frequency, Bandwidth, and Latency Defined

> The **wavelength** of the signal is the distance traveled from a zero value, to the highest positive value, back to 0, to the lowest negative value, and then back to 0.

Today, most information is still transmitted via analog signals (see Figure 4.1). Radio, television, cable, and satellite transmissions are in analog form. This means that a signal (sound, light, temperature, fluid motion, and pressure are measured and transmitted in analog form) is copied and transmitted via air or cable and received on the other end by a terminal that just repeats the signal it receives. For this reason we call televisions, phones, and radios "dumb terminals."

Figure 4.1:

An analog wave.

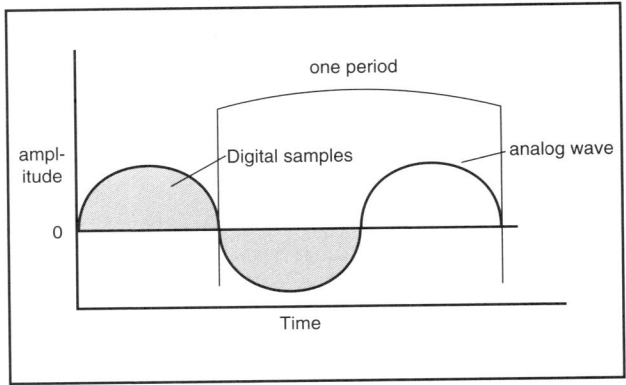

> **Frequency** is the number of times the cycle is repeated per second and is measured in hertz.

A signal is measured in wavelength and **frequency**. The **wavelength** of the signal is the distance traveled from a zero value, to the highest positive value, back to 0, to the lowest negative value, and then back to 0 (see Figure 4.2). The amount of time it takes a wavelength to complete its course is called a cycle. The number of times the cycle occurs per second is called the frequency. This is usually expressed in hertz after Heinrich Hertz, a German physicist. One hertz is one cycle per second, 1,000 cycles per second is one kilohertz and one million cycles per second is one megahertz.

Figure 4.2:

A wavelength.

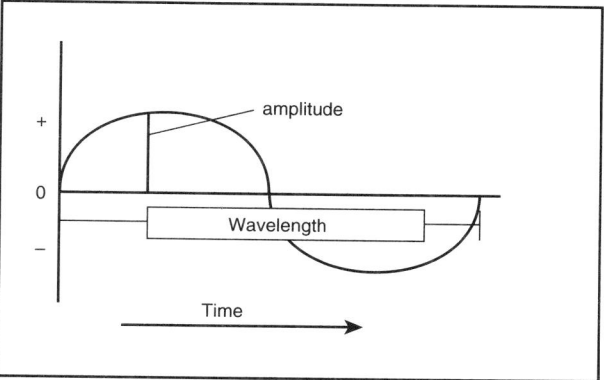

As these waves of information are transmitted, they are subject to some quality distortion, thus repeaters are placed along phone lines and amplifiers are used for television to clean the signal. Digital transmission of the same waves allows for the wave to be broken into a series of ones and zeroes that can be reassembled at the other end. This digitizing process involves breaking up a wave into a succession of digital representations of values for a predefined number of points on the wave. The more points on the wave that are sampled, the truer the digital representation is to the original signal. Digital transmission does not require repeaters or amplifiers. The signal is broken into values that are placed into packets of information that are transferred to the receiving end where they are reassembled.

Latency is the time it takes to send a packet and receive a response based on the contents of the sent packet.

"Latency" is the time it takes to send a packet of digital information and receive a response based on the contents of the sent packet. Hence if it takes 100 milliseconds to transmit a packet to a server, 25 milliseconds to process this packet, and 100 milliseconds to transmit a reply, the latency is 225 milliseconds. **Latency** greatly affects whether a user will be happy with the time it takes to view 3-D content.

In analog terms, the necessary bandwidth to transmit a given signal is equal to the maximum frequency of that signal. For example, 4kHz (4,000 cycles per second) is allocated for voice transmission. Thus any parts of the signal that go beyond that range are lost, but this is considered adequate for normal conversations. Stereo music, on the other hand, requires at least 20MHz to adequately represent the sounds discernible by the human ear.

Digital bandwidth is the transmission capacity per unit time of a given medium and is usually expressed in bits per second (bps).

The number of different packets that can be delivered at once over a given medium (coaxial cable, copper telephone wire, or fiber optic lines) is the **digital bandwidth**. When we refer to bandwidth from now on we will refer to this definition. Bandwidth is usually measured in bits per second (bps), and is normally expressed in kilobits, megabits, and gigabits per second.

Bits and Bytes

There are eight bits in a byte and a byte is sufficient room to express one alphanumeric character. For graphics, between eight and 32 bits are required, according to the number of colors being displayed, to instruct each pixel on-screen what color to produce. For frame of reference, a 640×480 screen has 307,200 pixels. This number must be multiplied by the number of bits per pixel to yield the digital bandwidth required to transmit a full-screen graphical element. For full-motion video that result must be multiplied by the 30 frames required per second. Without doing the math, you can already see that we are getting into high numbers. Remember also that it is not uncommon for high-resolution monitors to have one million pixels or more.

This problem is overcome today by limiting the size of the image and thus the number of pixels to limit this math somewhat. This is acceptable for viewing multimedia on computers, but consumers will accept nothing less than full-screen, high-quality images for video on demand. Expressed another way: we don't want to use a small portion of the real estate on our wide-screen TV. We want to use all of it.

Digital Compression involves limiting the number of bits required to represent a signal based on the idea that many of the bits are redundant.

Compression technologies are evolving that help alleviate this problem somewhat. **Compression** involves limiting the number of bits required to represent a signal based on the idea that many of the bits are redundant. These can be added back in later when the signal is reassembled. There are two kinds of compression: *lossless* and *lossy*.

Lossless compression remains truest to the original data but offers the lowest compression rates, while lossy compression permits greater compression at the expense of the quality of the reproduced data. Lossless compression offers ratios of 3 to 1, whereas lossy may offer up to 200 to 1 compression for full-motion video and 50 to 1 compression for still images. There are many standards for achieving this compression, but the two most common are MPEG-1 and MPEG-2 for video and JPEG for still images.

Although MPEG-1 delivers video quality equal to that of VHS tapes today, most experts agree that this will not be acceptable quality for the high-resolution displays of the near future. This means that a better standard and faster transmission methods will need to be created. MPEG-2 is now being adopted and promises to provide for a spectrum of resolutions and aspect ratios, and improves on the compression ratios of MPEG-1.

Today's 28,800 bps modems are definitely inadequate to deliver real-time 3-D events. At that speed, transmission of color images takes several minutes per image and three or four minutes of high-fidelity music takes up to an hour to transmit. Faster transmission methods are necessary.

Delivery

The burning question on everyone's lips then is by what means will we deliver this content? The options today are fiber-optic lines, plain old twisted-pair (POTS) copper wire, coaxial cable, or wireless satellite transmission. See Table 4.1.

Table 4.1

Approximate Bandwidths for Each Transmission Technology

Medium	Bandwidth
Copper wire	2.4Kbps
ISDN	2MB
Coaxial Cable	20Mbps
T3 Fiber Optic	42Mbps

Fiber Optic Transmission

Fiber-optic lines are made of a glass material refined from sand. The advantages of this transmission method are higher bandwidth, easier maintenance, lower weight, less environmental impact during manufacturing, and less susceptibility to wire-tapping[1]. Most telephone landlines are slowly being replaced with this medium, but the process is labor intensive and therefore more expensive than using existing cable lines. Nicholas Negroponte recently lambasted companies like CableComm for deterring or delaying fiber optic installation by promising to offer a cheaper solution using existing infrastructure. I see CableComm's approach as a logical evolutionary transition to a hybrid fiber/coaxial cable network that will eventually lead to an all fiber network once it becomes cost-effective.

Clearly, fiber optic transmission provides the greatest bandwidth, but with the high estimated costs for implementing this nationwide, this may not happen for quite some time. Bill Gates and his partner in Teledisc, Craig McCaw, are placing side bets on satellite transmission.

They plan to launch 840 satellites by the end of the century to help bring the Information Superhighway to the most remote regions of the Earth.[2] But there are severe bandwidth limitations with wireless communication as well. Furthermore, current satellite technology does not provide interactivity. One cannot send messages back to the satellite. Process of elimination leaves us with the next best choice: coaxial cable.

Coaxial Cable

According to Nicholas Negroponte, author of *Being Digital*, the data we currently send over wireless will be transmitted by landline in the future and vice versa.[3] This makes a lot of sense once one contemplates the limited spectrum of radio frequencies available for transmission. Some of this spectrum will be freed up once satellites stop broadcasting television signals and concentrate on paging and cellular communications.

Coaxial cable provides a reasonable amount of bandwidth while having the added benefit of already running within a stone's throw of 95 percent of the businesses and households in the U.S. In fact 60 percent of U.S. households already subscribe to cable services. Companies such as Motorola's CableComm, DEC, Intel, and General Instrument are working on cable modems capable of asymmetrical transmission speeds in excess of 10 megabits per second (compared to current speeds of 28.8 kilobits per second over phone lines). Referring to Table 4.1, you see that we still have room with coaxial cable to improve modem speeds to 20 megabits per second or 694.44 times the bandwidth we have with a 28.8Kbps modem today.

If this does indeed come to pass, bandwidth for real-time transmission of 3-D worlds will be possible very soon. We may find ourselves in the position of having the bandwidth available before the content. Cyberspace authors, please start your engines.

Barriers Overcome

The desire to offer next-generation, interactive services on the Information Superhighway has inspired extraordinary mergers in the cable and phone industries. But achieving this exciting new world of multimedia capabilities also requires that a key technical obstacle be overcome: namely, the capability of fiber/coax infrastructure to support two-way transmission and to offer interference-free communications.

Motorola Multimedia's CableComm

Just as it has in the past when it lead the industry in applying radio frequency to the world's most challenging opportunities, Motorola is leading the industry through the application of its RF expertise to this challenge. Today, Motorola Multimedia's CableComm stands a good chance of leading the way to the new era of true multimedia, 3-D interactive services on the Information Superhighway.

Creating a Two-Way Network

CableComm is Motorola Multimedia's strategy to use its expertise in radio frequency (RF) technology to create a two-way, interactive network out of the existing fiber/coax infrastructure, which enables network operators to overcome the interactive bottleneck of coax and to offer next-generation interactive services to subscribers.

The fiber/coax infrastructure now in place is used primarily for carrying broadband television downstream to the home and is within connecting distance of 95 percent of the 100 million homes in the United States. This infrastructure is mature, cost-effective, and widely supported. Motorola Multimedia's strategy is to use its expertise in radio frequency (RF) technology to create a two-way, interactive network out of the existing fiber/coax infrastructure. This enables a network operator to overcome the interactive bottleneck of coax and to offer next-generation interactive services to subscribers. The technology Motorola Multimedia has developed to accomplish this is called **CableComm**. CableComm can coexist with TV and other broadband services on the cable network in an extremely efficient manner, and can support enhanced telephone services and wireless personal communication.

The CableComm Layout

CableComm transforms a hybrid fiber/coax network that offers only basic CATV services into a fully interactive system for wired or wireless services. In a standard fiber/coax network today, the network delivers broadcast video entertainment services from the cable headend through a fiber node to coax, where it eventually terminates in a tap and a subscriber drop into a home. To install CableComm, a cable operator places the Cable Control Unit (CCU) into the cable headend. The CCU provides connectivity between the local phone switch and the cable system and supports both wired and wireless cable telephony.

At the subscriber end, a Cable Access Unit (see Figure 4.3) is installed in the home. The unit features standard interface connectors (RJ-11) for a conventional telephone and a coaxial connection for the cable interface.

Figure 4.3:

Motorola's cable access unit.

Within the home or office, CableComm provides high-speed data communications via Motorola's new CyberSURFR cable modem (see Figure 4.4). CyberSURFR is specifically designed for data communications for online services, Internet access, telecommuting, and other emerging services for home and business PC users. The modem offers throughput speeds of up to 10Mbps per user in the downstream direction over existing cable TV networks. Return upstream path throughput for the CyberSURFR modem is 768Kbps (compare to today's 14.4Kbps modems).

Figure 4.4:

Motorola's CyberSURFR modem.

Cable operators can also offer wireless services, including wireless local loop and pedestrian mobility, through the integration of various possible wireless system components into the CableComm System. Through this integration, CableComm subscribers can enjoy mobility within their home or business, or anywhere that coverage is provided.

This is a wonderful solution for increasing bandwidth into the home. The difficulty comes into play when we upload information or responses from the home back into the network. This *upstream path* uses radio frequencies with a limited spectrum of 5 to 42 megaHertz and is subject to *ingress* interference which seriously degrades the transmission quality. This interference comes from sources like shortwave transmitters, electric motors, vehicle ignition systems, and paging systems among others. Motorola's extensive experience in cleaning up these radio frequency signals gives them a clear advantage in the imminent interactive cable market. CableComm is already being tested in selected markets and should be widely available by 1997.

Figure 4.5:
Fiber/coax CableComm network.

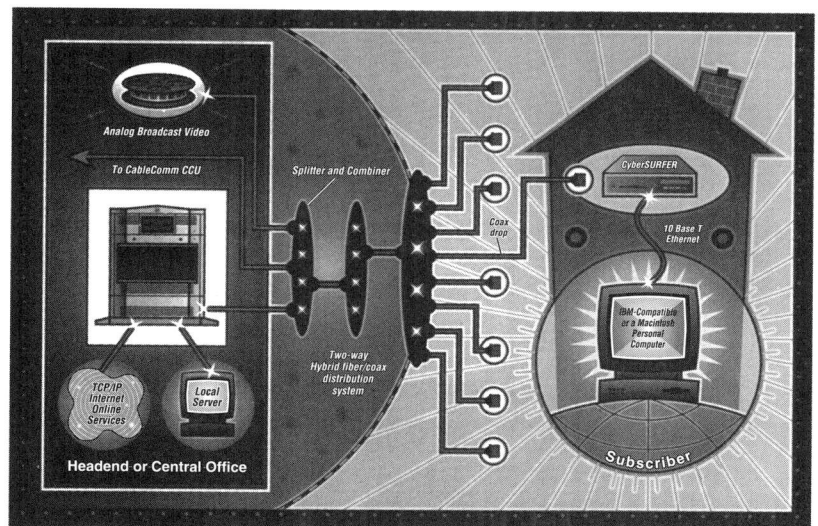

Processor Speed

A **topbox** is a computer resembling a channel converter that connects to the television.

Okay, so we finally have real-time, 3-D content capable connections in our home by 1997. Our clever set **topbox** or computer modem has unpacked the packets of data and they are resting comfortably in RAM awaiting only a few clicks of the mouse before revealing the wonders of a 3-D information landscape. Our unadorned 120 MHz Pentium processor roars to life and unveils a beautifully ray-traced town complete with a town square, shops, banks, an institute of higher experiential learning (IHEL), and various offramps heading into the cybermist at the edges of our rendered perception.

We decide immediately to go for a stroll and click at the top of the screen to begin our journey. A spinning world appears and five seconds later we move forward. Apparently bandwidth isn't the only issue we had to confront. Although the Pentium processor in our set topbox is a speed demon relative to its 486 predecessor, it still balks at content made for high-end workstations. Photo-realistic 3-D worlds are still beyond the purview of today's acceptably priced and widely available machines. It is still prudent to preach the gospel of evolution versus revolution. In order to make experiences in the information landscape available to everyone, we must create spaces that run on inexpensive hardware, with easy to use interfaces at affordable prices.

Making Do

For the time being, this means creating worlds with less expensive (computationally speaking) rendering options like flat shading, or Gouraud, or phong shading at the most extravagant. Our interest is in providing a sense of place as a container for information, it isn't necessary to create photorealistic worlds. At least, not until it is computationally trivial and inexpensive to do so.

Levels of Realism

Levels of realism in rendering in descending order are:

- **Radiosity:** Multiple light sources including ambient light and reflections and diffusions.

- **Ray tracing:** Traces the path(s) of light source(s) through the model. Allows for reflections. Each pixel can be a different color.

- **Phong shading:** Each polygon or surface can be multiple colors. This method also allows for specular reflections.

- **Gouraud shading:** Each polygon is compared to the light source and a linear interpolation of the effect is mapped to the polygon. Each polygon can be more than one color. This is also called "smooth shading" because it blends rough flat shaded edges.

- **Flat shading:** Each polygon can be only one color. If a room has one light source pointing down from the ceiling, the floor will be lighter than the walls, which are in turn lighter than the ceiling. Flat shading is fast, but less realistic.

It is important to keep in mind that there are trade-offs with each level of realism. Radiosity is still impractical for most home computers. Ray tracing looks good but still takes hours to render and does not allow real-time navigation. (Instead of frames per second you are looking at frames per hour.) Also, whenever an object or the observer is moved in a ray-traced scene, the entire scene must be rendered again, usually a good time for a long lunch break. If we remember that all we are doing is fooling the eye anyway, we can look for creative ways to achieve the most realism or suspension of disbelief with the most navigation speed and smallest file size.

The model shown in Figure 4.6 is an opera set created by set design author Darwin Payne in Virtus WalkThrough Pro. This is a flat-shaded navigable model that has been texture mapped to look ray-traced. Darwin applied lighting effects to his textures in Adobe Photoshop before applying them to his model. This is the kind of creativity that pays great dividends on the still bandwidth-impoverished Internet.

Figure 4.6:

Opera set model created by scenographer Darwin Reid Payne.

Conveying Depth

Several visual cues convey a sense of depth and of place. **Motion parallax** is the sensation of changing perspectives as one moves through a space. Naturally, the faster one is moving, the greater the suspension of disbelief from the fact that this is really a 2-D screen generated from a succession of 1s and 0s and not Rodeo Drive. Virtus VRML relies heavily on this cue to create the 3-D effect. Another cue is that of binocular vision. This creates depth even when one is not moving because each eye is sampling the space from a slightly different perspective. This is available in Virtus WalkThrough Pro 2.5 but does require additional processing power to draw an additional screen or extra lines (in the case of alternating line or field sequential stereo).

The visual cue relied on most by high-end renderers like 3D Studio and Lightwave 3-D is the shading of a space created by painstakingly tracing the source and path of every light ray in the space, as shown in Figure 4.7. Most programs take into account the effect that shiny or chalky surfaces in a space have on light refraction and diffusion. This is computationally very heavy-duty business, with rendering of each frame even on Pentiums and Power Macintosh computers requiring 30 minutes to an hour each. It is not recommended for real-time navigation.

Figure 4.7:
A ray-traced image of a scene from the upcoming computer game, Tom Clancy's First contact: Derelict.

The only real-time ray-traced 3-D space I have entered is Dr. Fred Brooks' splendidly rendered house courtesy of the multimillion dollar pixel planes five massively parallel computers at the University of North Carolina at Chapel Hill. This system uses one processor per pixel to render the scene in real-time. Each processor has only to notify its buddy pixel what color to generate 30 times per second. One day, this horsepower will be available on our sub $300 set topbox, but don't look for it this Christmas.

It is a set topbox and that is a piece of hardware that will enable your TV to communicate like a computer, a telephone, and a television set....

Competition Helps

One ray of light (pun intended) in the otherwise flat-shaded world of real-time 3-D is the heavy competition among graphics accelerator board makers like Creative Labs, 3-D Labs, S3, Matrox, and others that is pushing the cost for these polygon screamers below $300. The makers of these chips purport that they will offer 500,000 polygons per second performance for Gouraud, shaded and texture, mapped spaces. At this price it is conceivable that they will be bundled with top of the line multimedia systems in 1996 offering a tremendous boost to Pentium and Power Macintosh systems.

In the meantime, it is prudent to author worlds that cater to the mass of machines out there selling for less than $2,000. As someone once said, computers can count from one to zero, the rest is illusion.

The Interface Is the Thing

An interface is anything that allows two or more unlike things to communicate. I think we can all agree that asking a machine to create virtual universes from 1s and 0s is not necessarily a natural state of human communication skills. This feat requires some translation. "Ease-of-use" or "user-friendliness" are important factors affecting how well and widely the information highway will be adopted.

For UNIX jockeys accustomed to complex commands and communication protocols, interfaces like Netscape and Mosaic may seem incredibly easy to use. But for the majority of would-be cyber navigators who still have trouble programming their VCRs, the prospect of doing searches that turn up thousands of responses, or even having to type in addresses like http://www.virtus.com may be a bit daunting.

The 3-D Answer

Again, 3-D interfaces may provide a more friendly atmosphere from which to view information. Using the metaphor of a town or museum, destinations and content can be portrayed in spatial terms familiar to everyone.

General Magic, although still 2-D, has taken a stab at representing the information landscape using this metaphor. A possible 3-D version of the General Magic interface is shown in Figure 4.8. Using images to represent destinations rather than arcane lines of code helps make navigating the information landscape more friendly. Non-linear 3-D space also helps us with active thinking while we navigate versus mindless channel surfing.

Figure 4.8:
This 3-D Main Street includes a house that contains a 3-D desktop (and all of your files), entertainment section, communications building, and a software store.

3-D Browsing

Browsing is another area where 3-D can be of assistance. Because, as I determined earlier, more information can be represented with a 3-D interface, we can look at more information at any given time. Active newsgroups or databases with the most information or that contain the highest number of hits from a search will be represented by 3-D icons that make them easy to identify.

Figure 4.9:

Inside the house you find a 3-D desk complete with rolodex, telephone/ modem, scratch pad, in/out mailbox, and database.

I like the concept of a virtual world as an interface because it requires us to make conscious decisions about our movements through cyberspace. It will be very different from scanning text or flipping channels. A non-linear landscape populated with other unpredictable reflections of human consciousness in the form of 3-D avatars creates a dynamic space for the cultivation of emergent behavior. The social sciences will have a whole new category to add to the study of civilized society: cyberspace behavior.

The Future Is Near

Although we are facing serious obstacles to real-time 3-D information navigation on the Internet today, it certainly appears that many of them will be reduced or eliminated within the next eighteen months. In that time, processor speeds will have doubled and cable modems will have attached themselves remora-like to the outsides of our dwellings eager to draw the creative content generated from within into the veins of the Internet while eagerly delivering the life-sustaining entertainment and information we crave. On our way to this inevitability, we 3-D content authors will temper our worlds with judiciously applied shading and texture mapping in order to maintain the speed and navigability consumers will crave. We do this because our 3-D worlds are not made to be admired in their static glory, but to be explored in 4-D (x,y,z and time). 4-D is also considered virtual reality, especially when the navigator uses immersive equipment like a head-mounted display and a 3-D input device like a data glove.

In Chapter 5, we explore the issues and accouterments surrounding the nebulous world of virtual reality and how it will augment our virtual world exploration.

[1]Baran, Nicholas, *Inside the Information Highway Revolution*, 1995, Coriolis Group Books, pg. 84.

[2]*The Wall Street Journal*, July 29, 1994.

[3]Nicholas Negroponte, "Products and Services for Computer Networks," *Scientific American*, September, 1991.

5

What Is Virtual Reality?

No discussion of a virtual reality modeling language would be complete without the obligatory exercise of attempting to define **virtual reality**. In every MecklerMedia virtual reality conference spanning the last few years, we have all struggled with this chimera. Even today, you will find no more agreement among the conference faculty than among their watches on the definition of virtual reality. Most descriptions begin with the obvious remark that the term is an oxymoron and then the discussion degenerates into catcalls and *ad hominem* attacks from there.

Virtual reality is a computer system that can immerse the user in the illusion of a computer-generated world and permit the user to navigate through this world at will.

The extremists on one end vociferously maintain that unless every human sense is immersed and massaged in a cyber experience, it is not virtual reality. The extremists on the other end passively allow that any experience, even reading a good book or watching a movie, which allows one to suspend one's disbelief for a time should be embraced as virtual reality. Naturally, my own inclinations lie somewhere in the yawning expanse between. I have always preferred Myron Krueger's term *Artificial Reality*. His book by the same name is a good introduction into the field. I believe Howard Rheingold's Virtual Reality is the quintessential documentary of what virtual reality is all about. See the following sidebar for more information about Rheingold's Virtual Reality.

Howard Rheingold's Virtual Reality

Howard Rheingold agrees with Fred Brooks, an early and sage pioneer in the realm of computer graphics, who believes the function of the computer and of virtual reality is to augment the faculties of the human mind, not substitute a different reality. Brooks calls this doctrine intelligence amplification, or IA. The acronym begs for it to be compared to AI (artificial intelligence), but they are very different philosophies. Artificial intelligence seeks to reproduce the functions of the mind whereas intelligence amplification concentrates on those areas where the computer is better than the brain and adds those capabilities to those of the mind.

Brooks points out that the human brain far exceeds the capabilities of a computer in three areas: pattern recognition, context, and evaluation. The computer excels at calcula-tion and storing data. The ideal application for virtual reality, it seems, is to merge these capabilities into a bio-electronic entity that has all of these talents.

This is the promise of immersing humans in three-dimensional seas and landscapes of data. Cyberspace will consist of millions of connected databases of stored information and calculation capability that we humans will "jack into" via our TV or computer portals and navigate together using the innate capabilities of our minds in concert with the incredible power of distributed computers to amplify our intelligence. We will see new relationships among information and will be able to communicate directly with people from across the globe. This is what virtual reality is all about. It will serve as the interface to this bio-electronic entity.

Applying Virtual Reality

In North Carolina (what I used to jokingly refer to as the Silicon Valley of the South until people stopped laughing some time in 1993), we are fortunate to have some of the most advanced virtual reality labs and finest Internet access in the country, if not the world. At the University of North Carolina at Chapel Hill, Fred Brooks and Henry Fuchs preside over the fastest graphics computer on the planet, Pixel Planes V. The state government is busy completing the first completely fiber optic network among all of the education systems in the state.

Pixel Planes V, based on the pixel flow technology created by Brooks, Fuchs, and associates, is a massively parallel computer system that consists of one processor per pixel. The sole job of each processor is to answer its companion pixel's request "what color am I?" at the rate of thirty times a second. I imagine these processors getting very bored like Marvin the Robot in Douglas Adams' *HitchHikers Guide to the Galaxy* series. This is tremendous computing power and provides some enthralling virtual reality experiences.

Using the nanomanipulator, I was able to grasp molecules that I viewed in a head mounted display as I attempted to dock them together. The robot arm actually provided force feedback to help me feel the attracting and repelling forces between the molecules. I was also treated to an excursion through Fred Brooks' house in a ray-traced fully immersive simulation that allowed me to walk around in the room. The entire ceiling of the lab is covered with head tracking tiles.

Perhaps the most compelling and vital problem the lab is working on is aiding the cancer treatment center at the UNC hospital to visualize radiation treatments. In this simulation, the exact sighting of each of three radiation lasers is focused in 3-D space so that they converge only on the offending cancer cells and not on other vital tissue. These are the areas where virtual reality excels. Some problems, like molecular manipulation architecture and the modeling and rehearsing of tricky medical operations and procedures, really benefit from this technology.

In short, virtual reality enables us to:

- Visit inaccessible places

  Inside a volcano

  Outer space

  Inside a living patient

- Visit places that no longer or do not yet exist

  The battle of Hastings

  Kobe, Japan before the earthquake

  Mt. Rushmore in 2010 (included on your CD)

- Create impossible art

- Create virtual poetry

- Create worlds that defy physics

CD-ROM

Now that we have a handle on what can be accomplished with VR, let's look at what we need to participate in these experiences.

Components of VR

I certainly believe that a computer should be involved somehow and I would prefer it to provide a three-dimensional space. I also believe that the worlds created should be real-time and non-linear. Users should be able to move in six degrees of freedom at their own pace. I also know that I have no predilection toward having every sense embedded in a computer via an assortment of electronic orifices and appendages. The former extremists have an image of the future they call *wetware,* in which the human brain is directly wired to the processor. I am concerned about what would happen if my friend jokingly did a Control-Alt-Delete while I was "jacked in." (Yes, that's the sort of company I keep.) I am still paying for college and would consider it a shame to lose the benefits and memories of my education before having a chance to drink them away properly.

Immersive versus Window Worlds

Among those of us in the middle, the clearest dividing line is drawn between immersive and window worlds. These terms simply describe two methods for interacting with artificial geometry created in the computer. They are both virtual reality and are used in different ways:

- ■ Immersive worlds involve peripherals like head mounted displays (HMDs) and the dataglove, shown in Figure 5.1.

- ■ Window worlds provide interaction with virtual environments via a 2-D monocular interface like a monitor and usually provide input via a standard mouse.

Figure 5.1:

Virtual i-O is an example of a HMD (Head Mount Display) used for an immersive virtual reality experience.

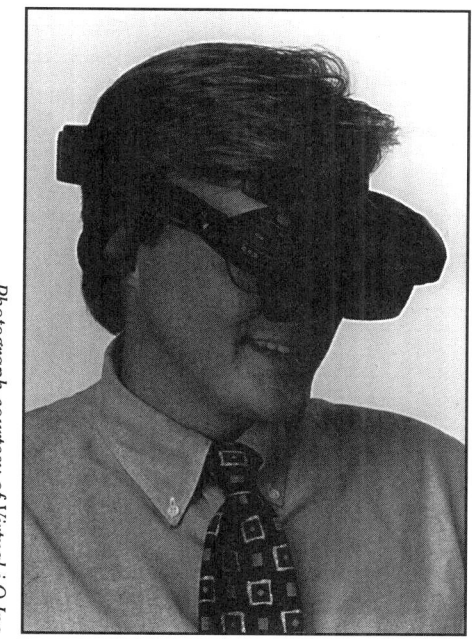

Photograph courtesy of Virtual i-O Inc.

Like 3-D graphics accelerator boards, stereo headsets are finally breaking the cost threshold that has kept them out of the hands of most of us until now. 1996 will probably see the first multimedia systems equipped with stereo head-mounted display peripherals. The dataglove may also make a comeback. They, too, should be priced reasonably because there must be a warehouse somewhere with stockpiles of them left over from Mattel. Like everything else, the pull-through that will bring these devices into the home is entertainment.

Stereo HMDs provide a depth that is definitely lacking when viewing with only a monitor, and the exclusionary nature of the helmet provides a more personal experience. But my own experiences with headsets compel me to question the prudence of wearing them for any length of time beyond a few minutes, as described in the following sidebar "What's Wrong with HMDs?". This would seem to exclude them from practical applications like computer-aided design. They may be appropriate for presenting a finished model, but almost certainly not for doing the actual modeling.

The dataglove is not much better than the HMD. Try this little test. Hold your arm straight out in front of you. Now see how long you can keep it there. As with any exercise program, please consult your physician first. You may feel a slight burning sensation after a few minutes. I'll wait.

After a while, carpal tunnel syndrome will seem like a paper cut. The muscles of our arms need resistance or they pull against each other. This is why the light pen failed as a peripheral, and why the dataglove will be used for short bursts of activity in games—but not for extended use in navigating cyberspace.

What's Wrong with HMDs?

The discomfort experienced when using HMDs comes from several sources. The first complaint comes from the encumbrance of the device. Besides the weight of the traditional helmet, you are also effectively cut off from the physical world and are subject to bumping into objects as you attempt to move in the artificial world. There are also valid health concerns stemming from the intimacy of enclosed helmets being worn by many people. When you take an enclosed headset from someone, you are also taking a headset from everyone who has ever worn that headset. The other frequently noted criticism of immersive experiences is the disorienting effect of lag.

Remember the concern about the processor being able to render the virtual worlds fast enough in one window? Stereo display requires two windows to be drawn and thus effectively cuts speed in half. In cases where the head tracker cannot render the frames as fast as you move your head, you are left with the disorientation of moving your head and waiting for the display to catch up. The resulting nausea has been called "simulator sickness" by Howard Rheingold. One would expect faster processor speeds to alleviate this, but Rheingold maintains that this malady occurs both from displays that are not good enough and those that are too good!

There has been rapid advancement in the last 12 months in the design of HMDs, and they are getting cheaper and less intrusive. The simulator sickness problem is with us for some time though. Like anything else, the experience is a personal one and the buying public will eventually decide whether these peripherals are widely adopted.

My affinity for window worlds stems from the fact that they meet the criteria for an evolutionary approach to technology: the concept of evolving with available hardware and paradigms. They do not require additional hardware or expense, and they build on existing user interface paradigms. I already know how to use my mouse and my monitor.

VR Is a Medium

Despite the exciting prospect of entering exotic worlds where people across the planet engage in thrilling multi-player games, the most elevating consequence of VR is the communication power inherent in information landscapes. In Chapter 3, we discussed the merits of 3-D for user interfaces and information containment. That same density of information is intrinsic in 3-D virtual reality worlds.

Better Representation of Ideas

Virtual reality is first of all a natural interface between the human and the computer and the human and information. We experience life spatially. Have you ever taken a picture of the mountains and been a little disappointed with the representation in the picture? A 2-D image is but an echo of the 3-D experience. Representing information spatially provides more detail and visual clues. We remember the spatial locations of our favorite destinations on the Internet easier than we remember the exact Unix file directory path.

All of the information for a project can be represented in 2-D and 3-D in a virtual room providing at-a-glance status reports. Because of the density of information in that space, and the fact that 2-D items like spreadsheets, charts, and pictures are included within the 3-D space, the whole experience can be emailed to someone else rather than sent piece by piece. The person with whom we have communicated will see how the data is interrelated.

Better Communication

With shared worlds, such information can be mass communicated and collaborated on. The same technology in your copy of Virtus VRML was used to create ICE: the Interactive Collaborative Environment (see Figure 5.2). In this networked 3-D space, collaborators can bring up 3-D white boards on which they can write, paste graphics, or even show real-time data feeds in fully functional applications. 3-D objects can be dragged and dropped by remote collaborators to illustrate a point or demonstrate a new product. Collaborators can copy unlocked data by simply dragging and dropping from the shared space. This topic is discussed further in Chapter 16.

Figure 5.2:

The Interactive Collaborative Environment (ICE) was a prototype project showing how two or more users could share the same virtual space and view the same information, sounds, and graphics simultaneously.

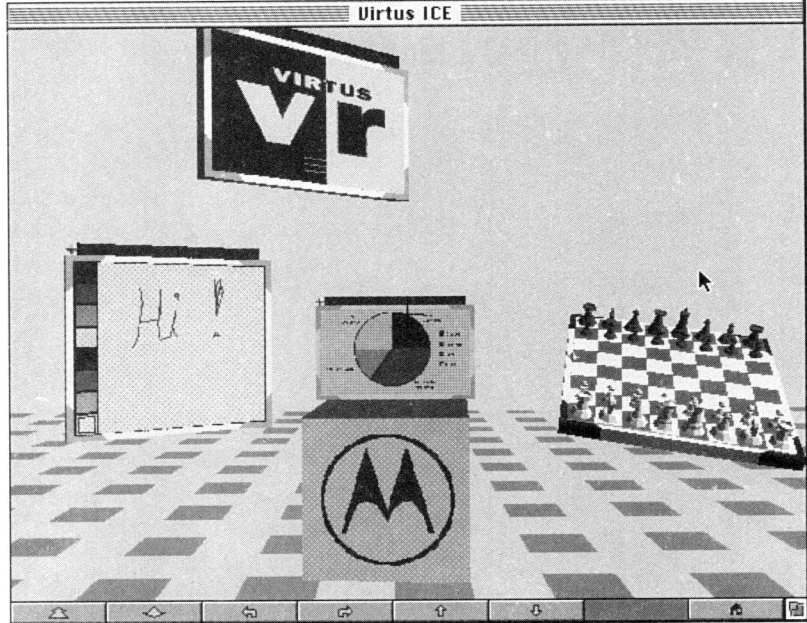

The human element is present here in live video feeds mapped to flying TV sets representing each of the collaborators as they move through the space. Because all aspects of 2-D and 3-D media are at the disposal of each participant in the conference, we truly are communicating with real-time multimedia.

Traditional window-based conferencing environments are still lacking the element of being able to show how information is interrelated through proximity, and certainly will not show the movements of all conference participants who can reveal which topics are of the greatest interest and therefore merit clicking the mouse and moseying over for a closer look. (My friends bet me I couldn't use the word "mosey" in a sentence in this book. Pay up, boys!)

Emerging Technology

The question that is cascading in rivulets of thought and just beginning to coalesce into the pool of a question in your mind is, "If 3-D virtual interfaces are so darn inevitable and good, why are there none yet?" I'm glad you asked. I had the distinct pleasure of speaking at the very last National Computer Graphics Association conference in Philadelphia at the behest of the industry-revered Dr. Joel Orr in 1993. In that year the association disbanded because it had become redundant.

In the days of DOS, computer graphics were a vision quest on the bleeding edge of computer performance. It wasn't until 1993 that people really began to have the horsepower on the low end to do more with their computers than word processing and spreadsheets on any grand scale.

Windows 3.0 and video- and image-compression standards also loosened the moorings that held us to the 1-D world of command lines. In 1995 we have finally seen machines on the low end capable of real-time 3-D display. The graphics accelerator cards mentioned earlier will also hasten this transition. We have made the journey from 1-D to 2-D and now are crossing the threshold into an inevitable world where 3-D graphics on the computer serve as our interface and our medium of choice for data communications.

Intelligence Amplification or Sensory Replacement?

One last interesting point to ponder is the growing debate about the advisability of immersing future generations in our artificial worlds. The question is just another remove from the concern regarding the alienation of our children from reality resulting from prolonged exposure to television imagery. This is a real concern and merits some discussion. As with any new technology, when creating virtual worlds we have a responsibility to pause after answering the question "Can we?" to ponder the question "Should we?"

The Duplicity of Virtual Reality

The essence of the question is that as we continue to remove ourselves from a subjective view of nature toward more abstract and objective viewpoints, are we in danger of alienating ourselves completely from the nature and humanity that makes us who we are?

Before Brunelleschi and Durer (see the following sidebar), artists were not aware of mathematical rules regarding three-point perspective. These renaissance men succeeded in reducing artistic representation of the real world to lines and mathematical constructs that consistently reproduce viewpoints realistically. The reason no one had made this observation before was because until the renaissance, people viewed the world subjectively from within it. The world was a mystical three-point perspective place of fairies, dragons, and spirits.

We have since succeeded in discovering scientific and mathematical explanations for much of the phenomena we witness. As we explain these mysteries away, our abstraction from those mysteries grows. This distance and objectivity has been very useful because it has enabled us to discover the laws that we exploited to put humans on the moon, and create computers capable of constructing artificial worlds and experiences within those worlds.

This objectivity has been very useful. But the danger, as we distance ourselves from the experience of nature through abstraction, is that we may end up creating worlds with proper three-point perspectives and mathematically accurate shading and even physical laws, but worlds that are spiritually and sensually dead. Are these the environments we want to greet the next generation?

The Origins of the Three-Point Perspective

In the fifteenth century in Florence, Italy, Filippo Brunelleschi, otherwise known for his architecture, shocked the art world by creating the first painting in true perspective. His method involved superimposing an imaginary pyramid from the eye of the artist over the scene to be painted and using the mathematical points of that pyramid to construct the objects in a painting of that space. Albrecht Durer, the German master of perspective, paid homage to these points saying they "are the beginning and end of all things."[1] From this point, we can trace the beginning of our abstraction from the natural world.

How Real Is It?

Just as the first movies were spiritually empty because they were made by the same technicians who made the cameras, so too will our virtual worlds, borne of the same well-ordered minds that created the algorithms, ring hollow, mere echoes of the experience the real world has to offer. Do we want to experience the world once or twice removed from it?

There are no easy answers to these questions. I will argue that we can do no worse than television, and may actually do better. Consider this and compare it to your own experience. When we watch video of our favorite nature shows on the Discovery channel, how intimate are we really with the reality of nature, red in tooth and claw? We have certainly seen some compelling and sometimes brutally violent footage of nature playing itself out on our 30-inch TV screens. But is our experience of those scenes sensually immersive or detached? Are we experiencing nature in the first person or the third?

The obvious answer is that with video we are detached and passive observers. The images before us are certainly photo-realistic analogs of events that are as emotionally charged as any modern human could expect to ever encounter. But we watch this while thumbing absent-mindedly through a *People* magazine. We do not feel our hearts throwing themselves against the bars of our rib cages as we strain to escape the brutal death that breathes its fetid breath on our fleeing haunches.

We do not identify with the gazelle fleeing the fangs and talons of outrageous fortune any more than we feel the biting hunger in the belly of the pursuing lioness, nor her dejected frustration when she fails to catch her prey. Our senses, because they are not immersed, are free to tell us that what we view is really 2-D. We do not have a sense of place or identification. We are free to view the emotionally charged experience with a sensual detachment.

On the other hand, when the experience we view responds to and demands our active participation, our first person perspective involvement, we are obliged to commit our senses to the experience. Even when that experience is playing itself out on a 2-D screen, if we have enough visual cues to convey that sense of place and first person perspective, our experience is much more compelling. When we play DOOM we sweat, our hearts race, and we are completely involved in the experience. Why?

Certainly our psyches are aware that we are not really in a dungeon populated with beasts who take exception to our very existence. Yet we manifest all of the symptoms of being under the physical and emotional duress that such an experience would evoke.

Pilots who have been shot down in or have crashed in flight simulators experience heart palpitations and extreme duress. Often they need counseling after the disaster[2]. The visual cues and perspective available in these immersive cockpits, even with primitive graphics, are enough to enable these pilots to suspend disbelief.

Moderation Is the Key

So virtual environments are capable of creating very real and compelling experiences analogous to real-world experiences. But should we allow them to replace real-world experience? Certainly not. Today, there is evidence that we are gaining experience in living with ambiguity. We can reconcile our subjective experience of the world with our objective detachment. This skill is a requisite for those who expect to flourish in the transition from the industrial to the information age. But whenever possible, real experience should take precedence over simulation.

Rather than trying to reproduce reality by getting hung up on ray tracing and radiosity and squeezing that last bit of realism out of our computers, we should use our minds and imaginations for what they were meant—to experience the reality around us—and use computers and virtual reality to amplify our intelligence to solve problems and view data. So, ask not how realistic your cyberspace experience will be, but ask what new insights can be gained on the human condition with these powerful new tools.

[1]Talbot, Stephen L., *The Future Does Not Compute,* O'Reilly and assoc., 1995, pg. 265.

[2]Rheingold, *Virtual Reality.*

6

The VRML Story

3-D and virtual reality provide better ways for us to communicate with each other and interact with information. If the primary purpose of the Internet is to provide communication and access to information, it seems it was a foregone conclusion that we would one day apply these paradigms to it.

It is also true that if everyone did unto others as they would have done unto them, we would have Peace on Earth. But the unfortunate reality of the human condition is that people are selfish and getting people to agree on a common good at the expense of some selfish end is difficult, if not impossible at times.

For this reason alone, if no other, everyone in the computer industry stands in awe of the sizable feat of diplomacy managed by Mark Pesce and Tony Parisi in gaining universal agreement on a 3-D standard for the World Wide Web. VRML, the virtual reality modeling language, has entered stage left to alter the course of human events for better or worse.

Agreeing on the Standard

To understand the difficulty of this achievement, we need only look at human nature and an extension of human nature—the corporation. Whether you agree completely with the tenet that human beings are naturally selfish, you must accept the fact that in a capitalistic society, corporations are not the most magnanimous entities.

They exist to provide their owners with profits and their customers advantages over competitive products as a means towards obtaining profits. In the frantically paced high-technology market, this usually means jealously guarding all proprietary technology and entering into agreements with potential competitors only as a last resort in the face of a dominating competitor.

When IBM, Motorola, and Apple met clandestinely in the Hotel De Anza in San Jose to forge the pact for the PowerPC processor, most of us initially viewed this as one of the seven signs of the Apocalypse. But in the end we understood this unnatural tete-a-tete as a necessary reaction to the domination of the x86 market by Intel.

But no such competitive pressure was present when Pesce and Parisi began to gather support for VRML. This was not a reaction to a daunting competitor in a tough market, but an act of foresight that was necessary in order to create a new market.

What made the Internet possible in the first place was its birth under the nurturing aprons of the U.S. government. Okay, so the government had its own selfish interests at heart when it created ARPAnet as a database with no central point so it could not be knocked out by a Russian atomic warhead. But what this single parent nurturing meant was that there was only one language or protocol for representing information.

VRML Trends to Follow HTTP Trends

Many compare *http* (the hypertext protocol used on the Internet) to DOS. This analogy holds up because of its 1-D interface as well as the way in which it grew. DOS became the market leading standard because it was an open proprietary standard adopted by many hardware and software developers. What has happened with HTML on the World Wide Web is that many companies (for example, Netscape) created their own proprietary flavor of browser with HTML as the core. Netscape has done an admirable job of positioning itself as a supporter of standards while it also says that it will add whatever functionality deemed necessary to improve the product even if it does not conform to the HTML specification. We can expect more of this double positioning with VRML in the future.

VRML 1.0

VRML 1.0 is a standard. Although it is the ideal starting point—it allows people to create static scenes and was "easy" to complete—it is far from a *real* Virtual Reality Modeling Language. Already we are splintering: WebFX has collision detection, VRML+ has chat & interaction, IVRML (from Chaco) is similar, and SGI is using features from Inventor.[1]

Tip If you are interested in the VRML 1.0 standard or other information on VRML's progress, visit the VRML Technical Forum at `http://vrml.wired.com/vrml.tech/`.

VRML will undoubtedly undergo many transformations over the coming years and there will be a variety of flavors, but we will all owe homage to the initial unifying force of Mark Pesce.

That Persistent Pesce

VRML is the brainchild of Mark Pesce, Anthony Parisi of Intervista software, and a host of other contributors. The full specification is public domain and available online at `http://www.vrml.com`. Mark has his own book, *VRML–Browsing and Building in Cyberspace* (New Riders Publishing, 1995), which gives a complete account of how he and pal Tony Parisi were able to gain support for the concept of a 3-D interface protocol for the Internet:

> "The ultimate goal of VRML is to model the Black Sun in Neal Stephenson's *Snow Crash*. This allows a more or less realistic environment with physics-based modeling, autonomous agents, multiuser (or shared spaces), and no excuses interaction. Hiro Protagonist can have a "real" sword fight; emotions are apparent in facial features...."
>
> —Jan Hardenbergh[2]

According to Pesce, he first approached Parisi about the idea in San Francisco on New Year's Day, 1994. The two got along famously and agreed to work together to make the dream of a 3-D Gibsonian/Stephensonian Metaversal cyberspace become reality. Parisi had just moved to the city by the bay after a stint with Lotus as a programmer for 1-2-3. Pesce is a former computer consultant and self-described technopagan. His initial impetus for wanting a 3-D interface for the Web was to come closer to realizing his dream of viewing the entire Earth in 3-D on the Internet.

First International Conference on the World Wide Web

Before going to the First International Conference on the World Wide Web in Switzerland in the Summer of 1994, Pesce and Parisi hacked out a prototype called Labyrinth that worked within Mosaic. It called up a 3-D banana and allowed them to flip back and forth from the 3-D banana space to other 2-D Web pages. Pesce's first act of diplomacy after recruiting Parisi was to convince Servan Seondjian and Kate Seekings of Rendermorphics to allow him to use their Rendermorphics Reality lab 3-D API (now owned by Microsoft) free to create the 3-D interface.

At the conference, Mark and a core group of enthusiasts who were instilled with the Black Sun and Metaverse vision met in a BOF (Birds of a Feather) confab that produced the nucleus around which VRML would be born. Pesce actually credits David Raggett with coining the phrase "virtual reality mark-up language" or VRML, although "mark-up" was later changed to the more appropriate "modeling."

Although **VRML** now stands for "virtual reality modeling language," the original description, adopted by the creators at the first International Conference of the World Wide Web, was "virtual reality mark-up language."

Encouraged by the enthusiastic response at the conference, Pesce and Parisi set up a Web page and a list server asking for help in defining the VRML standard. According to Pesce, they had more than two thousand subscribers the first week. You can visit this site today for the latest scoop at `http://vrml.wired.com`.

Open Inventor File Format Adopted

With these humble beginnings, VRML was born. Things accelerated quite a bit when Rikk Carey, Paul Strauss, and Gavin Bell of Silicon Graphics generously offered their Open Inventor file format to serve as the nucleus for the budding standard. In his book, Mark expresses his astonishment at the charity of SGI in allowing its proprietary format to be published in the public domain:

> "The Web community is a community committed to open standards. We could not adopt a standard owned by any company. SGI had to be committed to putting Open Inventor's file format into the public domain, without restriction, so that the Web community could build upon it, free from the fear of lawsuits or royalties. The folks at SGI understood this. They wanted to see Open Inventor, even as VRML, succeed."[3]
>
> —Mark Pesce

In the same chapter, he acknowledges that as a result of making Open Inventor the nucleus around which VRML could grow, "SGI would make a lot of hardware sales, and that SGI would have the inside track on VRML development."[4] Once again we are forced to acknowledge that the corporation leopard is not likely to change its spots for stripes, even though it may don them for public appearances. The "open standard" file format for VRML is in fact provided mostly by one company—SGI. And it is SGI who stands to gain the most from widespread adoption of the format.

> "If we don't agree on standards now, VRML will inevitably begin to fragment into a horde of competing specifications. The lack of unity, all too common in the VR and graphics industries, is anathema in networking. There would be no Internet, no Web, and no cyberspace."
>
> —Mark Pesce, *Scale: A White Paper submitted to the VRML Futures Planning Meeting,* August 19, 1995. [This and other

VRML white papers can be found at `http://`
`vrml.wired.com/future`].

This is not unlike the position that Microsoft enjoyed when Microsoft DOS began shipping with every IBM-compatible machine. At the time it was very useful for the industry to adopt standards in order for it to grow. Microsoft's gain was a gain for all of us. The same is true for 3-D on the Internet. Without everyone agreeing on a standard, growth will be slow.

Today Microsoft controls the operating system for the majority of computers on the planet. Will Silicon Graphics control cyberspace in the future?

Beyond VRML 1.0

The VRML 1.0 specification is public domain information and is available online at `http://www.vrml.com`. Although the spec serves as a dramatic stride in the direction of information landscapes, there is still much to be done. The thorny issue of interactivity was bypassed in this spec as were issues of efficient 3-D database handling. (When you have a $100,000 Silicon Graphics workstation, who needs to worry about efficiency?)

- Interactivity includes objects that move and buttons that attach to other items within the environment as well as rudimentary physics that allow us to pick up an object and throw it.

- 3-D database handling includes issues such as not drawing rooms or objects that aren't being looked at by the observer. Right now VRML wastes cycles by drawing all of the geometry, even when the observer is not concerned with it at that time. Why draw all of the buildings of New York City when the observer is in the subway? This efficient database handling feature is part of Virtus VRML and Virtus Voyager. When dealing with 3-D databases on the Internet, little things mean a lot.

These issues are being addressed in the current effort toward a 2.0 version, but as discussed previously, most companies aren't waiting around and are trying to get a jump on the competition with their own improvements to VRML. The flag has dropped, may the best horse win.

Summary

The fairly recent phenomenon of VRML has done a wonderful job of rallying everyone to the cause that Stephenson and Gibson first raised more than a decade ago. In addition to creating a format such that anyone can now program a VRML browser (another reason for them to be free), Pesce's efforts have instilled in the hearts and minds of a generation of 'cybersurfers' the dream of information landscapes.

This dream will take many forms as a host of companies scamper to the cause rattling the sabres of their new technologies. Although there is some promise that these diverging development efforts may be woven back into future VRML specs (3.0?), they will almost certainly create some incompatibility problems among tools and browsers in the short run. But beneath it all will lie the bedrock of VRML, and eventually one standard will emerge from these pioneering efforts.

It's nice to dream, but even nicer to have a hand in making dreams come true. Enter stage right the *Virtus VRML Toolkit.*

In Part II, we don our virtual hard hats and set about the business of creating some unreal estate for the information landscapes of the future. Ladies and gentlemen, please turn the page and boot your computers.

Information on current and future specs for VRML is located at `http://vrml.wired.com/vrml.tech/`.

[1]White Paper for VRML 1.x/2.0 18-AUG-95, YON—Jan C. Hardenbergh—jch@oki.com

[2]Ibid.

[3]Pesce, Mark, *VRML–Browsing and Building Cyberspace*, pg. 36, New Riders Publishing, 1995

[4]Ibid.

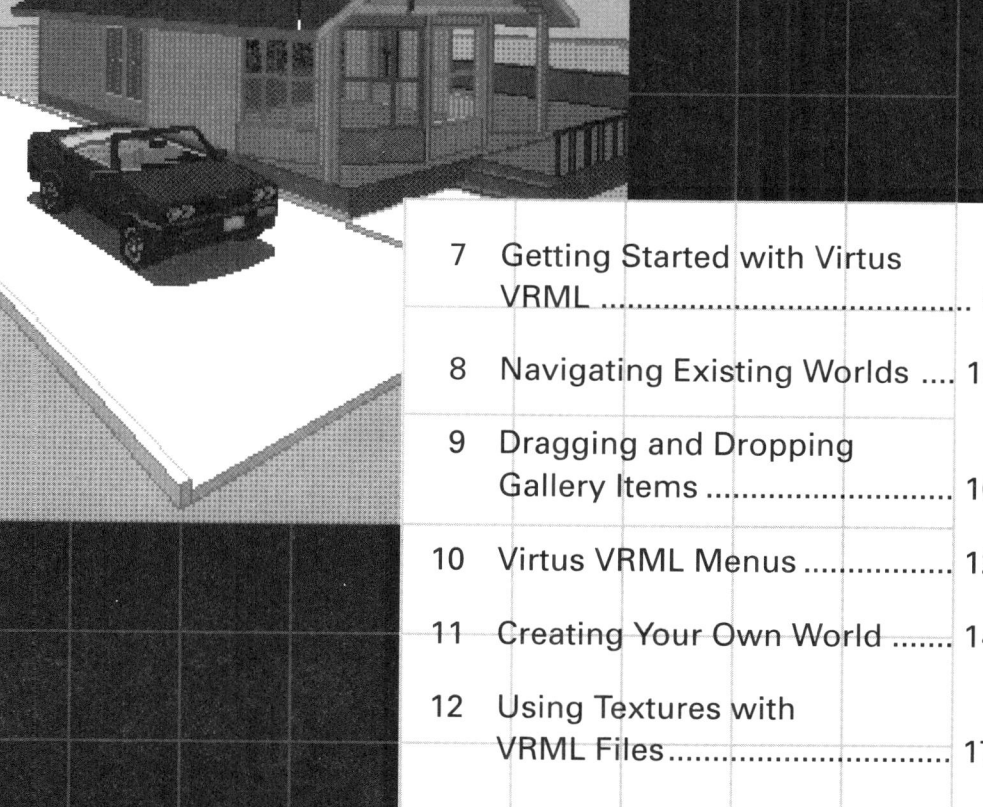

Constructing
VRML Worlds

Part II

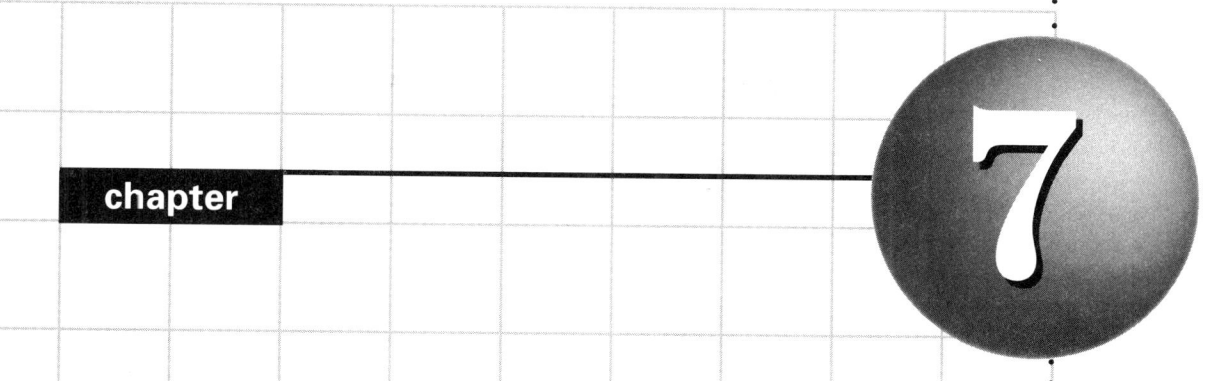

Getting Started with Virtus VRML

Now that you have a draconian background in the Zen of VRML, it's time to learn how to create these worlds for the Internet. The VRML language was developed to give visual interaction with multi-participants online and to give you the ability to hyperlink objects to other worlds or to HTML documents or other **MIME** (Multipurpose Internet Mail Extensions) types. VRML 1.0 allows for the creation of worlds with limited interactive behavior. Your level of control in the world may largely depend on the features of the VRML browser that you use, instead of the features you include in using your world-building software.

CD-ROM

Virtus Voyager is a VRML browser (included on your CD) that will enable you to view these great 3-D worlds that you and others will create. It is available for Macintosh, Windows 3.1, and Windows 95. If your version does not appear on the CD, you can download it from the Virtus home page at http://www.virtus.com.

With Virtus VRML, you can build worlds and create hyperlinks (using URLs) from your 3-D environment to a "2-D" browser (like Netscape or Mosaic). When you select a link to a VRML document from within a correctly configured WWW browser, a VRML viewer is launched, a VRML file string is downloaded, and the user has the experience of walking around in your model.

Virtus VRML is a unique 3-D modeling program that features a "drag-and-drop" approach to creating your own worlds for the Internet or just for your own computer. You don't have to build anything from scratch; to construct complex objects and structures, you just drag basic 3-D shapes from the program's object galleries and drop them into a 2-D design window. You may edit an object's shape, size and color; add textures (clouds, grass, carpet, wood, tile and more) and surface features (windows and doors, for example), and combine the object with other objects.

Immediately, any addition or change is rendered in a companion 3-D walk window where you can roam through and explore your model by navigating with your mouse. Despite the fact that your model might look great on your system, you'll have to do some testing to see whether the textures and the level of detail that you have given your model can be handled by your VRML browser.

Virtus VRML features one cubic mile of "cyberspace" in which to design, a set of construction tools, and various navigation techniques. Despite the fact that you have such a large construction area, until the day when we all have CableCom connections into our home or office, you will have to limit the size of your model. Limit it to what? Well, that's a tough question, but usually limiting a VRML space to one to three connecting rooms is all that can be handled for now. (Of course, we all know that as soon as this is in writing, I will be eating my words and you will be able to construct a model with a cozillion polygons with no problem.)

Know Your Audience

Never has the term, "know your audience" been more appropriate than when working on a project like this for the Internet. As when working with HTML documents, you have, no doubt, created a very clever Web page on your home or work system, only to see it displayed as a dismal concoction of pixels on someone else's system across town. Because displays and processors vary so much, and also because VRML is not exactly a speed demon, you have to be judicious with polygons when building a world that you want others to enjoy.

CD-ROM

Also included with your program on the CD are numerous galleries of 2-D surface features and textures, and 3-D objects that can be added to your Virtus VRML worlds. As well, two additional galleries, the Archaeology Gallery (just like it sounds) and the Home Remodeling Gallery (a collection of lots of home stuff) and pre-built "scenes" that illustrate the program's modeling, texture mapping, and real-time "walk through" capabilities that are provided on the CD.

Virtus VRML Galleries

Our growing collection of Virtus Galleries, sold separately from the Virtus VRML application, are extremely useful because they provide many pre-constructed 3-D objects and scenes that you can use in building your own models—whether it's an object or an entire room. Virtus Galleries are also compatible for use with Virtus WalkThrough Pro and the whole family of Virtus products.

The great thing about using galleries (either ours or yours) is that you don't have to start from scratch when you begin modeling. You can cut your design time drastically by using either rooms or objects that are already created. After you get up and running, you should be able to create a simple room and assign URLs in about five minutes by using the included galleries. Of course, if you'd like, you can add more detail to that model later without destroying the original design or the designated links to it. To date, Virtus gallery topics also include Home Remodeling, Interior Design, Office Design, and Science Fiction. Several more galleries are in the works.

Virtus WalkThrough Pro

Virtus WalkThrough Pro (v. 2.5+) is a professional-level 3-D visualization software with advanced modeling tools, advanced control editors, enhanced texture-mapping, industry-specific controls, and multiple file import/export formats. It is fully compatible with Virtus VRML files. For upgrade information contact Virtus Corporation, Sales Division: 1-800-847-8871.

Macintosh and Windows Documentation

Virtus VRML should be successfully installed on your computer before you begin. If you have installation questions, please refer to the Installation information in Appendix C at the end of this book.

This document is designed for both Macintosh and Windows users with basic operating knowledge of one platform or the other. Most of the features of Virtus VRML are identical in both the Macintosh and Windows versions. The differences are noted where there are slight variations; when dialog boxes or interfaces are significantly different, both versions are shown.

Overview

You're going to be able to create a world very quickly using this product, so you won't have to spend long hours reading manuals. It will, however, help to read through this part to understand how all of the windows work together. There are lots of little tricks that I throw in along the way and it's hard to get those if you don't read them.

Document Windows

There are three windows in Virtus VRML: Gallery window, Walk View window, and Design View window. Descriptions of these windows and a discussion of their functions follow. Figure 7.1 shows the basic interface.

Gallery Window

The Gallery window displays the 3-D library objects that you drag and drop to create your virtual environment. The gallery of objects can be changed by clicking the title button near the top of the window and selecting another gallery. Each item may be rotated in the Preview Area at the bottom of the Gallery window so that you can view it in more detail.

Walk View Window

The Walk View window is where you see and interact with the 3-D virtual environment that you create. Gallery objects that you drag and drop into the Design View are displayed in 3-D in the Walk View. You can navigate in, around, or through these objects using the navigation buttons at the bottom or the mouse cursor.

Note

Using the mouse cursor to navigate is what we call Virtus Standard Navigation, so if you want to be like the seasoned professionals, use that technique.

Figure 7.1:
Virtus VRML interface.

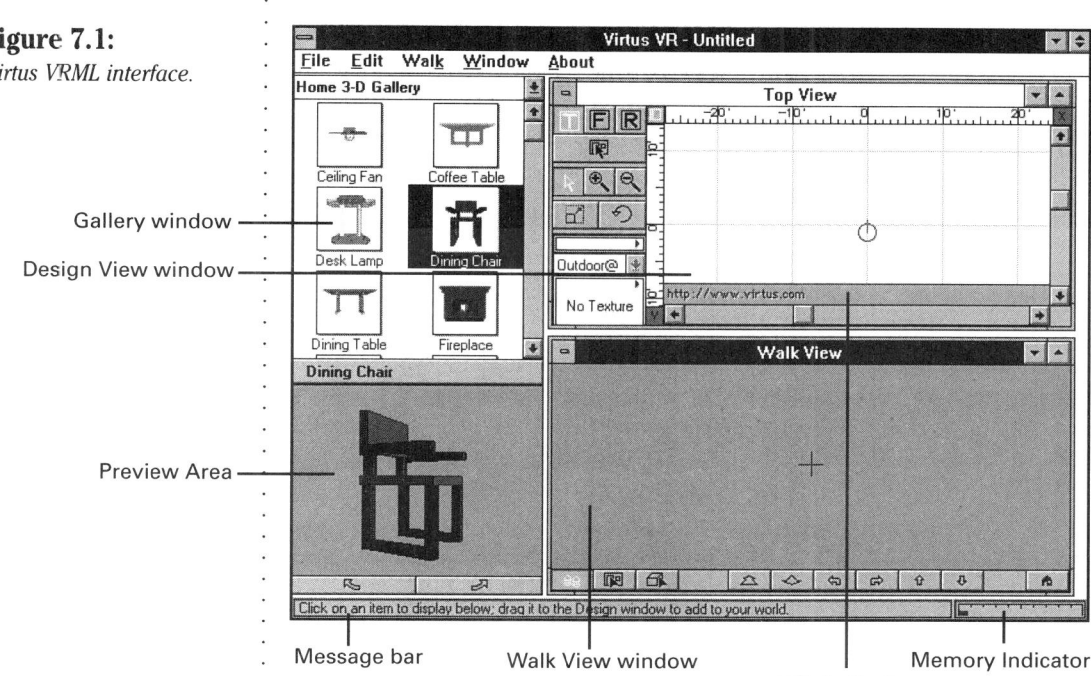

Gallery window

Design View window

Preview Area

Message bar   Walk View window

URL Indicator

Memory Indicator

Message Bar

A Message bar is displayed at the bottom of your computer screen. Within the Message bar, you see information associated with the operations that you perform. For example, if you select a particular tool in the Tools pad, the Message bar will display the tool's purpose and how the tool is used.

URL Indicator

An URL Indicator is located at the bottom of Design View that displays the address of a linked document or model. After you select an object in the Design View, you may type in the cell or paste an address to an HTML document, a valid MIME, or to another VRML file. After you have assigned an object an URL, if you place the cursor over that object, the URL address will display in the URL Indicator panel.

Memory Indicator

There is a memory indicator to the right of the Message Bar, at the lower right corner of your screen. It contains a colored bar that alternately shrinks and grows, displaying the amount of memory currently available to Virtus VRML. If the memory is below 75 percent, the bar is blue; if not, it is red.

Macintosh users, if you are running low on memory, try quitting the application and allocating more RAM to Virtus VRML. Remember you can use Virtual Memory if you are running low....

Active Window

The active window is the window in which you are working. The Gallery window is always active, that is, you can always select objects and press buttons within the Gallery window. The Design View and the Walk View windows are not always active. If you are working in the Design View, it is the active window. If you are working in the Walk View, it is the active window. Either the Design View is active or the Walk View is active. A window can be made active by clicking anywhere in or on the window.

An active window is distinguished by horizontal lines in the title bar (Macintosh) or a highlighted title bar (Windows). The title bar is at the top of a window.

If a window is not active, its buttons and tools are grayed and not selectable.

Adjusting a Window

All windows may be moved and resized. The Design View and the Walk View windows can be adjusted horizontally and vertically. (See your computer documentation for standard Macintosh and Windows operating system procedures regarding windows.)

Tools Pad

Within the Design View is the Tools pad. The Tools pad displays the tools that you use to edit objects and object surfaces as well as buttons that you use to change the Design View. Figure 7.2 shows the Tools pad.

Figure 7.2:

Virtus VRML Tools pad.

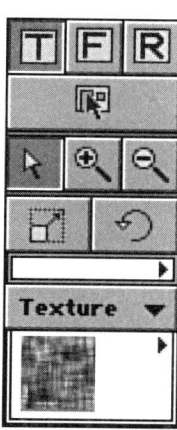

View Selector Buttons

The Tools pad buttons: T is the Top View, F is the Front View, and R is the Right View. Clicking one of these buttons changes the Design View perspective.

Surface Editor Tool

The Surface Editor Tool opens the Surface Editor, which allows you to edit a selected surface. A surface is a single side or face of an object.

Select Object Tool

The Select Object Tool is used to select objects to be edited. With the Select Object Tool, you point to an object and click it to select it. A selected object displays handles at its **vertices**. A selected object with handles is illustrated in Figure 7.3.

A **vertex** is where two object surfaces, or faces, meet.

Figure 7.3:
A selected object displays handles (black squares) at its vertices.

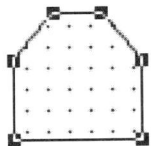

Magnify Tool

The Magnify Tool increases the apparent scale of the Design View. If you select the Magnify Tool by clicking it once, and then point to the area that you wish to zoom toward and click, the apparent scale of the Design View doubles.

Zoom-Out Tool

The Zoom-Out Tool decreases the apparent scale of the Design View. If you select the Zoom-Out Tool by clicking it once, and then point to the area that you wish to zoom away from and click, the apparent scale of the Design View decreases by a factor of two.

Resize Object Tool

The Resize Object Tool resizes an object about its center or about a specified anchor point. Objects can be resized uniformly along all three axes or non-uniformly along a single axis.

Rotate Object Tool

The Rotate Object Tool is used to rotate an object. This tool works in any view (Top, Front, Right), allowing rotation on more than one axis.

Color Bar

The Color Bar allows new colors to be selected, created, and assigned to objects. You can select from many color variations.

Texture Bar

The Texture Bar allows you to apply textures to objects.

Texture Button

The Texture button appears at the top of the Texture bar; the arrow indicates that a drop-down list appears when you click it. When pressed, the button displays a list of Texture Palettes.

3-D Movement

Movement in the Walk View is accomplished by using the standard Virtus navigation cursor techniques (shown in Figure 7.4) or the Navigation buttons along the bottom of the Walk View (see Figure 7.7). Figures 7.5 and 7.6 show the advanced navigation modes for Macintosh and for Windows, respectively.

Figure 7.4:

Normal Mode navigation.

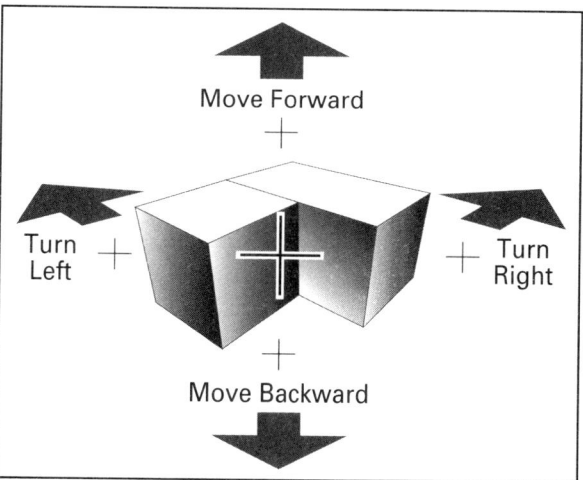

Standard Virtus Navigation

Movement through the Walk View is a response to your movement of the mouse pointer relative to the crosshair in the center of the Walk View screen. It takes a little practice to get the hand-eye coordination right, but after you master it, you'll have the ability to walk anywhere and look anywhere in your world.

Press the mouse button to begin movement and release the mouse button to stop.

Figure 7.5:
Advanced Macintosh navigation.

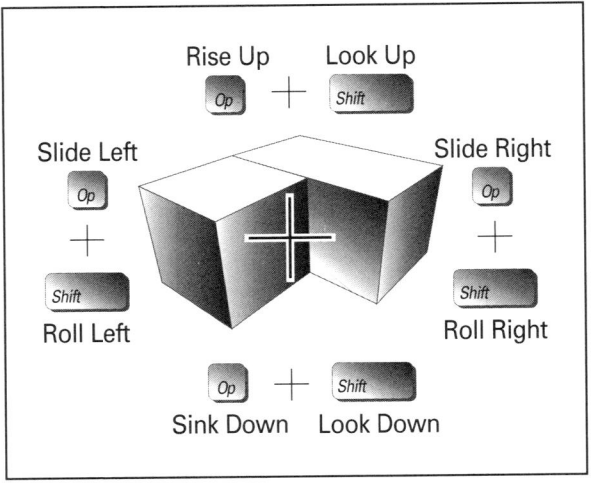

Figure 7.6:
Advanced Windows navigation.

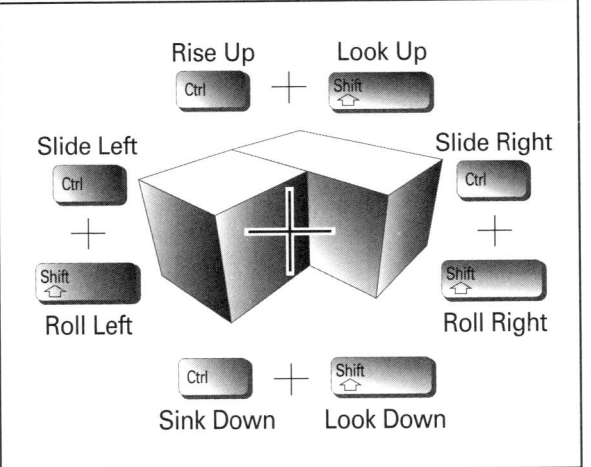

The farther away from the crosshair the cursor is positioned, the faster the walk speed is.

Direction is determined by the position of the pointer relative to the crosshair, as illustrated in Figure 7.7.

Figure 7.7:

Direction is determined by the position of the pointer relative to the crosshair.

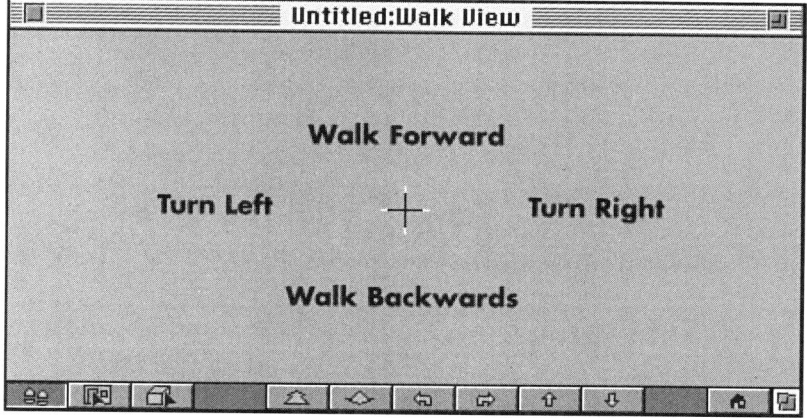

By using a combination of the Ctrl and Shift keys plus the Option key (Macintosh) or Ctrl key (Windows) with the mouse, movements like tilting your head, sliding from side to side, or increasing and decreasing your altitude are also possible. These key combinations are also illustrated.

Navigation Buttons

The Navigation buttons (shown in Figure 7.8) are always active when the Walk View is active. By pointing to a Navigation button and clicking, you move in a direction according to the button's function. If you hold down the mouse button while pointing to a Navigation button, you move continuously.

Figure 7.8:

Navigation buttons are located along the bottom of the Walk View.

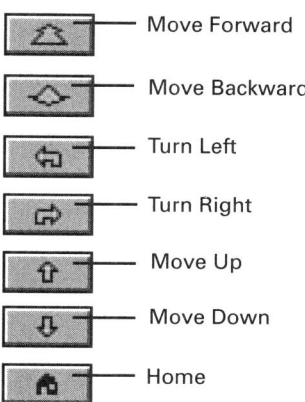

The exception to holding down the mouse button and moving continuously is the Home button. This button needs to be clicked only once to perform its function. When you click the Home button, your position in the virtual environment is returned to the 0,0,5.25 feet coordinate (about eye level).

Walk Mode Buttons

The Walk Mode buttons are displayed to the left of the Navigation buttons along the bottom of the Walk View. The Walk Mode buttons determine what happens when you click with the mouse cursor in the Walk View.

The Walk Mode buttons from left to right are Walk, Select Surface, and Select Object. Only one Walk Mode button can be selected at any time.

If the Walk button is selected, the mouse cursor functions like the Navigation buttons, depending on where you position the cursor around the crosshair in the Walk View.

If the Select Surface button is selected, the mouse cursor will select a surface of an object that you click and open the Surface Editor within the Design View.

If the Select Object button is selected, any object that you click with the mouse cursor in the Walk View appears in the center of the Design View.

Walk Button

When the Walk button (shown at left) is pressed, you can move freely around the Virtus VRML world using either the Walk Mode buttons or the standard Virtus navigation techniques.

If you use either the Select Surface button or the Select Object button, you must then select the Walk button again before navigation (walking) is enabled.

3-D Surface Selector Button

The 3-D Surface Selector button (at left) allows you to quickly access a surface in the Walk View to edit; you can change the surface's color or texture, or add surface features such as doors, windows, or a painting on the wall.

3-D Object Selector Button

The 3-D Select Object button (at left) allows you to select an object in the 3-D Walk View and have it become highlighted and centered so that you can edit it in the 2-D Design View. This is extremely useful when you are working on a complex drawing and cannot select the correct object in the Design View because another object is blocking it. (Another way around this is to change views to the Front View or Right View, select the object, and then return to the Top View to move or edit the object.)

Figure 7.9 shows the Surface Editor. After selecting the 3-D Surface Selector button and clicking the front gable of the roof, the gable's surface was selected and displayed in the Surface Editor. Now the color of the surface can be changed or textures can be added.

Figure 7.9:

Editing surfaces and textures.

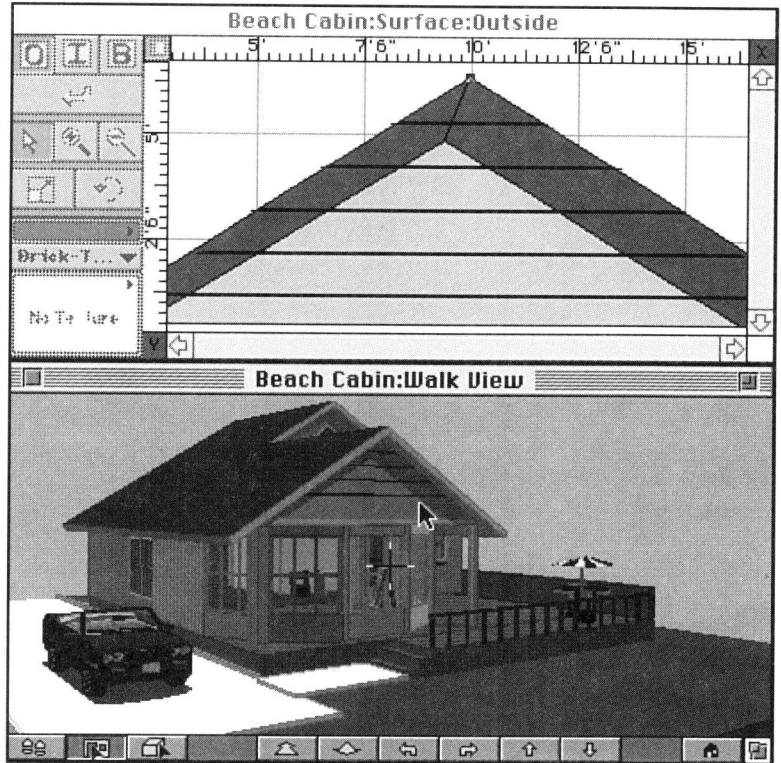

Observer

The Observer (at left) represents your location in the virtual environment. The Observer is represented by a circle with a line. You can move the Observer in the Design View by clicking and dragging it with the screen cursor. To change the view of the Observer, hold down the Option key (Macintosh) or Control key (Windows) and point to the center of the Observer; then drag to a new direction.

Also, you may adjust the point of view of the Observer (the direction the Observer's eyes are looking) by holding down the Option key (Macintosh) or the Control key (Windows), and then pointing to the center of the Observer and dragging in the direction that you wish to view. Figure 7.10 shows this action in process.

Figure 7.10:
Adjusting the point of view of the Observer.

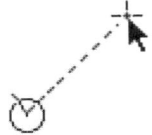

Design Concepts

The following design concepts are discussed in this section:

- ■ Containment
- ■ Auto Connection
- ■ Placement Depth

The following design concepts are actually the most fundamental features of the program. The property of containment is important because objects that you create must occupy only *one space* at a time; that is, a sofa cannot be inside of the house and outside at the same time (you can actually do this, but you're not suppose to...).

Auto connection is an invisible feature that allows you to *push* two objects together (with parallel surfaces) and have them magnetically attach to each other. This attachment allows for doors, windows, and so on, to be used as "shared" features.

Placement depth is the concept that every object that you drop into your world will go automatically to ground zero (0). That is, everything goes to the lowest point and you must move the object up manually (in the Front or Right Views) to see it elevated.

Containment

Every object in Virtus VRML knows what objects it contains and what object contains it. **Containment** provides some important benefits. For example, if you move a container, all objects contained within it also move and retain their orientation to each other.

Containment is a property that objects must occupy only *one space* at a time (as opposed to an object overlapping another) or all objects that are contained in one space must be wholly contained.

In Virtus VRML, containment is an all-or-none state; an object is either fully contained within another object or it is distinct from other objects. Objects cannot overlap (but they can be joined at a common surface). It is possible to draw overlapping objects and unfortunately the program does not warn you if you do this; however, the result of overlapping objects is that three-dimensional objects may appear twisted when rendered in the Walk View.

If you drag a small object into a larger object, a state of containment will exist when the mouse pointer reaches the interior of the large object. The program indicates containment by displaying small blocks called containment markers at the vertices of the containing object. These markers disappear when you release the mouse button.

Figure 7.11 shows containment markers displayed while a small object is being dragged into a larger object; the corners of the larger object change into containment markers so that you know when an object is wholly contained inside of another.

Figure 7.11:
A smaller object is being dragged into a larger object.

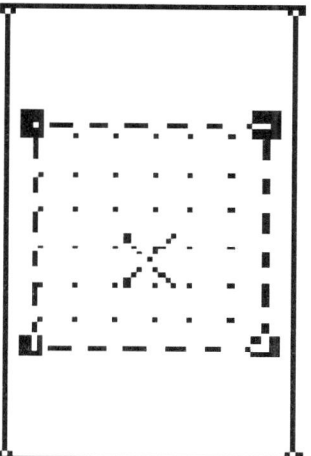

Auto Connection

Virtus VRML uses **auto connection** to make an adjacent surface share the
surface attributes of a current one. For example, if you drag two objects
(such as rooms) toward each other, the auto connection feature attaches
the two parallel surfaces when they touch. Any surface feature or surface
attribute, including textures, can be shared between adjacent surfaces
with the auto connection capability of Virtus VRML. Figure 7.12 illustrates
this concept.

Figure 7.12:

*Two objects connect
automatically when you
move one closer to the
other and then release.
Now their parallel sur-
faces (walls) can be
shared.*

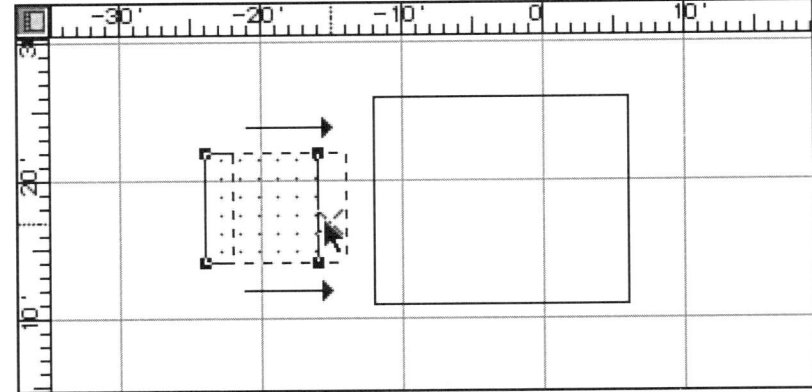

Placement Depth

When you drag and drop an object into the Design View, it automatically
drops to 0 feet in the dimension that you cannot see. For example, if you
drop an object in the Top View, you can position it anywhere in the Top
View by dragging. But change to the Front View and you will see that the
lowest point of the object is at 0 feet. What if you wanted the object to be
10 feet off the ground? You would change views to the Front View and
manually drag the object up to 10 feet, using the Select Object Tool. This
is how you stack objects on top of each other (for example, a lamp on a
desk, a roof on a building).

Because the Design View is two-dimensional, you can see only two dimensions at a time; you will find that you must often change views to position
objects as desired. After you do this a few times, it will become second
nature to you. Figure 7.13 illustrates placement depth.

Figure 7.13:

Change to the Front View (F) to move an object up or down.

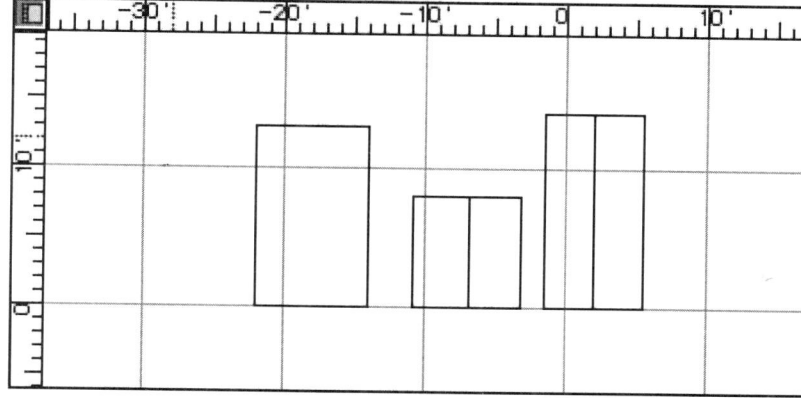

Summary

These are the basics that you need to know in order to begin creating your world for the World Wide Web. All of these are very important, especially the concepts of containment, automatic connection, and placement depth. After you have those down, you're just about ready.

In the next chapter, you learn all the ways to navigate in the Virtus VRML world and how you'll navigate later when you create worlds for the Internet.

8

Navigating Existing Worlds

Before you begin creating your own 3-D space, let's take a look at some of the models that have already been created and get the feel of how to navigate. As well, you'll be able to understand how models are created by looking at examples of others. You can do this from your local machine (computer) instead of jumping out onto the Net for now.

In this chapter, you learn:

- How to open an existing file and walk around in it.

- Standard Virtus navigation techniques.

- Novice Mode navigation techniques.

- Playing a recorded path using a model.

- How to use existing files and galleries to save valuable design time.

If you haven't already installed the program, follow the instructions in Appendix A to install the software on your hard disk. Launch the application by double-clicking the application icon.

Opening an Existing File

To open an existing model, choose Open in the File menu and use the standard Macintosh or Windows Open dialog to select the Virtus VRML file that you want to open (review Figure 7.1 for the opening screen).

For this example, navigate to the Scenes folder and open the file: **House Squared** (Macintosh) or **housesq.vvr** (Windows). After the file opens it should appear something like what you see in Figure 8.1.

Figure 8.1:
House Squared interface.

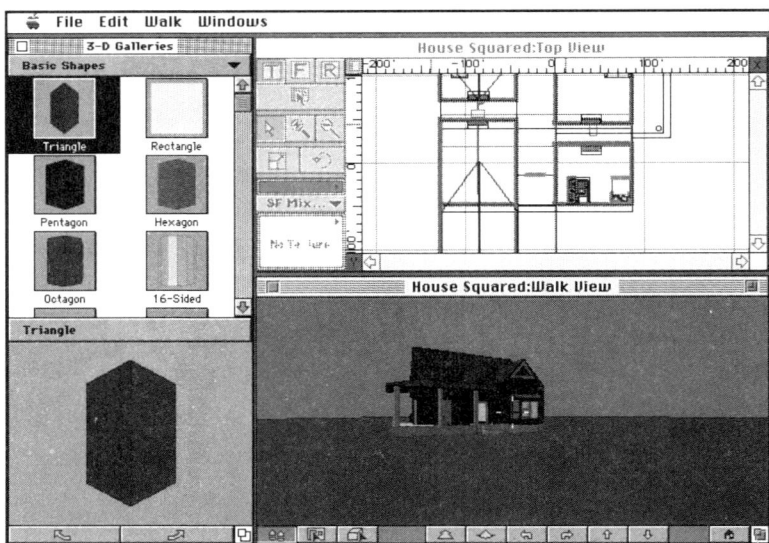

From the Walk menu, select Wide Angle. This will change the apparent Walk view from a standard lens (like a 35mm camera lens) to a wider view so that you can see more. Figure 8.2 shows the Walk menu.

Figure 8.2:
*Walk menu with Wide
Angle checked.*

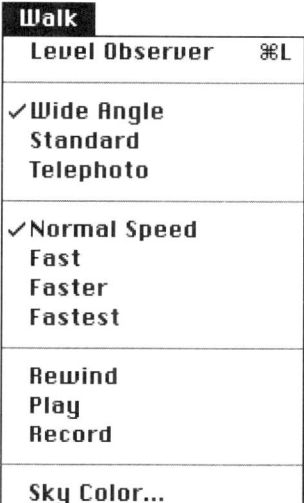

3-D Movement

To begin navigating or walking around in this model, you have two choices. You may either use the row of Novice Mode navigation buttons along the bottom of the Walk View or use the more preferred standard Virtus navigation technique, which I explain in the following sections.

Novice Mode Navigation

The Navigation buttons are always active when the Walk View is active. By pointing to a Navigation button and clicking, you move in a direction according to the button's function. If you hold down the mouse button while pointing to a Navigation button, you move continuously.

From left to right along the bottom of the Walk View, the Navigation buttons are Move Forward, Move Backward, Turn Left, Turn Right, Move Up, Move Down, and Home. These buttons are illustrated in Figure 8.3.

Figure 8.3:
Novice Mode navigation buttons.

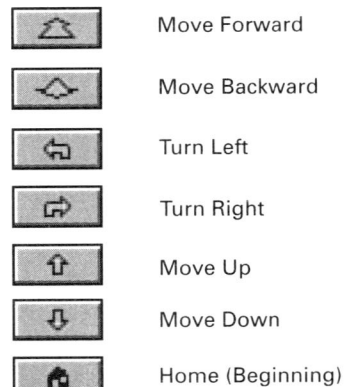

Move Forward

Move Backward

Turn Left

Turn Right

Move Up

Move Down

Home (Beginning)

The exception to holding down the mouse button and moving continuously is the Home button (shown in the margin). This button needs to be clicked only once to perform its function. When you click the Home button, your position in the virtual environment is returned to the 0,0,5.25 feet coordinate (about eye level).

Standard Virtus Navigation

Movement through the Walk View is a response to your clicking the mouse in a position relative to the crosshair in the center of the Walk View screen. It takes a little practice to get the hand-eye coordination right, but after you master it, you'll have the ability to walk anywhere and look anywhere in your world. Figure 8.4 shows the Normal Mode navigation keys.

Figure 8.4:
Normal Mode navigation keys.

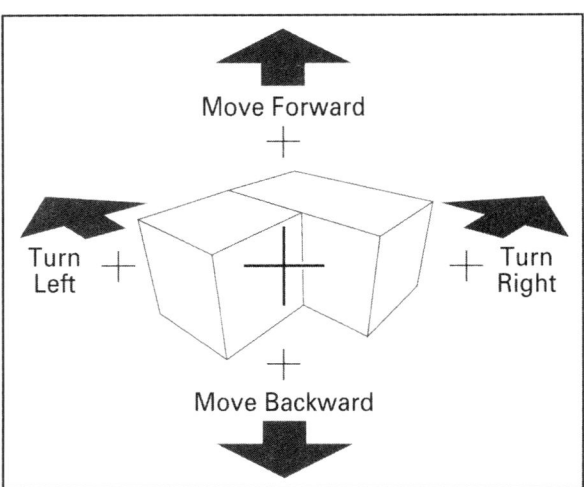

Click the mouse button when the pointer is near the crosshair to begin movement and release the mouse button to stop. Clicking the mouse button to the right of the crosshair moves your view right; clicking the mouse button to the left of the crosshair moves your view left. Clicking above the crosshair moves the scene closer, and clicking below the crosshair moves the scene farther away. Of course, you can move in many different directions by clicking in any direction around the crosshair—for example, below and to the right a bit moves you farther away and right.

Tip

The farther away from the crosshair the cursor is positioned, the faster the walk speed is.

Remember from Chapter 7 that direction is determined by the position of the pointer relative to the crosshair.

By using a combination of the Shift keys plus the Option key (Macintosh) or Ctrl key (Windows) with the mouse, movements like tilting your head, sliding from side to side, or increasing and decreasing your altitude are also possible. These key combinations are also illustrated in Figures 8.5 and 8.6.

Figure 8.5:
Advanced Macintosh navigation.

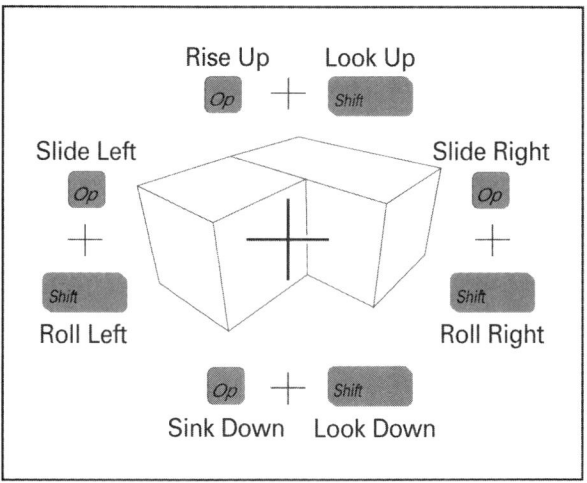

Figure 8.6:

Advanced Windows navigation.

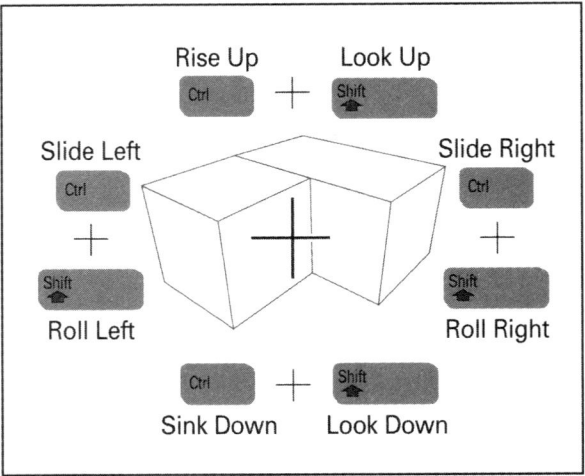

Practice a little with this model using both of these navigational techniques. You decide which is more convenient for you, although I push you to use the standard Virtus technique (with the mouse), because it is really quicker.

Playing a Recorded Path

Now that you've experimented with your new "walk skills," lets play a recorded path that the creator of the file made when it was built:

1. From the Walk menu, select Play (try this, for instance, with the House Squared scene).

2. To stop playing, click anywhere in the Walk View screen. Figure 8.7 shows the Walk menu in Play mode.

The recorded path will begin to play and you will now get to see what the 3-D artist *intended* for you to see. That's important because, in the House Squared scene, you might miss the fact that there is actually another miniature house in the back bedroom of this larger house! So the recorded path is important for that reason, but having the ability to walk around by yourself is equally or more important. Maybe you want to see the back area or another view of the model that you would be unable to see in a linear playback mode like a Windows FLC file or a QuickTime movie.

Figure 8.7:
Selecting Play from the Walk menu begins automatic movement through the scene.

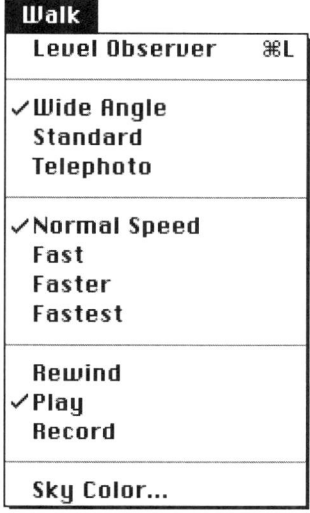

Walk
Level Observer   ⌘L
✓ **Wide Angle**
Standard
Telephoto
✓ **Normal Speed**
Fast
Faster
Fastest
Rewind
✓ **Play**
Record
Sky Color...

If you ever get really lost or lose your altitude while walking, select the Home button to reorient yourself.

Open up a couple of more scenes and try moving around them using the standard Virtus navigational technique. Also, make sure you practice the advanced navigational techniques so that you can tilt your head up and down and rise up and down.

Use Existing Gallery Items

An important consideration when building your 3-D worlds is to use existing items in the galleries before building something yourself. Why spend the design time to build a special chair if the chair is already available in a model that you saw? Or why build a certain living room when you can copy the room (with all of its furnishings) and then paste it into your model? We haven't really started talking about constructing worlds yet, but keep in mind that anything that you see in these sample files, you can use in your world.

Summary

Now you are an expert in navigating in and around your Virtus VRML scenes and have an understanding of several different ways that you can do it. It *does* take a little practice to really become proficient, so don't feel badly if your hand-eye coordination needs a little work. A good way to practice is to have a file with only one simple box in it and practice walking up to it, around the side of it, flying over it, flying under it, walking inside of it, and turning around and around.

In Chapter 9, you learn how you can save valuable time (like we have all the time in the world to read books...) using pre-created models, scenes, and objects contained in Virtus Galleries. Start dragging.

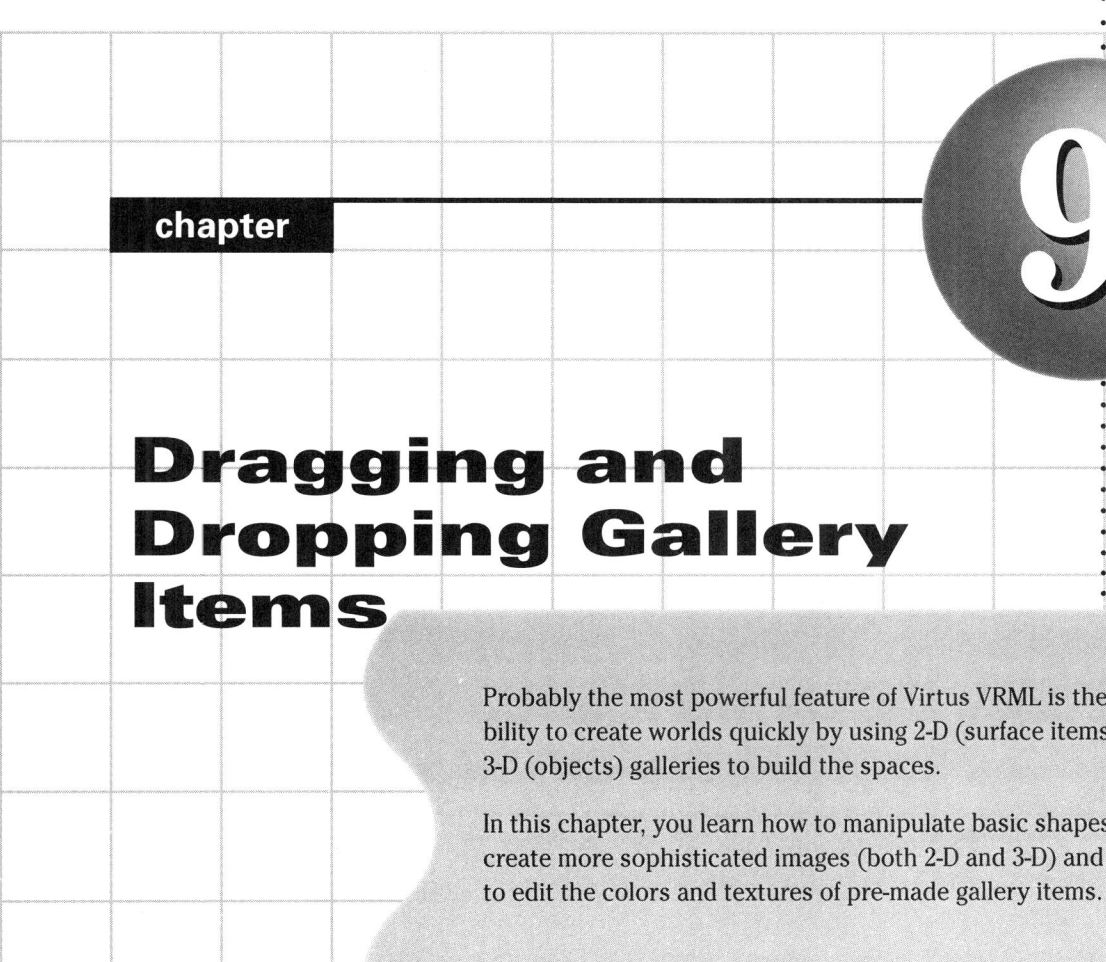

Dragging and Dropping Gallery Items

Probably the most powerful feature of Virtus VRML is the capability to create worlds quickly by using 2-D (surface items) and 3-D (objects) galleries to build the spaces.

In this chapter, you learn how to manipulate basic shapes to create more sophisticated images (both 2-D and 3-D) and how to edit the colors and textures of pre-made gallery items.

As a default, you will notice that the window on the left side of the screen is the galleries window and loads with a simple polygon gallery called Basic Shapes. This is a selection of cubes, cylinders, pyramids, triangles, pentagons, and so on that represents at least one simple building-block shape available to you to simply drag and drop into the Design View. Many more complex galleries are available to you that will later increase your ability to design quickly. These galleries are located on the CD in the 3-D Galleries folder. They all load automatically at startup.

If your version of Virtus VRML doesn't load the Basic Shapes gallery, you have the item deselected in the Window menu as a default.

Manipulating Basic Shapes

To begin creating, you have to have some 3-D objects. Luckily for you, the default galleries window loads with the Basic Shapes gallery—a collection of 3-D objects just for this purpose. This is a group of objects that were created from the same *view* (more on this later), but used different extrusions like cones, pyramids, cylinders, cubes, triangles, and so on.

Changing Object Color

The colors are different, but you may alter any of the colors by following these steps:

1. Select the object you want to change.

2. Click the Select Object Tool (shown in the margin).

3. Click the Color Bar (shown in the margin) and click and drag your mouse over to find a new color that you prefer, and then release the mouse button.

For more detailed information about changing color, see the section "Using the Color Bar" later in this chapter.

Changing Object Size

The sizes of the objects are relatively the same, but they can be edited using the Resize Object Tool (shown in the margin). You also can resize objects by selecting one of the sides or corners of the object with the Select Object Tool (the arrow icon shown in the previous section) and pulling the object out or pushing it in toward its center.

Note

The default gallery is called Basic Shapes T because the objects were originally created in the T or Top View. This is important to you because you can edit this object with the Select Object Tool only when in the Top View. Similarly, there is a gallery called Basic Shapes F that can only be edited in the F or Front View, and so on.

Selecting a New Gallery

You can have only one gallery open at a time, but you can change them easily by clicking the gray Gallery Window bar (in Figure 9.1, it is called "Home Sampler"). When you click it, a pop-up list of the Virtus VRML object galleries appears in your main folder/directory. To select a new gallery, drag down the list to highlight the desired gallery name and release the mouse button, as shown in Figure 9.1. The Gallery will then load.

Figure 9.1:

The Gallery pop-up list.

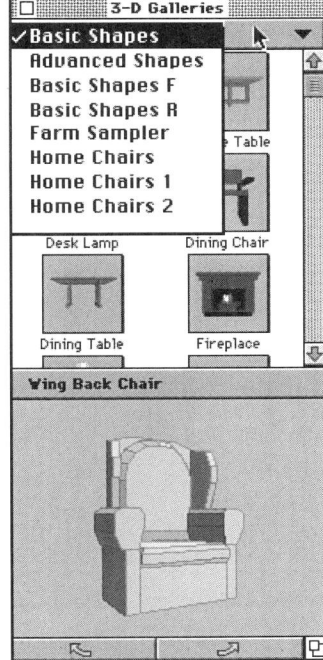

The selected gallery object is displayed in the lower portion of the Gallery window (in the Preview area).

Adding Galleries

Galleries are stored within the Virtus VRML folder/directory in folders/directories specific to their use. There are three gallery folders/directories: 2-D Galleries, 3-D Galleries, and Textures. If you ever install new galleries, you must restart Virtus VRML before it recognizes the new galleries.

Selecting a Gallery Object

To create a virtual environment in Virtus VRML, you want to select objects to add to your world. Point to an object in the Gallery Window, and click to select it. At the bottom of the Gallery Window, you see a 3-D representation of the highlighted object, as shown in Figure 9.2. By clicking the Rotate buttons at the bottom of the Gallery Window, you can rotate the highlighted object in 3-D.

Figure 9.2:

Drag an object from the Gallery Window and drop it in the Design View.

Gallery window

Preview area

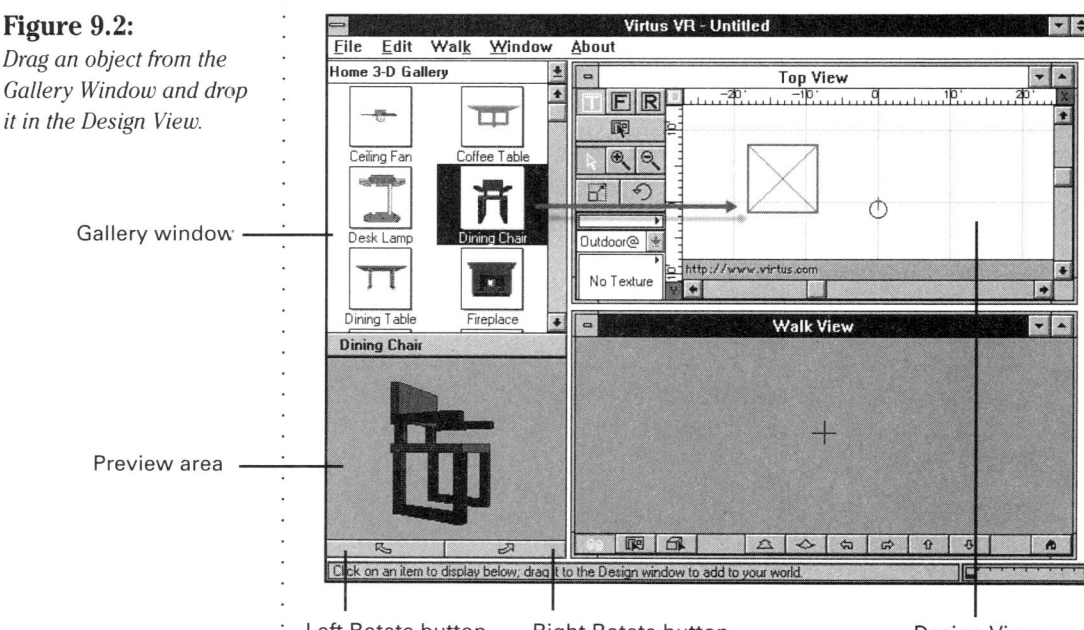

Left Rotate button   Right Rotate button   Design View

Note

The Design View window is the white gridded window. A Top View and Right View and Front View are all subsets of the Design View. The Walk View is the 3-D window that you walk around in.

Using Drag and Drop

To move the selected gallery object to the Design View, click and drag the icon from the Gallery Window to the Design View. Position the object where you want it, and then release the mouse button. A 2-D object outline appears in the Design View where you released the mouse button. *(See Placement Depth in Chapter 7.)*

Modifying an Object

After an object has been dropped into Design View, you may move it by dragging it with the mouse. You can also edit the object's color, scale, rotation, and surface opacity with the following tools and procedures.

Selecting an Object

Before editing an object, you must select it. A selected object displays handles at its vertices. You can select an object in Design View (Top View) or in Walk View.

Selecting an Object in Design View

Click the Select Object Tool in the Tools Pad, point to the object that you want to select, and click.

Selecting an Object in the Walk View

Click the 3-D Object Selector button in the screen cursor buttons at the bottom of the Walk View (shown in Figure 9.3), point to the object in the Walk View that you want to select, and then click. The object appears in the center of the Design View and is selected. You'll realize how important this feature is when you have a complex model with lots of objects and you find it difficult to select a specific item in the Design View.

Figure 9.3:

To select an object in the Walk View, click the 3-D Select Object Button and touch the object (the table here) that you want to select. Look up in the Design View and the object is centered and selected for you.

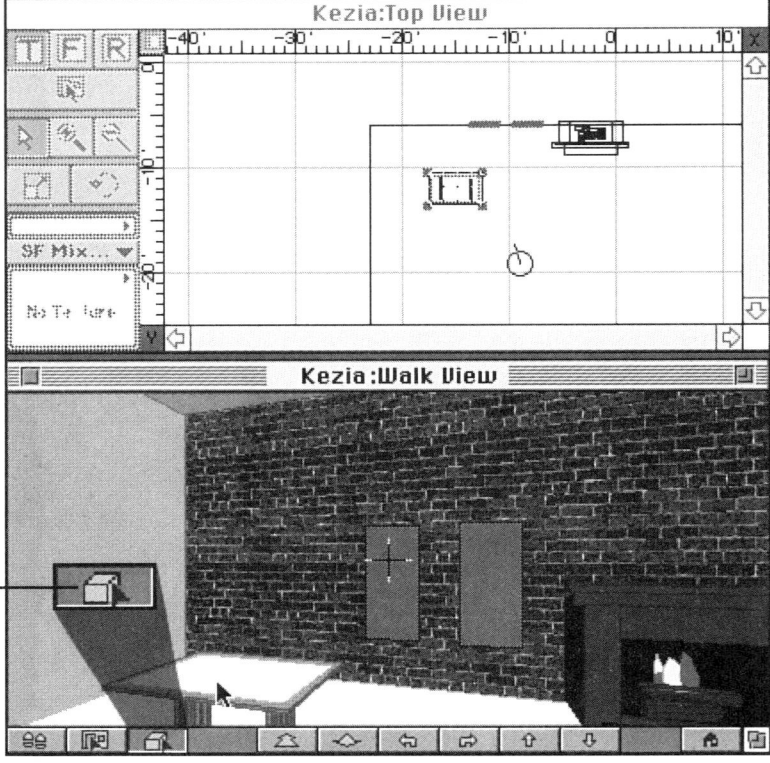

3-D Select Object Button

Reshaping and Rotating Objects

In addition to selecting objects, the Select Object Tool (shown in the margin) is also used to reshape objects. If you point with the Select Object Tool to an object handle and drag the handle, you can reshape the object. Figure 9.4 shows how different objects can be reshaped. You can also drag a line between two handles to reshape an object.

Figure 9.4:

To reshape an object, point to a solid handle, click, and drag it in any direction.

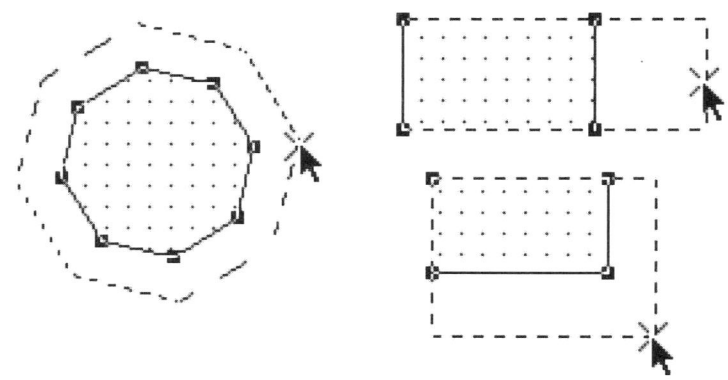

Tip

If an object is grouped, the Select Object Tool cannot be used to re-shape the grouped object. The grouped object must be ungrouped (with the Ungroup command from the Edit Menu) before the Select Object Tool can reshape it or its pieces.

Limitations of Reshaping

Depending on what dimensions you are viewing in the Design View (**T**op, **F**ront, or **R**ight), the reshaping capability of the Select Object Tool may be limited. Object handles indicate to what extent an object can be reshaped:

- ■ Solid handles can be manipulated by dragging either the handles (vertices) or the lines.

- ■ Hollow handles are limited as to how they can manipulate an object. If hollow handles exist, the object is editable in only one direction.

- ■ Gray handles indicate a grouped object (which must be ungrouped before you can edit it).

Figure 9.5 illustrates the different handles.

Figure 9.5:
Solid, hollow, and gray handles have different sizing capabilities.

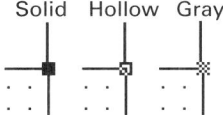

When dragging a handle, an object maintains its type. For example, if you drag the handle of a rectangular object, the object remains rectangular. If you drag a handle of an eight-sided polygon, the object remains an eight-sided polygon. This is true for regular-shaped objects; however, irregular-shaped object handles move individually.

Tip

If you hold down the Option key (Macintosh) or Control key (Windows) while you drag a handle of a regular-shaped object, the object becomes irregular.

In addition to dragging a handle, you can also drag a line between two handles, depending on the type of handles. Hollow handles limit the Se-lect Object Tool's modifying capability, and gray handles indicate a grouped object.

Resize Object Tool

The Resize Object Tool (shown in the margin) scales or resizes an object about its center or about a specified anchor point. Objects may be resized independently along any of the three coordinate axes (dimensions). Objects may also be resized uniformly in all dimensions (X, Y, and Z) by holding down the Shift key before dragging.

When an object is resized, its contents and any surface features are resized with it. If this effect is undesirable, you may want to use the Select Object Tool to resize or reshape the object.

To resize an object about its center, follow these steps:

1. Select the object to be scaled.

2. Select the Resize Object Tool.

3. Point to a reference point (such as a corner), and drag to the new position. Figure 9.6 illustrates this concept.

Figure 9.6:

Resizing an object about its center.

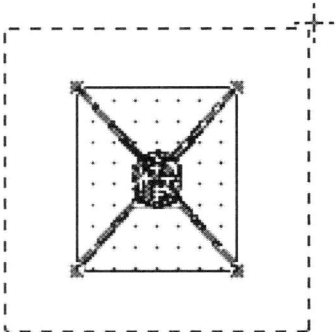

To resize an Object about a specified anchor point, follow these steps:

1. Select the object.

2. Select the Resize Object Tool, and point to the desired location of the anchor point.

3. Hold down the Option key (Macintosh) or Control key (Windows) and click to establish the new anchor point.

4. Point to a reference point and drag to a new location. Figure 9.7 illustrates this concept.

Figure 9.7:
Resizing an object about a specific point.

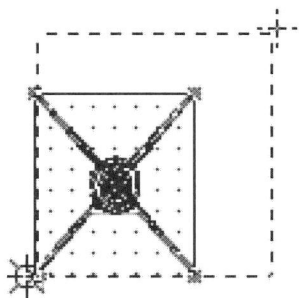

If you resize an object and then add a surface feature to it, the surface feature will automatically resize to match the new scale of the object.

Rotate Object Tool

The Rotate Object Tool (shown in the margin) is used to rotate an object. When rotating an object, this tool works in any view (Top, Front, Right), thus allowing rotation on more than one axis.

To rotate an object:

1. Select the object that you want to rotate.

2. Select the Rotate Object Tool and point to any location in the Design View to establish the center of rotation.

3. Drag the pointer away from the center of rotation. A dotted line will appear between the pointer and the center of rotation.

   As you drag the pointer farther from the center of rotation, you gain finer control over the angle of rotation.

4. Drag the pointer in an arc around the center point to rotate the object. Figure 9.8 illustrates this process.

Figure 9.8:
Drag from the center of rotation outward, and then drag in an arc.

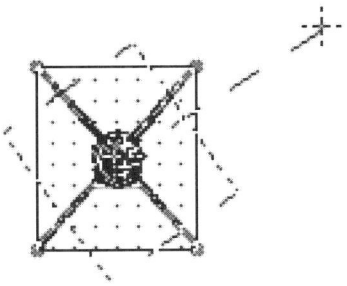

Remember that a **contained object** is one that is entirely contained inside of another object.

If Snap to Grid is selected when you rotate the object or surface feature, the rotation snaps to five-degree increments. If you hold down the Shift key when you rotate the object, the rotation is constrained to 15-degree increments.

Contained objects are rotated with the container unless you hold down the Option key (Macintosh) or Control key (Windows) when you rotate an object. Holding down the Option key (Macintosh) or Control key (Windows) rotates the container, but not the contained objects.

Using the Color Bar

The Color Bar (shown in the margin) allows new colors to be selected, created, and assigned to objects. Colors can be applied to translucent as well as opaque objects and surfaces.

Changing the Color of an Existing Object

Select the object and double-click the Color Bar to give the object the default color. (The default color is the color that appears in the Color Bar.) Or select the object and select a new color from the Color Selector by clicking the Color Bar to reveal the Color Selector. Drag to select a new color. Figure 9.9 shows the Macintosh Color Bar.

Figure 9.9:
The Macintosh Color Bar is identical to the Windows Color Palette, with the exception of an icon.

Each time that you select a new color, the color appears as a small square across the top of the Color Selector. This section of the Color Selector is the Color Palette. If you have selected several colors since you started the program, each of those colors will be displayed as a small square in the Color Palette. This helps you keep color selections consistent. By recording the last 30 colors that you selected, the Color Palette allows you to select the same shade of color for the same types of objects.

For example, you might select a light shade of blue from the Color Selector and apply that color to a glass window. Every time that you create another glass window, you will be able to give it exactly the same shade of blue by selecting from the Color Palette, rather than from the Color Selector. Figure 9.10 shows the Windows Color Selector.

Figure 9.10:

The Virtus VRML Windows Color Palette.

Click the palette icon to define a custom color.

This Color Palette shows the last 30 colors that you selected.

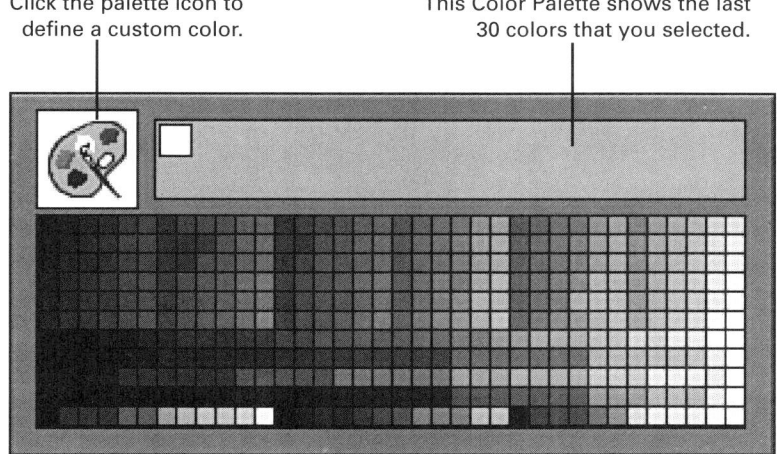

If the colors in the Color Palette do not contain the desired color, click and drag the mouse to the icon in the upper-left corner of the Color Palette and release. This displays the standard Macintosh Color Wheel or Windows Color Selector.

To select a new color from the Macintosh Color Wheel or Windows Color Selector, point to the desired color and click.

Defining a Custom Color

To define a custom color, point to a shade of color in the Color Wheel/Selector and click. On the right of the Color Wheel/Selector dialog is a brightness control. You can slide the brightness control up or down to change the shade of a color, thus creating a custom color. Figure 9.11 shows the Macintosh Color Wheel and Figure 9.12 shows the Windows Color Selector.

Figure 9.11:
The Macintosh Color Wheel.

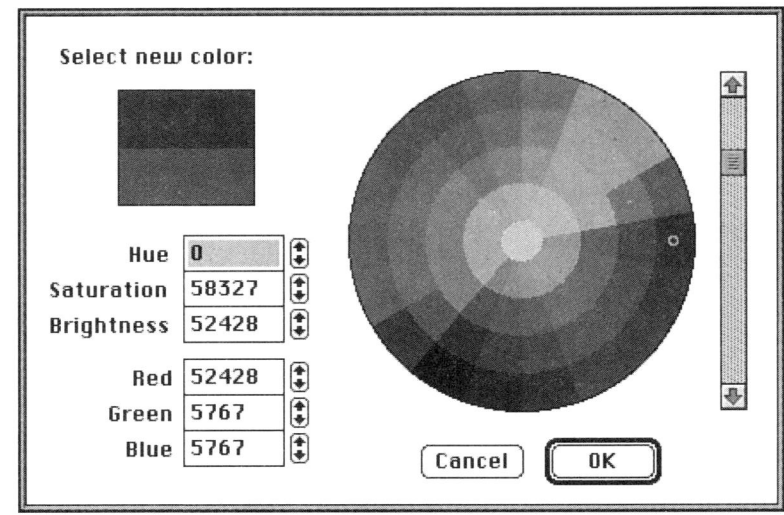

Figure 9.12:
The Windows Color Selector.

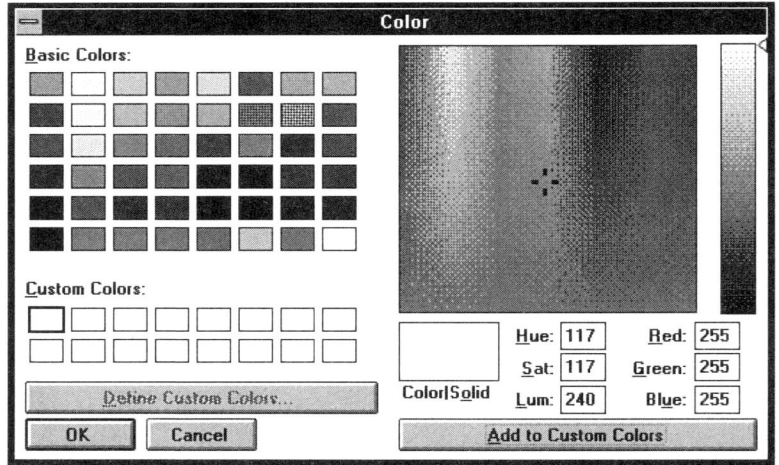

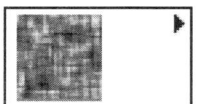

Using the Texture Bar

Clicking the Texture Bar (shown in the margin) reveals the Textures Palette (shown in Figure 9.13). The Textures Palette displays thumbnails of textures that you can apply to objects. Texturing objects can add realism to your 3-D environments.

Applying a Texture to an Object

Select an object in the Design View by clicking it. Then click the Texture Bar to reveal the Textures Palette, as shown in Figure 9.13. Click and drag the screen cursor to highlight the desired texture, and then release the mouse button. The texture that you selected will be displayed on the object in the 3-D Walk View.

Figure 9.13:

Click and highlight the desired texture on the Textures Palette.

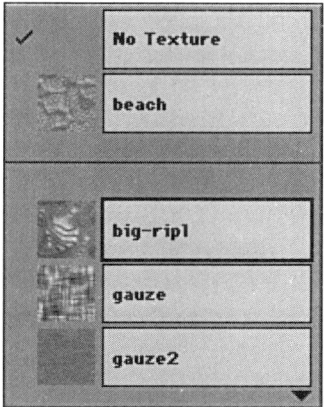

Removing a Texture from an Object

Select the textured object, click the Texture Bar, and drag to select "No Texture." The textures in the Textures Palette can be changed by selecting another palette to replace it, as explained in the next section.

Selecting Another Textures Palette

Click the Texture button to reveal the names of the Texture Palettes in your Textures folder/directory within the Virtus VRML folder/directory (see Figure 9.14). Drag to select the desired Textures Palette.

Figure 9.14:
Click the Texture button to reveal a list of other Textures Palettes available.

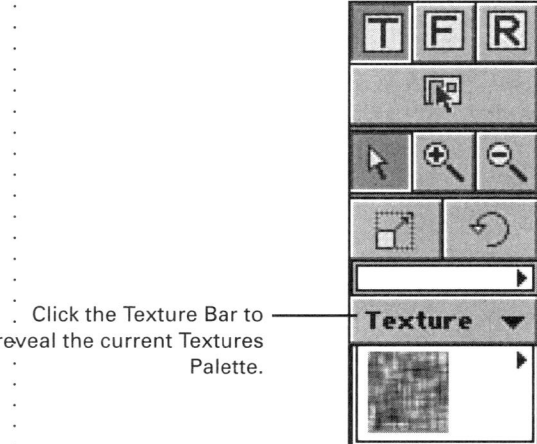

Click the Texture Bar to reveal the current Textures Palette.

Additional textures are included with each Virtus VRML Gallery, which are sold separately from the Virtus VRML application. You may also create your own textures with a paint program, and then move these into your Virtus VRML Textures folder/directory for use with the program.

Included on the CD-ROM are bonus galleries and textures, including the Archeology and Home Remodeling Galleries. Check the ReadMe file on your CD for additional gallery information.

Don't forget to restart Virtus VRML after new textures have been added so that the program will recognize them.

Modifying an Object Surface

In addition to entire objects, individual object surfaces can be modified. Surface color can be changed, and a surface feature with a specific opacity or texture can be dragged from a 2-D gallery and dropped onto the surface.

Before editing an object surface, you must select it—see Figure 9.15. Like an object, a selected object surface displays handles at its vertices. You can select an object in the Design View or in the Walk View.

Figure 9.15:

A selected surface in the Surface Editor.

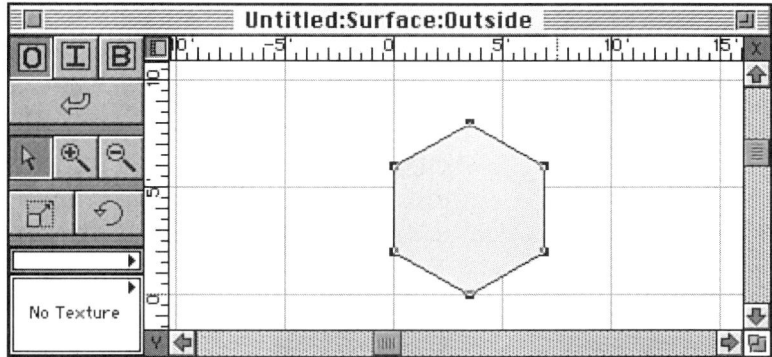

To select an object surface in Design View, click the Surface Editor Tool, and then click the surface that you want to select. You can select a surface that is perpendicular to your view or you can select a line representing a surface that is perpendicular to your view.

To select an object surface in Walk View, click the 3-D Select Surface button (shown in the margin), and then point to the 3-D surface in the Walk View and click.

A selected surface is displayed in the Design View and is aligned perpendicular to your view. When the surface is displayed, you will notice that the title bar of the window has changed and the Tools Pad has also changed. This set of tools and window is called the Surface Editor.

Understanding the Surface Editor

The Surface Editor (shown in the margin) appears in the Design View when a surface is selected and it allows you to edit the selected surface. Many of the tools in the Tools Pad for the Surface Editor are the same as those available in the Design View.

The tools exclusive to the Surface Editor are the Placement buttons (shown in the margin). **O** is the outside surface; **I** is the inside surface; **B** is both the inside and the outside surfaces. The selected button determines where the color, texture, or surface feature is applied to the surface.

The Return Button (shown in the margin) closes the Surface Editor and returns you to the Design View.

Using 2-D Surface Galleries

When the Surface Editor is open, the Gallery Window changes to show a collection of 2-D surface features. There are many types of surfaces that range from a plain sheet of translucent glass to a pair of ornate French doors. A surface feature, like an object, can be dragged from the Gallery and dropped into the Surface Editor Window on a selected surface. Once dropped, a surface feature can be rotated with the Rotate Object Tool or scaled with the Resize Object Tool. Surface feature colors can be changed with the Color Bar and textures can be applied with the Texture Bar.

To edit the opacity of an object's surface, for example, drag the desired shape and opacity from the 2-D Surface Gallery to the Surface Editor Window, as shown in Figure 9.16.

Figure 9.16:

Using the 2-D Surface Galleries.

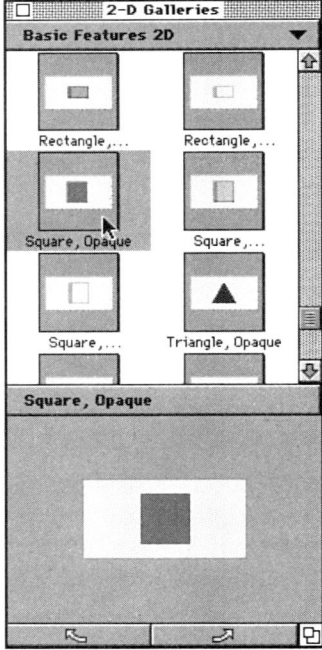

Summary

Now you should have an understanding of the basic tools and the editors that you use to create your exciting 3-D world for the Internet. You now know how to use a 3-D Gallery object to cut your design time by quickly dragging and dropping an item into a Design View. As well, you know that you can edit those objects and customize them to suit your particular situation.

Colors and textures play an exciting role in creating a realistic virtual world and you now know how they can be added (or removed) easily from your model.

In the next chapter, you learn all about the Virtus VRML menus—which will give you more control over the technical aspects of the program. So turn the page and let's get going.

10

Virtus VRML Menus

This chapter covers all of the menu items in Virtus VRML. It is especially important because it gives you more technical information about some areas of the program. You might want to just skim it and use at as a reference.

The File Menu

Many of the Virtus VRML File menu options and commands are standard for the Macintosh and Windows operating systems. These include New, Open, Close, Save, Save As, Revert to Save, Page Setup/Print Setup, Print, Snapshot, and Quit/Exit. Figures 10.1 and 10.2 show the Macintosh and Windows File menus, respectively.

Table 10.1 offers a brief description of the simpler File menu options and the sections that follow explain the more complex ones.

Figure 10.1:

The Macintosh File menu.

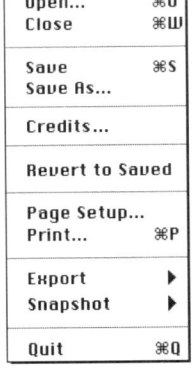

Figure 10.2:

The Windows File menu.

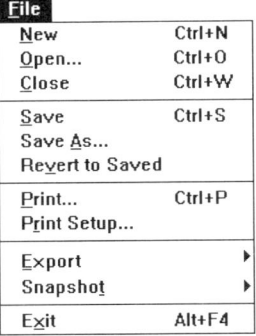

Table 10.1

The File Menu Commands

Command	Purpose
New	Creates and opens a new Virtus VRML file.
Open	Displays the standard Macintosh and Windows Open dialog box from which you can select an existing file to open.
Close	Closes the current file. If you made any changes to the file since the last time you saved it, you are prompted to save the changes before the file is closed.
Save	Saves the current file with the currently used name.
Save As	Opens the Macintosh and Windows Save dialog box, which allows you to save the current file with a new name.
Credits	Allows you to customize your model by adding a custom splash screen to your file. In addition to text, you may add a PICT (Macintosh) or BMP (Windows) graphic to enhance your custom credit screen.
Snapshot	Allows you to save a view of a Virtus VRML model in another file format (see the following sections for more information).
Revert to Saved	Opens the last saved version of the current file. If you select this option, any changes made to the model since the last time that you saved it are lost unless you first use Save As... and save the changes to the file with another name.
Page Setup (Macintosh) Print Setup (Windows)	Opens the standard dialog with which you choose printout size, paper orientation, and other printing features.
Print	Prints the active window centered on the page and enlarged within the constraints of the page.

continues

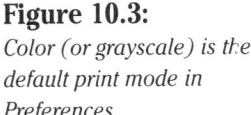

Table 10.1

Continued

Command	Purpose
Quit (Macintosh) Exit (Windows)	Exits Virtus VRML. If a model is open and changes were made since the last time it was saved, you are prompted to save any changes before exiting.
Export VRML	Allows you to save your file as a VRML file, which may be used on the Internet with an appropriate VRML browser (see following sections for more information).

Other Printing Issues

Printing an entire Design View

Select the Design View to make it active, zoom out until you can see all the objects (you may also resize the window), and then choose Print.

Printing the Walk View

Navigate in the Walk View to the desired viewing angle, and then choose Print.

Figure 10.3 shows the default print mode.

Figure 10.3:
Color (or grayscale) is the default print mode in Preferences.

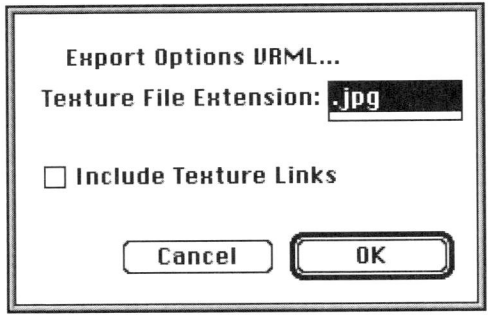

When printing the Walk View, if your printer does not print grayscale, you may want to print black object frames with white shading. This gives you a clean, black-line drawing.

Printing objects with black frames and white fill

In the Preferences dialog, click B & W Print Mode (see Figures 10.4 and 10.5).

Figure 10.4:
B & W Print Mode selected in Preferences.

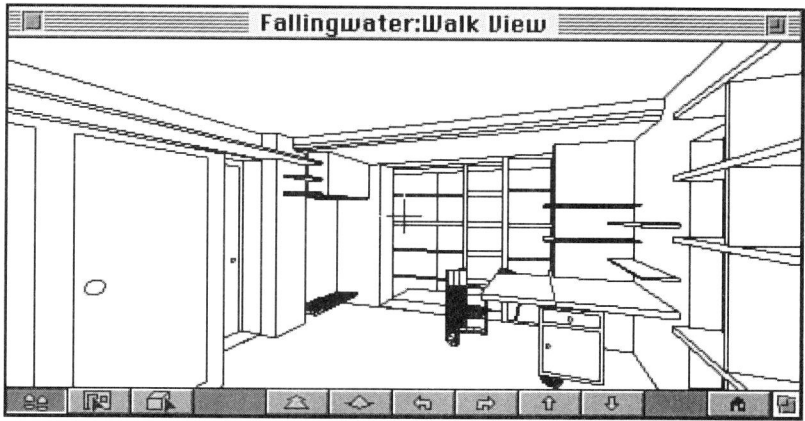

Figure 10.5:
For a clean, black-line drawing, select B & W Print Mode.

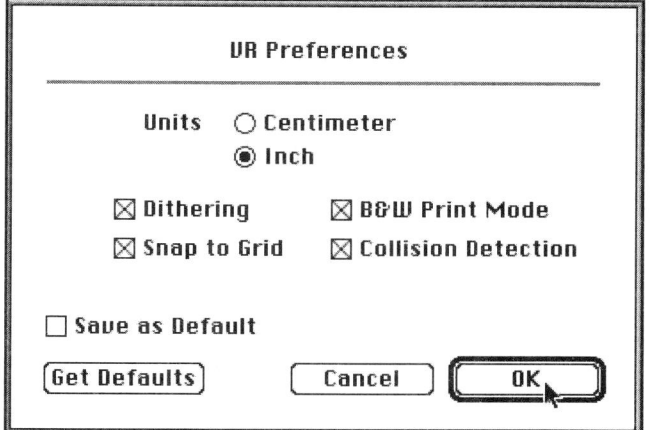

Export Command Issues

The Export VRML command allows you to save your file as Virtual Reality Modeling Language, which may be used for distribution on the Internet using an appropriate VRML browser like Virtus Voyager.

When you export your model, you are asked to change the *internal* extension of those textures to JPEG (.jpeg) or GIF (.gif)—file extensions that can be used on the Internet. This feature changes the internal resources that look for the textures in your model. It does *not* create new texture files for you that have been converted to JPEG or GIFs. You must do that manually to use those textures in your model. (See Chapter 12, "Using Textures with VRML Files.")

Check the box "Use texture strings" if you want to include the texture information with your model. If you do not want to save the texture information with your model, leave the box unchecked.

Remember that if you use a browser that does not read textures, it might become confused and not open at all if the texture information is included.

Snapshot Issues

Snapshot allows you to save a view of a Virtus VRML model in another file format. The saved view can be a particular perspective in the Walk View, the drawing in a Design View, the Surface Editor window, or a recorded walk path.

Snapshot displays a pop-up menu listing possible file formats in which to save the snapshot.

Taking a Snapshot

Click the window that you wish to take the snapshot of (to make it the active window), and then select Snapshot and a file format. Select the desired options for the snapshot and click OK. The options for each snapshot are described in Figures 10.6–10.9. After all options are selected for Snapshot, the standard Save As dialog appears, from which you can select a file name for your snapshot.

Macintosh snapshot formats and Windows snapshot formats are different and are described next.

PICT Options (Macintosh)

Figure 10.6 shows the Snapshot options for PICT.

Figure 10.6:
Snapshot options for PICT format.

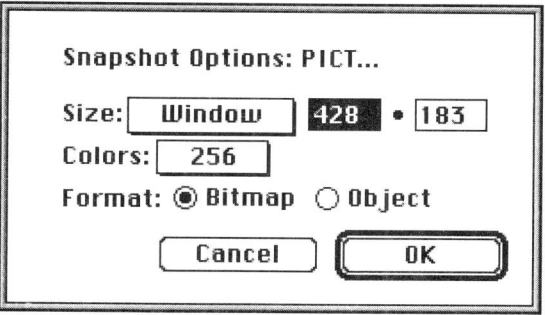

The Macintosh (PICT) options are as follows:

■ **Size** is a pop-up menu with a list of common screen sizes, measured in pixels, from which you can choose a size for the snapshot. Also on the pop-up menu is the **Custom** option, which allows you to enter a custom pixel width and height in the text boxes next to the pop-up menu.

■ **Colors** displays a pop-up of 2, 16, 256, or millions from which you can select a color mode. Also displayed is the **Grayscale** check box, which saves the snapshot in shades of gray if your monitor supports this mode. The number of shades of gray depends on which option is selected in the pop-up.

■ Selecting the **Bitmap** check box gives you a PICT image limited to bitmapped or pixel graphics. These graphics are ideally suited for multimedia-based use.

■ Selecting the **Object** check box gives you a PICT image that is converted to vector lines. Vector-based graphics are better suited for printer output.

PICS and QuickTime (Macintosh)

Before taking a snapshot in PICS or QuickTime format, you must have a recorded walk path of the open model. If you do not have a walk path recorded, the PICS and QuickTime options are grayed. Also, if you do not have QuickTime installed properly on your machine, the QuickTime option in the snapshot pop-up is grayed.

Figure 10.7 shows the Snapshot options for QuickTime.

Figure 10.7:
Snapshot options for QuickTime.

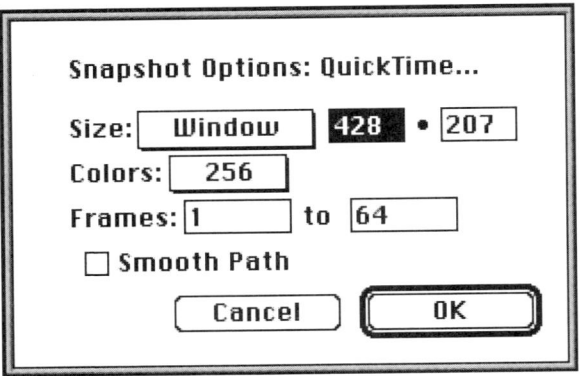

The options for PICS and QuickTime are as follows:

■ **Size** is a pop-up menu with a list of common screen sizes, measured in pixels, from which you can choose a size for the snapshot. Also on the pop-up menu is the Custom option, which allows you to enter a custom pixel width and height in the text boxes next to the pop-up menu.

■ **Colors** displays a pop-up of 2, 16, 256, or millions from which you can select a color mode.

■ **Frames** allows you to select a range of frames from the recorded walk path to be saved in QuickTime/PICS format. The default is for all frames to be saved, but you may type a new range in the text boxes.

Smoothing is the process of calculating the difference between pairs of frames and inserting additional frames, if necessary, to make the recorded path smoother.

■ **Smoothing**, if selected, calculates the difference between pairs of frames and inserts additional frames, if necessary, to make the recorded path smoother. The disadvantage of smoothing is that it can easily quadruple the file size of your snapshot. And smoothing may not even be helpful at all, depending on the size of the steps in the walk path.

BMP Options (Windows)

Figure 10.8 shows the Snapshot options for BMP.

The options for BMP are as follows:

■ **Size** is a pop-up menu with a list of common screen sizes, measured in pixels, from which you can choose a size for the snapshot. Also on the pop-up menu is the **Custom** option, which allows you to enter a custom pixel width and height in the text boxes next to the pop-up menu.

Figure 10.8:

Snapshot options for BMP.

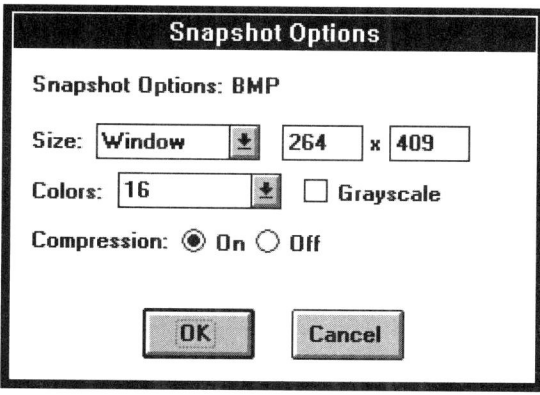

- **Colors** displays a pop-up of 2, 16, 256, or millions from which you can select a color mode. Also displayed is the **Grayscale** check box, which saves the snapshot in shades of gray if your monitor supports this mode. The number of shades of gray depends on which option is selected in the pop-up.

- **Compression** options are On or Off. The default is On. Most software capable of reading BMP format can deal with compressed format; however, some software cannot. If you have trouble reading a BMP snapshot into another program, try turning off compression.

Animator Pro Options (Windows)

Figure 10.9 shows the Snapshot options for Animator Pro.

Figure 10.9:

Snapshot options for Animator Pro.

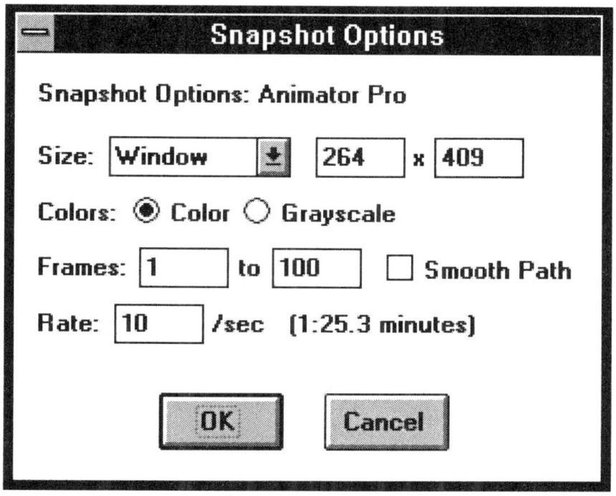

To take a snapshot in Animator Pro, you must first record a walk path. If you have not recorded a walk path, the Animator Pro format option is grayed and unselectable. The options are described as follows:

- **Size** is a pop-up menu with a list of common screen sizes, measured in pixels, from which you can choose a size for the snapshot. Also on the pop-up menu is the **Custom** option, which allows you to enter a custom pixel width and height in the text boxes next to the pop-up menu.

  The true Animator format size is 320×200; any other size is considered Animator Pro format. This is important to users who want to play back the snapshot with an older Animator player. Some older players read only Animator format (320×200).

- **Colors** offers two options for the Animator Pro file, Color or Grayscale.

- **Frames** allows you to select a range of frames from the recorded walk path to be saved in Animator Pro format. The default is for all frames to be saved, but you may type a new range in the text boxes.

- If selected, **Smooth Path** compares frames in the recorded path and inserts more frames where necessary to make the path less jerky when played back. The disadvantage of smoothing is that it can easily quadruple the file size of your snapshot. And smoothing may not even be helpful, depending on the size of the steps in the walk path.

- **Rate** allows you to enter a rate of frames per second for Animator Pro to play back the file. Your machine is limited to how fast that it can play back frames. For example, you may set the Rate option at 32 frames per second, but your machine may only be fast enough to play back six frames per second.

Edit Menu

Figures 10.10 and 10.11 show the Macintosh and Windows Edit menus, respectively.

Table 10.2 offers a brief description of the simpler Edit menu options and the sections that follow explain the more complex ones.

Figure 10.10:
The Macintosh Edit menu.

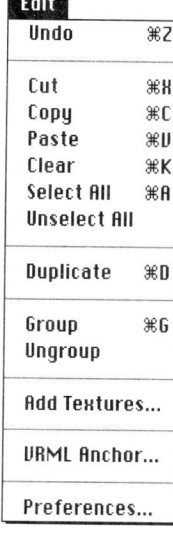

Figure 10.11:
The Windows Edit menu.

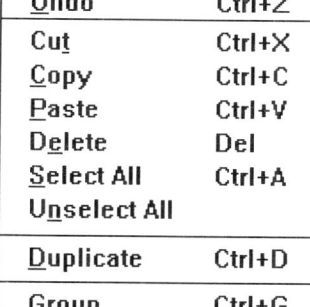

Table 10.2

The Edit Menu Commands

Command	Purpose
Undo	Undoes the last operation.
Cut	Removes any selected objects and places them in the Clipboard. Cut objects can then be pasted with the Paste command.

continues

Table 10.2	Command	Purpose
Continued	Copy	Copies any selected objects to the Clipboard. The difference between Copy and Cut is that Copy leaves the original in place, and Cut removes the original. Copied objects can then be pasted with the Paste command.
	Paste	Puts the contents of the Clipboard into the model.
	*Clear (Macintosh) Delete (Windows)	Removes or deletes selected objects, surface features, or slices without placing them in the Clipboard. Selected objects can also be deleted by pressing the Delete key or the Backspace key. The difference between Cut and Delete/Clear is that Delete/Clear removes objects completely, whereas Cut moves objects to the Clipboard so that these may be pasted again.
	Select All	Selects all objects (displays all handles).
	Unselect All	Unselects objects or surface features (handles are removed). Another method of unselecting is clicking the background in the Design View or Surface Editor.
	Group	Groups selected objects and treats them as one.
	Ungroup	Ungroups a selected object if it was previously grouped with the Group command.
	Duplicate	Makes an exact copy of any selected object or surface feature and places it on or near the original. (See the following section for more information.)
	Add Textures…	Displays a dialog box that enables you to select a bitmapped texture, PICT (Macintosh) or BMP (Windows), and add it to the texture palette.
	VRML Anchor…	Displays a text box to type (or copy and paste) the URL of a linked file.

Command	Purpose
Preferences	Allows you to set preferences for the appearance of Virtus VRML. (See the following sections for detail.)

*If you Delete, Cut, or Clear something accidentally, immediately choose Undo from the Edit menu to reverse the action.

Duplicate Command Issues

Duplicate makes an exact copy of any selected object or surface feature and places it on or near the original. Duplicate does not copy to the Clipboard as does the Copy command.

Duplicate duplicates objects as well as object placement, scaling, and rotation. For example, you can create an object, duplicate that object, and position the second object on the right side of the original so that the objects appear to be touching. Then you can select Duplicate again and an identical third object, joined on the right side of the second object, appears; you have a line of three identical objects spaced the same distance apart. The duplicate's position relative to the object that it duplicated is maintained as long as the original object remains selected. If you continue choosing Duplicate, the objects continue duplicating to the right until you have a line of identical objects. This can be extremely helpful in modeling objects such as staircases.

When you create the first duplication, it retains the original object's position, scaling, and rotation information. The object must remain selected until the next duplication is made or the information is lost.

Changes to object type are not duplicated. For example, if you create an object 10 feet tall and then duplicate it and increase the height of the duplication to 15 feet, subsequent duplications have a height of 15 feet—they do not grow in height by increments of five feet. If you wish to accomplish the effect of an incremental increase in size or shape, you must use the Resize Object tool to adjust the size or shape of the first duplication, and then duplicate it.

The Duplicate command duplicates manipulations only of the entire object. It does not duplicate edits to part of an object.

Group Command Issues

Group joins any selected objects so that they are treated as a single object—that is, they can be moved, rotated or scaled together and selected with a single click (see Figure 10.12). Grouped objects can be ungrouped with the Ungroup command. Figure 10.13 shows an ungrouped gallery object (all objects are selected separately).

Figure 10.12:

A grouped gallery object.

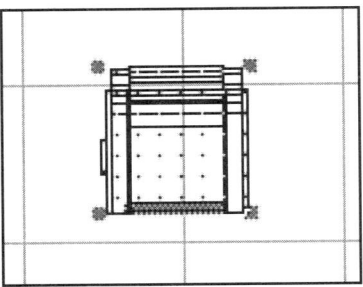

Figure 10.13:

An ungrouped gallery object (all objects are selected).

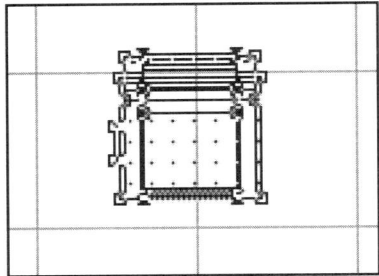

When working with a model of a complex item (like an armchair or a computer), grouping an object allows you to select the entire item easily instead of having to marquee the image each time you want to move it. Often in a model that has many pieces, it may even be *impossible* to successfully marquee the entire image because of all of the objects behind or in front of it.

The Preferences Command

Figures 10.14 and 10.15 show the Macintosh and Windows Preferences dialog boxes, respectively.

The Preferences dialog box allows you to set preferences for the appearance of Virtus VRML. Each time you save a Virtus VRML model, any changes that you made to the preference settings are saved with it. When you open the model again, its preferences are restored.

Figure 10.14:
Macintosh Preferences dialog box.

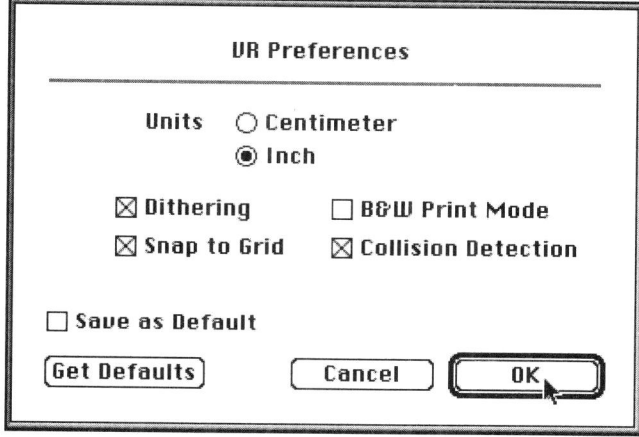

Figure 10.15:
Windows Preferences dialog box.

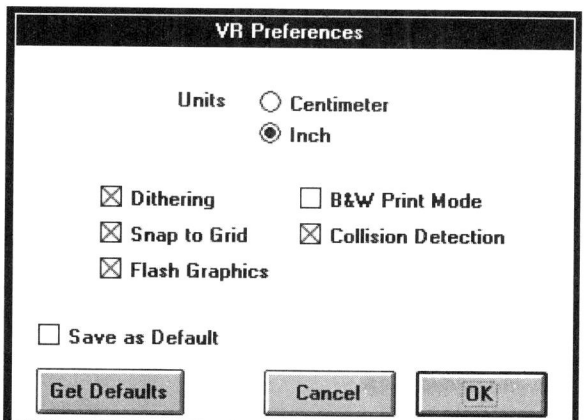

Table 10.3 describes the preferences you can adjust.

Table 10.3	Preference	Meaning
User and Program Preferences	Units: Centimeter/Inch	Determines the units of the ruler in the Design View.
	Dithering	Activated by default. The disadvantage of Dithering is that the screen appears more grainy.

continues

Table 10.3

Continued

> **Dithering** is a technique that allows more colors in an object, which results in more color-accurate renderings.

Preference	Meaning
Snap to Grid*	Snaps objects to an invisible grid when they are placed or moved. The grid is based on the ruler tick marks in the Design View and Surface Editor.
B&W Print Mode	Prints objects with black lines and white surfaces. The printed result is a clean, black-line drawing. This is a great way to print your files if you don't have access to a color printer (see Figure 10.16).
Collision Detection	Prevents you (the Observer) from walking through walls or surfaces where no hole or doorway is present. If this option is not selected, you are free to navigate through object surfaces.
Flash Graphics (Windows)	Turns on Virtus VRML's drawing routines and uses those routines instead of the standard Microsoft Windows drawing routines. Flash Graphics substantially speeds up the Virtus VRML application. Usually, Flash Graphics is turned on by default; however, some video boards are not compatible with Flash Graphics. The Virtus VRML application checks for compatibility with your system when you install, and if a conflict is detected, Flash Graphics is grayed.
Save As Default	Saves the current preferences as the application default preferences. Application default preferences apply to all new models that you create. If you open an existing file, that file's preferences override the application defaults.
Get Defaults	Resets the Preferences dialog box to the original preferences settings.
Cancel	Voids changes that you made to the preferences settings.
OK	Applies any Preferences changes to the current model.

*If you zoom in or out while using Snap to Grid, the ruler tick marks change; therefore, the invisible grid changes. For example, if each tick mark represents one inch, handles snap to the nearest inch. If each tick mark represents one foot, handles snap to the nearest foot. If Snap to Grid is not selected, the capability to place and move objects is constrained only by screen pixels. Snap to Grid also affects object rotation. If Snap to Grid is selected and you rotate an object, the rotation snaps to five-degree increments.

Figure 10.16:

B & W Print Mode selected in Preferences.

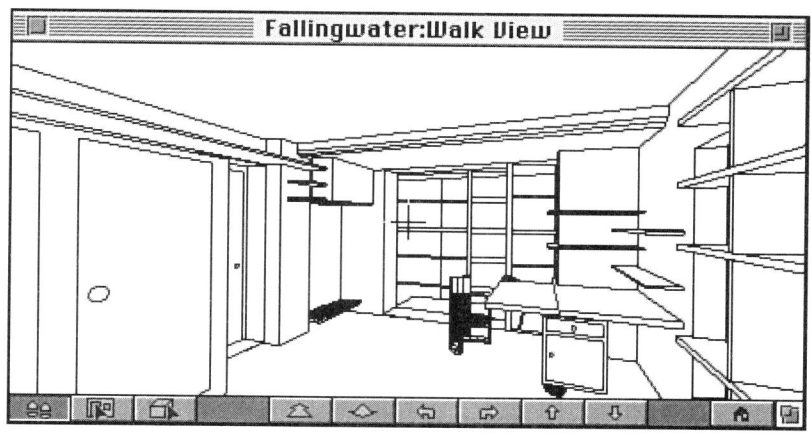

Walk Menu

The Walk menu is available only when the Walk View is active. Figures 10.17 and 10.18 show the Windows and Macintosh Walk menus, respectively.

Figure 10.17:

The Windows Walk menu.

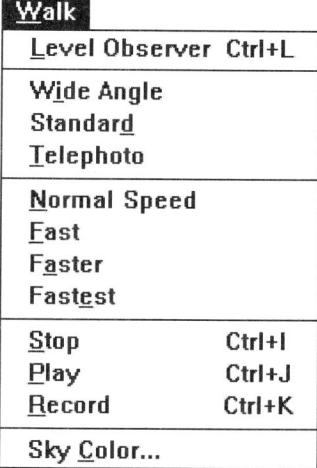

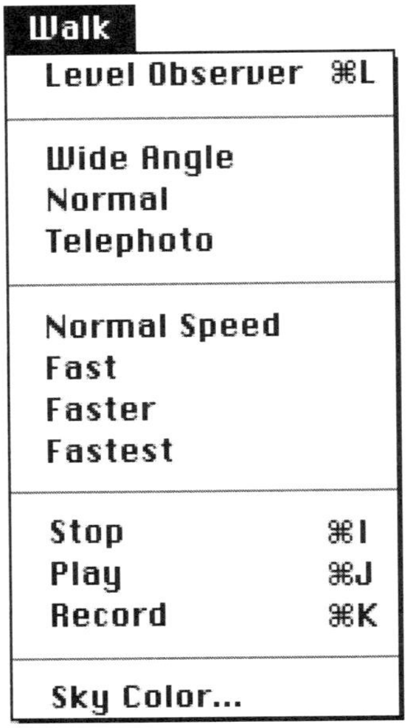

Figure 10.18:
The Macintosh Walk menu.

```
┌──────────────────────────────┐
│ Walk                         │
│ Level Observer       ⌘L      │
│                              │
│ Wide Angle                   │
│ Normal                       │
│ Telephoto                    │
│──────────────────────────────│
│ Normal Speed                 │
│ Fast                         │
│ Faster                       │
│ Fastest                      │
│──────────────────────────────│
│ Stop                 ⌘I      │
│ Play                 ⌘J      │
│ Record               ⌘K      │
│──────────────────────────────│
│ Sky Color...                 │
└──────────────────────────────┘
```

Table 10.4 describes all of the Walk menu options for Windows and the Macintosh.

Table 10.4

The Walk Menu Commands

Command	Purpose
Level Observer	Orients the line of sight in the Walk View, making it level if it has been altered with the Shift key during navigation.
Wide Angle	Changes the Walk View to give the effect of looking through a 15mm, wide-angle camera lens (see Figure 10.19).
Standard	Displays the Walk View normally (35mm), that is, not wide angle or telephoto (see Figure 10.20).
Telephoto	Changes the Walk View to give the effect of looking through a 135mm, telephoto camera lens (see Figure 10.21).
Normal Speed	Displays all translucent and transparent object surfaces and surface features, and displays object color fill, wire frames, and textures.

Command	Purpose
Fast	Displays all translucent and transparent object surfaces and surface features, and displays object color fill and wire frames, but does not display textures. This display increases your walk speed somewhat.
Faster	Increases your walk speed by not allowing you to see through transparent or translucent object surfaces or surface features, and by not displaying textures.
Fastest	Speeds up your navigation by displaying only wire frames of objects. No object color fill, surface features, or textures are displayed.
Stop	Allows you to stop the recording of a walk path. If a walk path is playing, you can stop it by clicking the mouse button. Once the playback is stopped, selecting Stop rewinds the recording to its starting point. If you select Play without first rewinding with the Stop command, the playback continues from the point where it was stopped.
Play	Allows you to play back a recorded walk path. Walk paths are recorded with the Record option.
Record	Allows you to record a walk path. When you select Record, any movements that you make in the Walk View are recorded. You can then play back the recorded walk path or save it with the Snapshot option.
Sky Color	Allows you to change the background color of the Walk View. Selecting Sky Color displays the Macintosh Color Wheel or Windows Color Selector so that you can choose a new color.

Figure 10.19:
Wide Angle view selected.

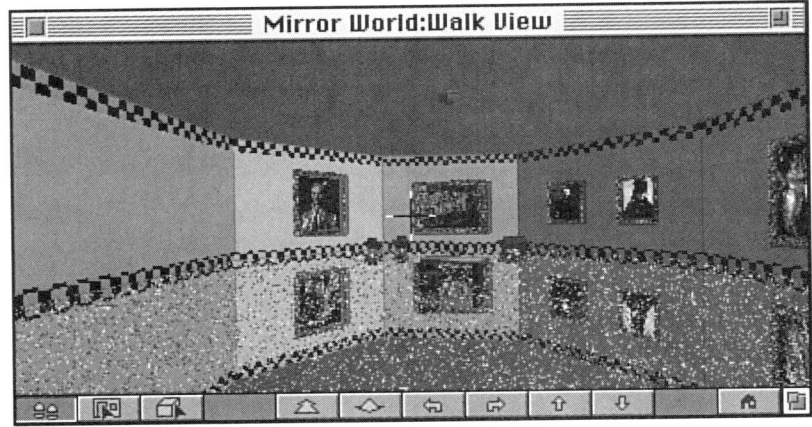

Figure 10.20:
Standard view selected.

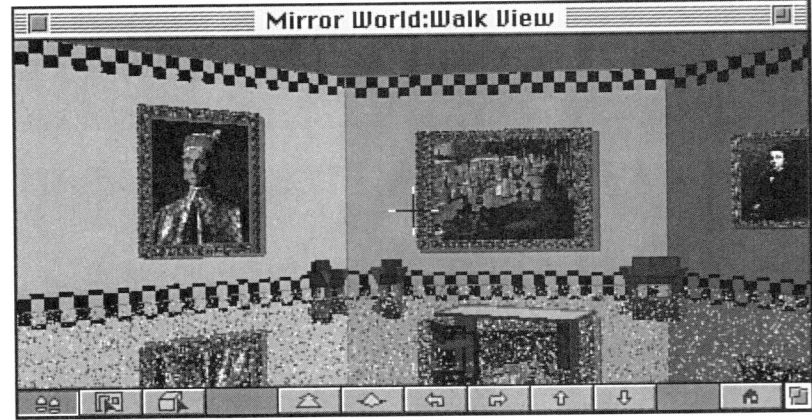

Figure 10.21:
Telephoto view selected.

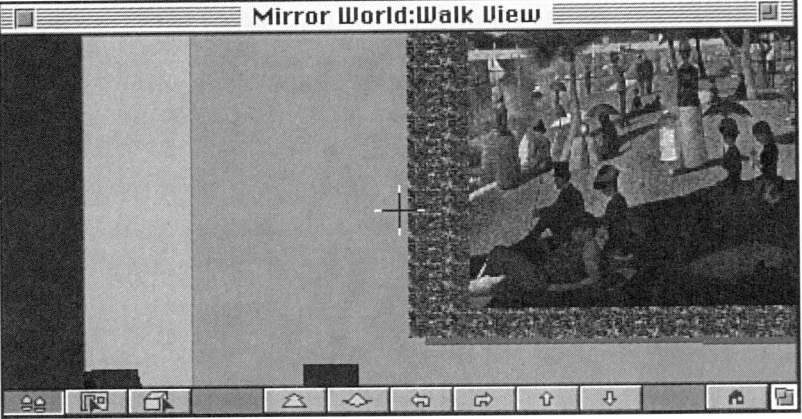

Windows Menu

The Windows menu contains commands for displaying the different windows in Virtus VRML. Figures 10.22 and 10.23 show the Windows and Macintosh Window menus, respectively.

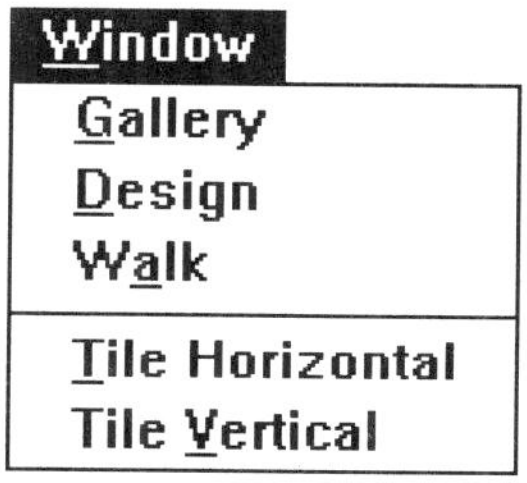

Figure 10.22:
The Windows Window menu.

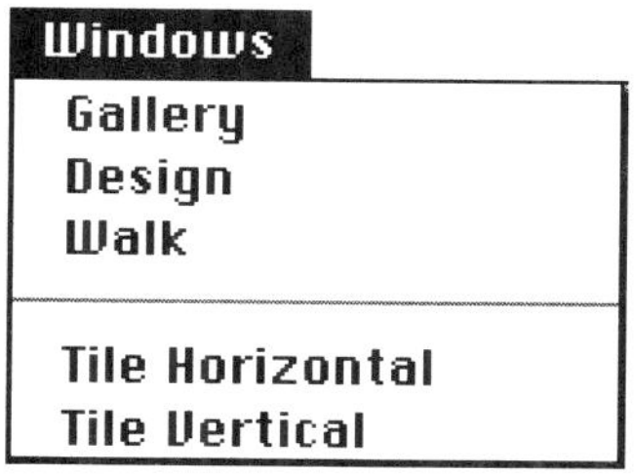

Figure 10.23:
The Macintosh Windows menu.

Table 10.5 describes all of the Window menu commands.

Table 10.5

The Window Menu Commands

Command	Purpose
Gallery	Displays or hides the Gallery Window.
Design	Displays or hides the Design View.
Walk	Displays or hides the Walk View.
Tile Horizontal	Positions the Design View above the Walk View, and both windows are stretched horizontally to fit the monitor. The Gallery Window is positioned normally—that is, to the left of the other windows.
Tile Vertical	Positions the Design View to the left of the Walk View and both windows are stretched vertically to fit the monitor. The Gallery Window is positioned normally—that is, to the left of the other windows.

Summary

After reading this chapter, you have a breadth of knowledge ready to apply to building 3-D worlds. There is a lot of information here, so I encourage you to use the Index to retrieve any information that you need while working with the program. Each of these features are important and, if you understand them and use them properly, they will enable you to work more effectively.

In the next chapter, you'll build on this new knowledge and begin creating your first environment. But before you begin reading, make sure you have loaded Virtus VRML. If you have installation questions, please turn to Appendix A.

11

Creating Your Own World

Okay, now that you have the basics down, you can learn how to create a 3-D world, furnish it, and link it as a VRML file.

This chapter acquaints you with the basics of Virtus VRML by guiding you through a series of hands-on exercises. You perform the following tasks in this chapter:

■ Construct a two-room dwelling and decorate it with pre-built furniture supplied with the program.

■ Model additional furniture and a mailbox from scratch.

Then in the next chapter, you embed URLs and file names and link objects.

The first part of the chapter gives you an overview of the program's basic capabilities, including computer information with which you may already be familiar. In the second part, you learn how to create realistic models.

So let's get started. First, we'll take a look at some terms that you'll encounter when working with the tutorial.

Mouse Movements

It is important to understand the following terminology in order to use this tutorial effectively:

Point—Move the pointer (the cursor that looks like an arrowhead) onto an item on the screen.

Drag—With the pointer on an object, press and hold down the mouse button. Then with the button still down, move the mouse to drag the object to another location.

Click—Press and release the mouse button once.

Double-click—Quickly press and release the mouse button twice.

Select—Point to and click a tool, object, window, menu option, and so on, to choose it or to make it active.

Drag-and-Drop—In Virtus VRML, a feature that allows you to click and hold down an object in the Gallery Window, drag the object to the Design View, and then release the mouse button to drop the object in that window.

VRML Features

For further explanations and definitions, see Appendix B, the glossary.

Active Window—Although you may have several windows open on your screen, this is the one in which you're currently working.

Coordinates—These pinpoint the location of objects on your screen. In the Top View of Virtus VRML, X represents the horizontal units of measure on the screen (from left to right) and Y represents the vertical units (from top to bottom). When you switch to the Front View, X still represents the horizontal units of measure and Z represents the vertical units. Finally, when you switch to the Right View, Y represents the horizontal units of measure and Z represents the vertical units.

For example, coordinates –5,20 in the Top View translates to –5 feet on the X axis and 20 feet on the Y axis. In the Front View, you'll see that –5,20 again translates to –5 feet on the X axis, with 20 feet represented on the Z axis. And in the Right View, –5,20 translates to –5 feet on the Y axis, with 20 feet represented on the Z axis.

Depth—This can be a source of confusion for those who are new to a 3-D visualization program such as Virtus VRML. Here's an example that may be useful in thinking about depth:

You're in the Top View in the Design View. You drag over a rectangle from the Gallery Window at the left, drop it into the Design View, and then stretch it (using the Select Object Tool) to measure 30 feet by 40 feet. As you look at the rectangle in this view, pretend that you're sitting in a helicopter and looking down at the top of a building. You can see what size the building's roof is from left to right and from top to bottom, but those are measurements for the top of the roof only. How tall is the building? Is it one story high, or is it a skyscraper? In this view, you can't tell. To find the answer, switch to the Front View (or Right View). Once in the new view, look to the left along the Z axis—if the building stretches from 0 to 50, for example, it's 50 feet tall.

Design View—The Virtus Design View offers two ways to work:

- Choosing a Top, Front, or Right View allows you to edit 3-D objects (furniture, and so on). When in any of these views, you see a gallery of 3-D objects.

- Activating the Surface Editor tool allows you to edit 2-D surfaces (windows, doors, and so on). The window's title bar carries the word "Surface," and a 2-D gallery appears on your screen.

Gallery Window—Displays a collection of either two- or three-dimensional objects, depending on whether you've chosen to work with a Virtus VRML 2-D Gallery or 3-D Gallery. Any object in a gallery can be dragged and dropped into the Design View and edited.

Handles—When you click (select) an object, you'll see that small square boxes appear around it. These are called handles and in Virtus VRML, these can be black, white, or gray.

Recall from Chapter 9 the subtle difference between the handles, as follows:

- Solid black handles can be manipulated by dragging. If all handles are black, it means the object was created in the current view.

- Hollow handles indicate that the image is limited as to how it can be manipulated. If all handles are hollow, it means the object *was not* created in the current view, so the object can be edited in only one direction. This is why there are three different Basic Shapes Galleries; each one created in a different view; **T**op, **F**ront, and **R**ight.

- Gray handles indicate a grouped object (which must be ungrouped before you can edit it).

Navigate—You can walk around in your Virtus VRML model by either of these methods:

- Clicking the navigation buttons at the bottom of your Walk View.

- Clicking in the Walk View at any location around, or distance from, the crosshair.

See Chapter 8 for more detailed information about navigational techniques.

Observer—In the Design View, it's the circle with a line extending from its center (shown in the margin). The tip of the line (outside of the circle) points in the direction in which you're looking while in your model's Walk View.

Surface—A single side or face of an object.

Surface Editor—Allows you to create and edit surface features while in the Design View.

Surface Feature—A two-dimensional feature (window, door, and so on) on an object's surface.

Tools Pad—Located on the left side of the Design View, it displays the program's tools.

Walk View—Displays a three-dimensional rendering of the two-dimensional items that you place in the Design View. In this window, you can navigate through (walk through) your model.

Walk View Buttons—Buttons along the bottom of the Walk View; includes object editing buttons and novice mode navigation buttons.

Virtus VRML Overview

After you install Virtus VRML, double-click the Virtus VRML application icon to start the program. You'll see the spinning Virtus VRML splash screen and the program will load into your computer's memory. Figure 11.1 shows the working screen.

Figure 11.1:
The Virtus VRML working screen.

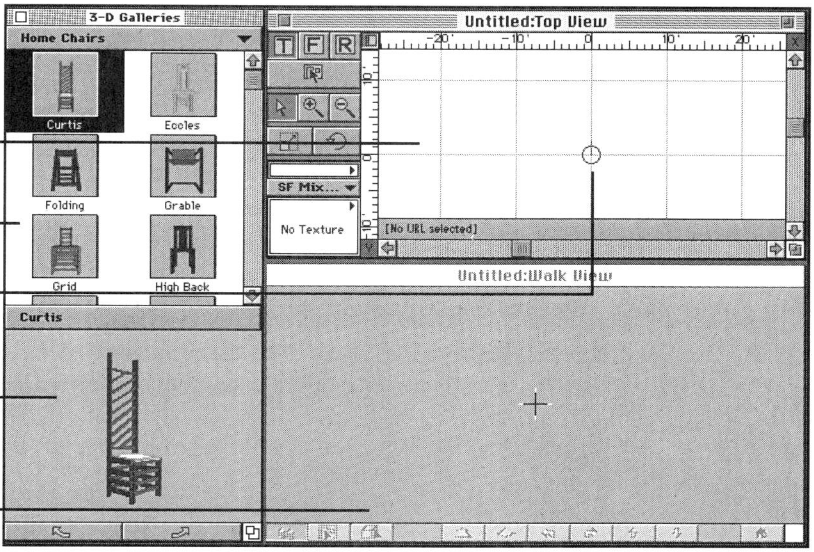

Design View Window
Gallery Window
Observer
Preview Area
Walk View Window

Views, Windows, and the Menu Bar

When Virtus VRML opens, you see three windows:

- At the left, the Gallery Window displays the Basic Shapes Gallery (Macintosh) or Basic 3-D Gallery (Windows) used in building models.

- To the right at the top, the Design View displays the Top View, one of that window's three views in which you can edit 3-D objects such as furniture. (The other two Design View views are Front and Right.) Also, activating the Surface Editor while in the Design View allows you to edit 2-D surfaces such as windows and doors.

- Below the Design View is the Walk View, an empty window with a blue background. As you add objects to your model, the Walk View shows you a three-dimensional rendering of them.

Only one window can be active at any time. Click once in the Design View (Top View). Notice that the title bar at the top displays horizontal bars or becomes a bolder color. This indicates that the window is *active*. Then click anywhere in the Walk View and notice how it becomes the active window.

Tools and Buttons

By now, we hope you're acquainted with the tools and buttons in Virtus VRML. From this point in the tutorial, we assume that you're familiar with their functions.

Memory Indicator

There is a memory indicator to the right of the Message Bar, at the lower-right corner of your screen. It contains a colored bar that alternately shrinks and grows, displaying the amount of memory currently available to Virtus VRML. If the memory is below 75 percent, the bar is blue; if not, it is red. To learn more about memory and memory management, please read your computer's documentation.

Macintosh users, if you are running low on memory, try quitting the application and allocating more RAM to Virtus VRML. Remember to allocate more RAM, quit the program, and from the desktop, select the Virtus VRML icon, and from the File menu, select Get Info. In Memory Requirements, change the Minimum and Preferred Requirements to 8,000K (or more if you have it…).

Manipulating the Observer

The small circle in the center of the Top View is called the Observer; it represents where you're standing in the virtual world. When you start Virtus VRML, the Observer is positioned at the 0,0 coordinate—see Figure 11.2.

Click the Select Object Tool in the Tools Pad. Point to the center of the Observer, and then click and drag the Observer to the lower-left corner of the Top View. The Observer "sticks" to the cursor as you move the mouse, allowing you to reposition the Observer.

Figure 11.2:

Point to the center of the Observer, hold down the Option key (Macintosh) or Ctrl key (Windows), and then click and drag in the direction that you want to view.

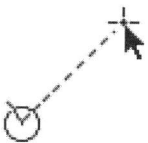

Notice the black line in the middle of the Observer. This line represents the direction of the Observer's view—your line of sight in the model. Point to the center of the Observer, click, hold down the Option key (Macintosh) or Ctrl key (Windows), and drag to the right of the Observer.

Notice the dotted line that appears between the mouse cursor and the Observer. Still holding down the Option key (Macintosh) or Ctrl key (Windows), stretch this line to the upper-right corner of the Top View. Release the mouse button and the Option key (Macintosh) or Ctrl key (Windows). Notice that the black line in the center of the Observer is now pointing to the upper-right corner of the Top View. This is how you manually rotate the Observer (change the line of sight of the Observer). Leave the Observer in this position.

Creating Objects

Virtus VRML is different from other graphics applications in that, with our program, you don't create objects from scratch. Instead, you're provided with pre-built galleries of 3-D and 2-D objects to use in constructing your models. To create a simple 3-D rectangle, follow these steps:

1. Select "Rectangle" from the Basic Shapes Gallery (Macintosh) or Basic 3-D Gallery (Windows).

2. Click it, hold down the mouse button, and then drag and drop the rectangle into the Design View just above (not on top of) the Observer, as shown in Figure 11.3.

Figure 11.3:

Creating a simple 3-D rectangle.

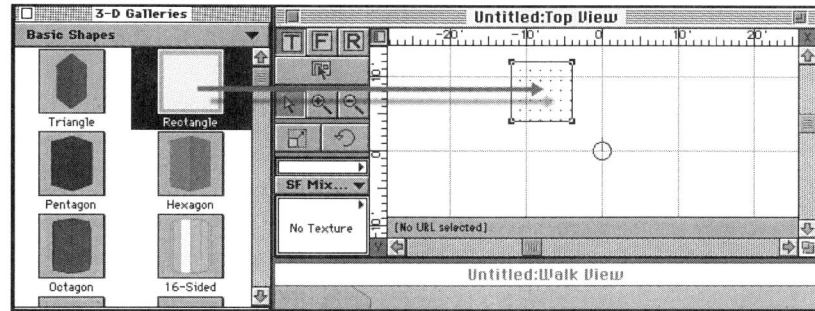

You just created an 8' × 8' rectangular object that is visible in the Walk View. If it's not visible, navigate to a position where you can see it.

3. Dragging the rectangle, position it so its lower-left corner is at the 0,10 coordinate (the window automatically scrolls as you drag an object off an edge).

4. Click and drag the upper-right handle to the 30,20 coordinate, as shown in Figure 11.4.

Top View selected

Figure 11.4:

Click and drag the upper-right handle to the 30,20 coordinate.

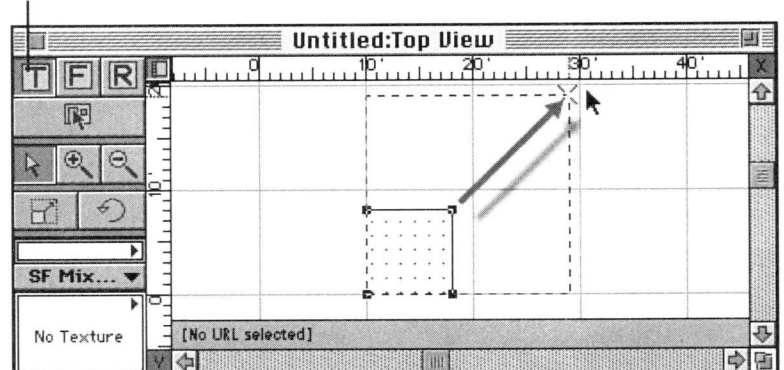

In Figure 11.4, you now have a 30' × 20' rectangular object (room) that can be viewed from the outside, as well as from the inside.

5. Make the Walk View active and navigate around the inside of the rectangle—just walk right through a wall. The height of the rectangle is eight feet; let's make it taller.

6. Make the Design View active and select the F button to switch to the Front View. Scroll the window so you can see the top edge of the rectangle. See Figure 11.5.

The ruler at the left, along the Z axis, should indicate that the height of the room is eight feet. That's because the default size of the Basic Rectangle is 8' × 8' × 8'. All objects in the Basic Shapes and Advanced Shapes galleries are about this size.

7. Click and drag the top edge of the rectangle until its height reaches 15 feet. The Walk View immediately updates to reflect any changes made in the Design View, allowing you to check your work as your model progresses.

Figure 11.5:

After changing to the Front View, click and drag the top edge of the rectangle until its height reaches 15 feet.

Front View selected

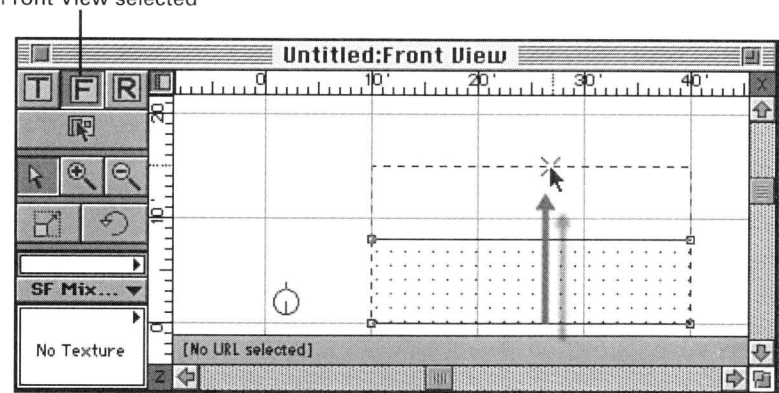

Understanding Handles

In Virtus VRML, one of three types of handles appears when you click an object. The specific type of handle gives you information about how the selected object can be edited or manipulated. The types are black, white, and gray handles.

Black Handles—Black handles can be manipulated in any direction to change the object's shape. When you're in the Top View, all objects from the Basic Shapes and Advanced Shapes galleries show black handles when the objects are selected. (In the Front and Right Views, white handles are shown). See Figure 11.6.

Figure 11.6:

Black handles.

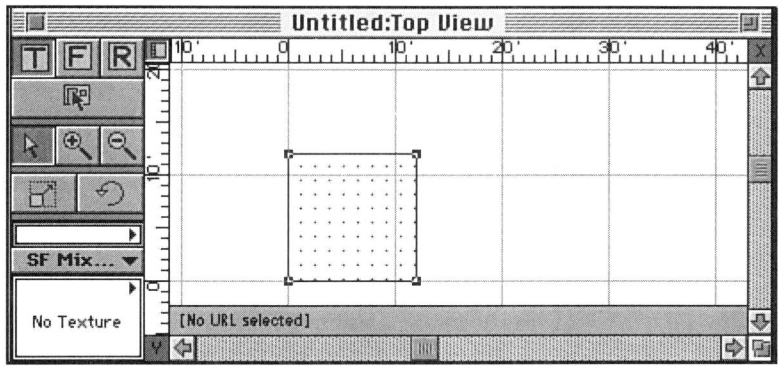

White Handles—A selected object showing white handles tells you that only the depth of the object can be manipulated. (You adjusted the depth of the rectangle while in the Front View by moving the top edge of the rectangle from 8 to 15 feet.) See Figure 11.7.

Figure 11.7:
White handles.

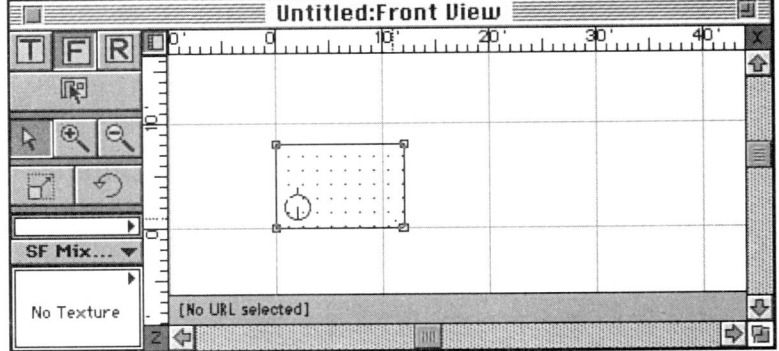

Gray Handles—Grouped objects (two or more objects selected and then joined with the Group command from the Edit menu) show gray handles when selected. Remember that grouped objects must first be ungrouped (with the Ungroup command from the Edit menu) before these objects can be manipulated. See Figure 11.8.

Figure 11.8:
Gray handles.

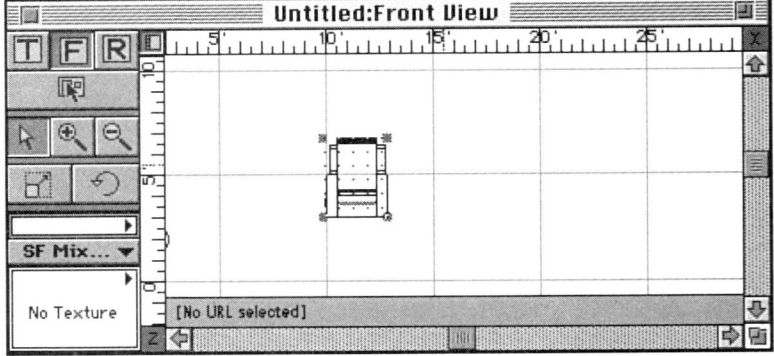

For extra practice later, experiment with objects from the Basic Shapes and Advanced Shapes galleries to get a feel for working with handles. Edit different objects in all three views—Top, Front, and Right—then look at them in the Walk View. Also, switch to the Home Remodeling Gallery (Macintosh) or Home 3-D Gallery (Windows) and ungroup "Bookcase" to see how it's constructed.

Choosing Gallery Objects

Basic Shapes and Advanced Shapes—Objects in these galleries always display black handles (can be manipulated in any direction) in the Top

View, and white handles (only the depth can be changed) in the Front or Right Views.

Basic Shapes F and Advanced Shapes F—Objects in these galleries always display black handles (can be manipulated in any direction) in the Front View and white handles (only the depth can be changed) in the Top or Right Views.

Basic Shapes R and Advanced Shapes R—Objects in these galleries always display black handles (can be manipulated in any direction) in the Right View and white handles (only the depth can be changed) in the Top or Front Views.

As you build a model, you'll often use shapes from more than one Virtus VRML Gallery. For instance, you might want to use "Rectangle" from the 3-D Galleries Basic Shapes (Macintosh) or Basic 3-D Gallery (Windows) to create a room, and then use "Triangle" from the Basic Shapes F or R galleries to create the roof.

Using Virtus VRML

Because of some of the complex issues regarding the Internet, it is important to maintain "digital integrity" when saving your files. If they are not saved properly, they may not be suitable for viewing on the WWW or may even 'crash' some browsers.

Although it would be hard for me to chide you for "saving too often," it is a problem if you save incorrectly. If you need to save before completing the tutorial (about 30 minutes), turn to the end of this chapter at the appropriately titled section, "Saving Your File" and do it right the first time....

Modeling a Bedroom with a Tiled Bath

I have to give you an example of something that you can identify with, so that's why you need to build a bedroom and bathroom. It could just as easily have been any surreal cyberworld, a shopping mall, an airport, or any world imaginable. If you work through these examples, I promise you will know the basics and you can create anything.

To begin:

1. Close any open Virtus VRML file (choose Close from the File menu), and then create a new file (choose New from the File menu).

2. In the 3-D Galleries Basic Shapes (Macintosh) or Basic 3-D Gallery (Windows), click and hold down "Octagon," and then drag and drop it into the center of the Top View (centered over the Observer at 0,0).

3. With the octagon still selected, click and hold down the Color Bar, and then point to a bright green color and release the mouse button. Now look in the Walk View to see the octagon's new color. (To view the entire octagon in the Walk View, click repeatedly below the crosshair in the Walk View until all of the octagon can be seen.)

4. Choose Save from the File menu. Save the file to your Virtus VRML folder, naming the file "Tutorial." Remember to save at regular intervals as you work.

5. Switch to the Front View (click the F button to press it) and drag the octagon until its top edge is at 0 feet high.

6. Switch back to the Top View (click the T button). Drag the middle-right handle of the octagon to the right, away from the octagon's center, until the octagon is 200 feet in diameter. (The Design View automatically scrolls as you drag objects or handles past the window's edge.) If necessary, use the Zoom-Out Tool and scroll to see the entire octagon (see Figure 11.9).

Figure 11.9:

Switch to the Front View (click the F button) and drag the octagon until its top edge is at 0 feet high.

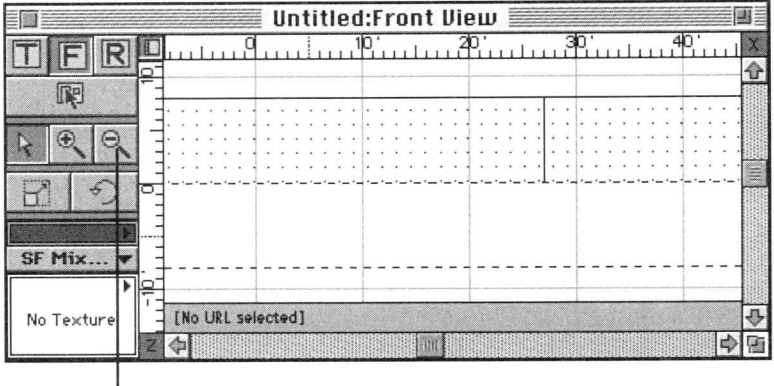

Zoom-Out Tool

You have just created a big yard (ground), so now you can build a room on it (later you might want to make a really large ground plane or maybe not have one at all for your Internet models):

1. From the 3-D Galleries Basic Shapes (Macintosh) or Basic 3-D Gallery (Windows), drag and drop a "Rectangle" into the center of the Design View (Top View). It will land at 0 feet high, on top of the ground, as shown in Figure 11.10.

Figure 11.10:

From the 3-D Galleries Basic Shapes (Macintosh) or Basic 3-D Gallery (Windows), drag and drop a "rectangle" into the center of the Design View (Top View).

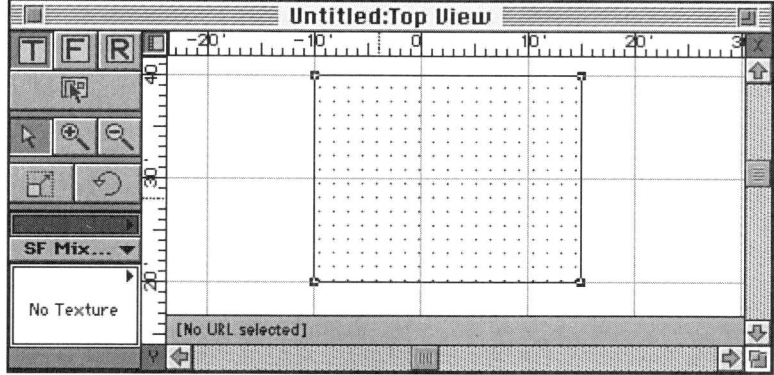

2. If the 0,0 coordinate is not visible, scroll the Design View until you see 0,0. Place the rectangle so that its lower-left corner is at –10,20. (Remember, that's –10 on the horizontal X axis and 20 on the vertical Y axis.)

3. Drag the handle in the rectangle's upper-right corner to 15,40.

To provide more working room on your screen, hide the Gallery Window by choosing Gallery from the Windows menu. Then choose "Tile Vertical" from the Windows menu.

4. Take a moment to walk around inside and outside of your bedroom by repeatedly clicking in the Walk View, or by clicking the navigation buttons along the bottom of the Walk View.

   When you've finished walking, click the Home button in the lower-right corner of the Walk View. Doing so returns your position in the model to the 0,0,5.25 coordinate (approximately eye level).

5. It's time to add the bathroom. Select the bedroom rectangle and duplicate it (Duplicate from the Edit menu). With the duplicate object still selected, move it to the right of the original, placing the left wall of the duplicate against the right wall of the original, as shown in Figure 11.11.

Figure 11.11:

Select the bedroom rectangle and duplicate it.

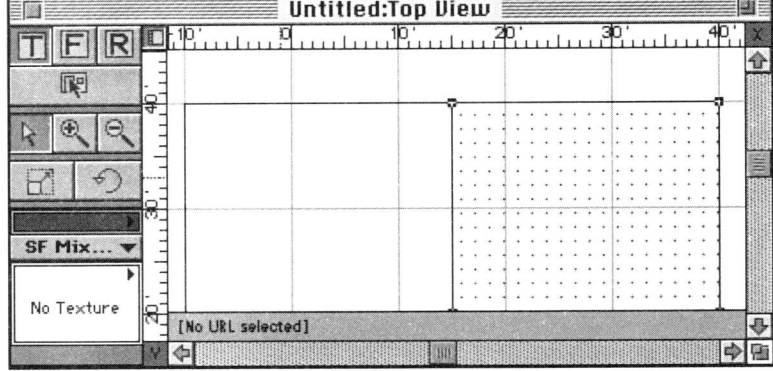

(Be careful not to overlap objects, which could prevent the program from rendering the objects properly in the Walk View.)

6. Drag the lower-right corner of the bathroom until that handle is at 25,30 (see Figure 11.12). The bathroom is now 10 feet wide and 10 feet long.

Figure 11:12:

Drag the lower-right corner of the bathroom until that handle is at 25,30.

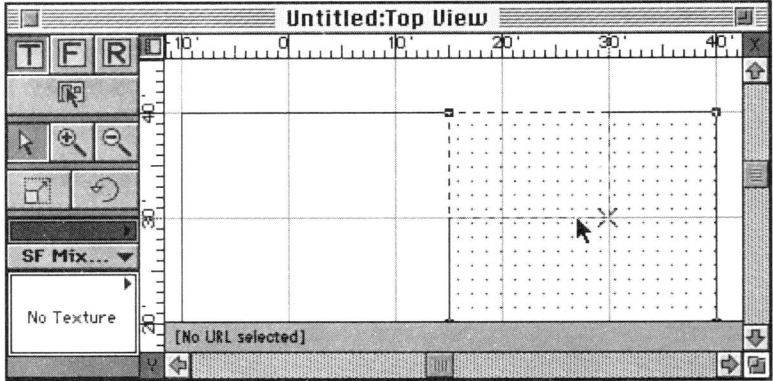

Adding Doors and Windows (Surface Features)

You need the Gallery Window again, so choose Gallery from the Windows menu and then choose Tile Horizontal from the same menu.

Make the Walk View active by clicking anywhere inside it, and then clicking the 3-D Select Surface button. You should see the front outside wall of the bedroom, as shown in Figure 11.13. This method of selecting a surface always shows you the outside of the surface. However, working with the 'I, O, and B' buttons, you can make your surface edits affect the inside (I), outside (O), or both sides (B) of a surface.

Another way to select a surface to edit it is to use the Surface Editor in the Design View and place your cursor on the segment that you want to access, as illustrated in Figure 11.14.

Remember that if you use either the 3-D Select Surface button or the Select Object button, you must then select the Walk button before navigation (walking) is enabled.

Figure 11.13:
The front outside wall of the bedroom.

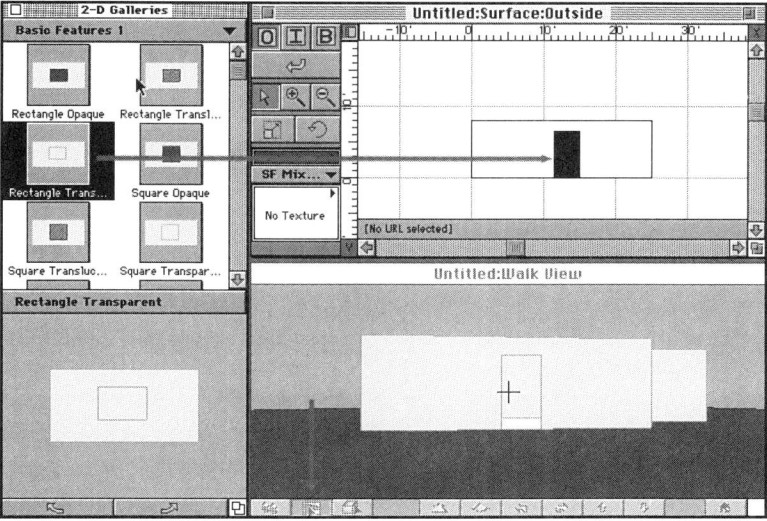

Figure 11.14:

You can also select a surface to edit by using the Surface Editor in the Design View and placing your cursor on the appropriate segment.

Surface Editor

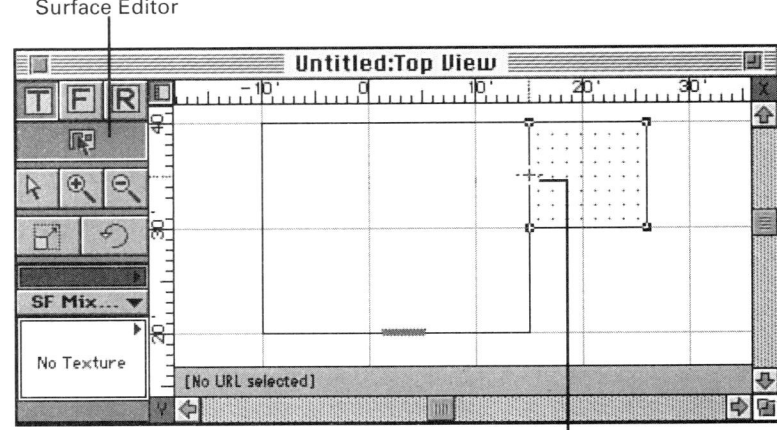

Place cursor here and press mouse

Next, you can add a door to this wall:

1. Click the Select Surface button at the bottom of the Walk View.

2. Move the cursor into the Walk View and click the front wall of the bedroom. The Design View title bar reads "Surface:Outside" because you selected the outside surface of the bedroom's front wall, which activated the Surface Editor.

   Now notice that the 2-D gallery named Basic Features 1 (Macintosh) or Basic 2-D Gallery (Windows) has appeared. (To see the names of additional 2-D galleries, click and hold down the bar that reads "Basic Features 1.") Whenever you select a surface to edit, the Gallery Window loads the 2-D galleries for you.

3. Click "Rectangle Transparent" in the Gallery Window. Then drag and drop it onto the front wall of the bedroom in the Design View.

4. Click and hold down the rectangle, and then move it until its bottom edge is even with the bottom of the wall.

5. Then size it, using the handles, until the transparent rectangle is 6.5 feet high and 3 feet wide. (To more easily accomplish this task, use the Magnify Tool and scroll as needed.) Position the door five feet to the right of the left side of the wall.

6. In the Design View, click the Return button to close the Surface Editor. Notice that you've returned to the 0,0 coordinate in the Top View and that the Gallery Window again displays 3-D objects.

   If necessary, scroll up until you see both rooms in the Design View.

Now we're going to work with the bathroom, and you can use Virtus VRML's second method of selecting a surface:

1. If not already selected, click the bathroom with the Select Object Tool from the Tools Pad, and then click the Surface Editor Tool.

2. Position the crosshair on the line that represents the bathroom wall—the wall shared with the bedroom—then click once to select it. The wall appears in the Surface Editor (Design View), and the "O" button appears pressed (selected).

3. Now you can add a transparent rectangle (door) to the bathroom. Drag and drop "Rectangle Transparent" onto the surface (wall), and then size it to 6.5 feet high by 3 feet wide. Position it in the middle of the wall, and then click the Return button. In the Walk View, you can now see into either room from the other room.

Let's add a window to the bedroom:

1. Scroll in the Top View until you can see the two rooms.

2. Select the front wall of the bedroom using the Surface Editor button in the Design View, or by using the Select Surface button at the bottom of the Walk View.

3. Click and hold down the 2-D Galleries Basic Features 1 (Macintosh) or Basic 2-D Gallery (Windows), and then select Window Sampler 1 (Macintosh) or Windows 2-D Gallery (Windows).

4. Click "Casement A Translucent" and view it in the Preview Area of the Gallery Window. Drag and drop the window onto the surface (wall) and position it five feet to the left of the right wall, and center it from top to bottom.

5. Click the Return button (shown in the margin) to go back to the Top View.

6. Scroll until you can see the two rooms. Notice that small bars showing the location of your doors and window appear in the Design View.

Adding Textures

Textures add realism to models, so it's good to enhance your rooms with a little tile and wood:

1. In the Walk View, navigate until you're inside the bathroom. (If clicking inside the Walk View doesn't move you around, make sure that the window's Walk button is pressed.)

2. To make it easier to see the entire room, choose Wide Angle from the Walk menu. Next, click the Select Surface button, and then click any bathroom wall to select it. See Figure 11.15.

Figure 11.15:

Click any bathroom wall to select it.

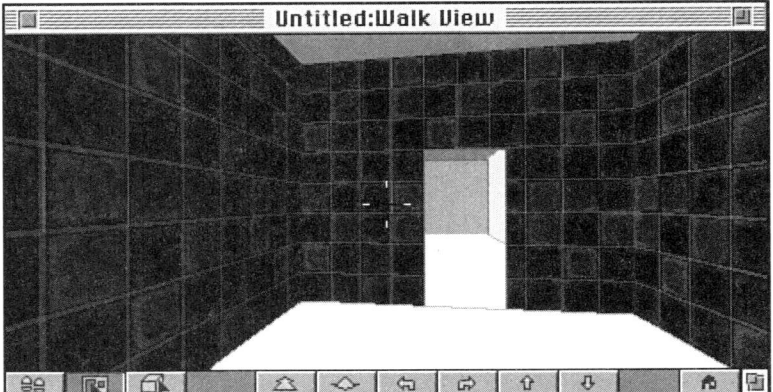

3. In the Design View, click the Texture Button. Click and hold down the Texture Button and choose the texture palette named Brick-Tile Shaded (Macintosh) or Brick@ (Windows). Then click and hold down the Texture Bar (the area below the Texture Button) and choose "Tile-Blue Shaded."

   The tile texture is applied to the wall; you'll see it both in the Surface Editor (Design View) and in the Walk View.

4. Using what you just learned, select the remaining three walls and apply the same texture to each. Finally, select the bathroom floor and apply a color of your choice from the Color Bar.

5. In the Walk View, navigate into the bedroom and select the floor.

6. In the Design View, choose the Textures Palette named Exterior Shaded (Macintosh) or Exter@ (Windows), and then apply the "Planks-Fir Shaded" texture to the floor.

7. Click the Return button to switch to the Top View. Scroll up until you can see both rooms. See Figure 11.16.

Figure 11.16:

Viewing what you have done.

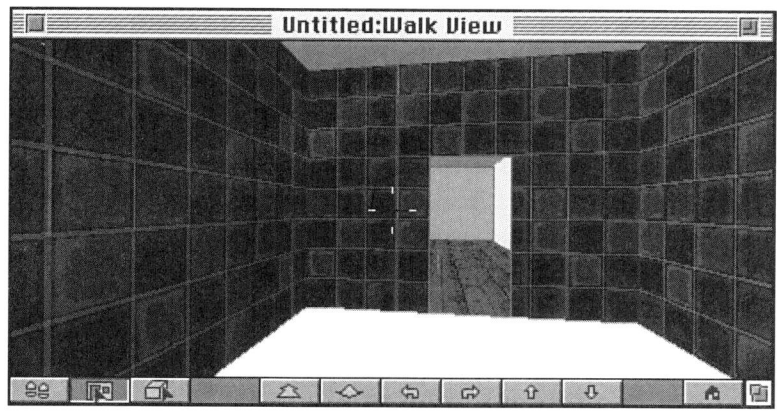

Adding Gallery Objects

Click and hold down the bar at the top of the 3-D Gallery Window that reads "Basic Shapes" (Macintosh) or "Basic 3-D Gallery" (Windows). Now choose the Home Remodeling Gallery (Macintosh) or Home 3-D Gallery (Windows) from the list of 3-D galleries. Drag and drop "Ceiling Fan" into the middle of the bedroom. Your screen should look something like Figure 11.17.

Figure 11.17:

Viewing the ceiling fan in Top View.

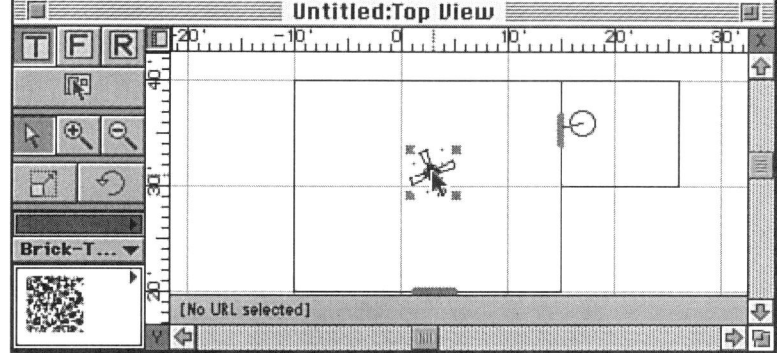

1. Because everything that is dropped into the Top, Front, and Right Views lands at 0 feet in the Design View, the ceiling fan is sitting on the floor.

2. Switch to the Front View, and then zoom in on the ceiling fan. Drag the fan up until it touches the ceiling, as shown in Figure 11.18.

Figure 11.18:

Moving the ceiling fan to the ceiling.

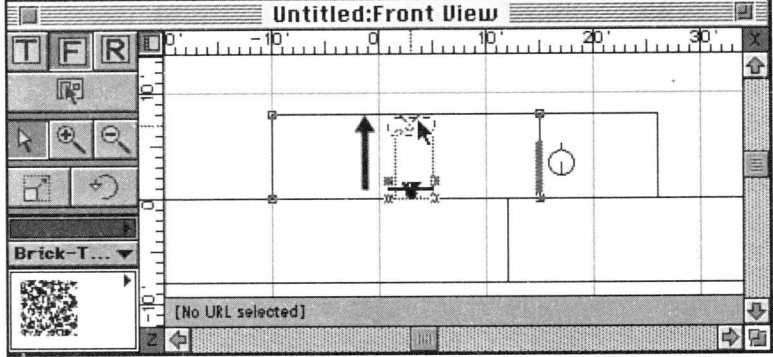

The bottom of the fan's light fixture is hanging pretty low, about 6.5 feet from the floor. Zoom out until you can clearly see the bedroom ceiling.

3. To make the ceiling higher, select the bedroom, click and drag the room's top surface until it's at 10 feet. Zoom in and move up the fan to meet the ceiling. Return to the Top View.

Also from the Home Remodeling Gallery (Macintosh) or Home 3-D Gallery (Windows), add "Platform Bed," "Side Table," "Study Desk," "TV with Stand", and "Wooden Bookcase" to your bedroom. You have to rotate some of the furniture to match our arrangement (shown in Figure 11.19).

To do this:

1. Choose an item with the Select Object Tool, and then click the Rotate Object Tool.

2. Position the cursor in the middle of the object you want to rotate, and then click and drag outward to create a handle.

3. Still holding down the mouse button, move the handle in an arc until the object is rotated as desired. Holding down the Shift key as you move the handle helps you keep the object from becoming skewed as it is rotated.

The various objects that make up a surface feature (a door or window) can't be grouped, so the window you're working with is actually a collection of objects. If you want to move the entire casement window, first make sure that all of its parts are selected. If you accidentally move some of the objects apart that make up the window, immediately choose Undo from the Edit menu. To move this window while in the Surface Editor, select all of its parts using the marquee method, or individually select each item while holding down the Shift key until all are selected.

Figure 11.19:
The final outcome.

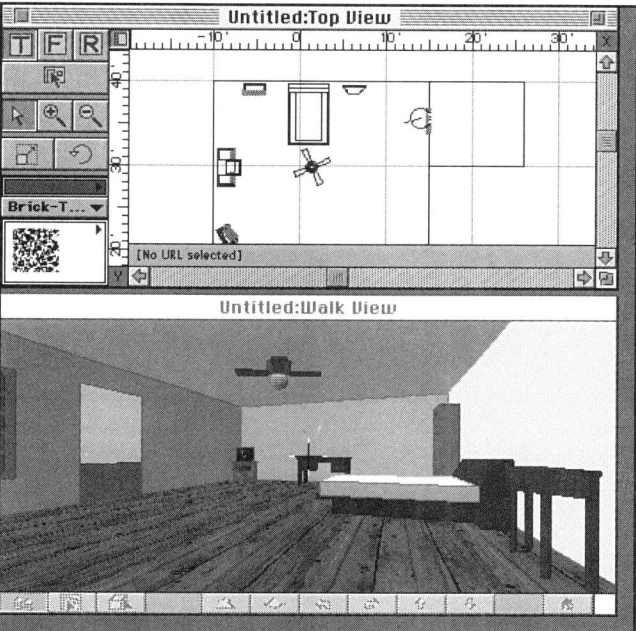

Modeling Your Own Objects

Dresser with Drawers—Neither the Home Sampler Gallery (Macintosh) or Basic 3-D Gallery (Windows) includes a dresser, so let's make one:

1. First, switch back to the 3-D Basic Shapes Gallery (Macintosh) or Home 3-D Gallery (Windows). Drag and drop a "Rectangle" into the Top View of the Design View. (If you place the rectangle outside of the rooms, on the ground, it is easier to work with it. If you inadvertently select the ground or other object while working outside the rooms, choose Unselect All from the Edit menu.)

2. In the Top View, size the rectangle so it's 5 feet wide and 2 feet deep. In the Front View, size it to a height of 2.5 feet. Change the color of the rectangle to brown. In the Top View, move the dresser to the location shown in Figure 11.20.

Figure 11.20:

Moving the dresser.

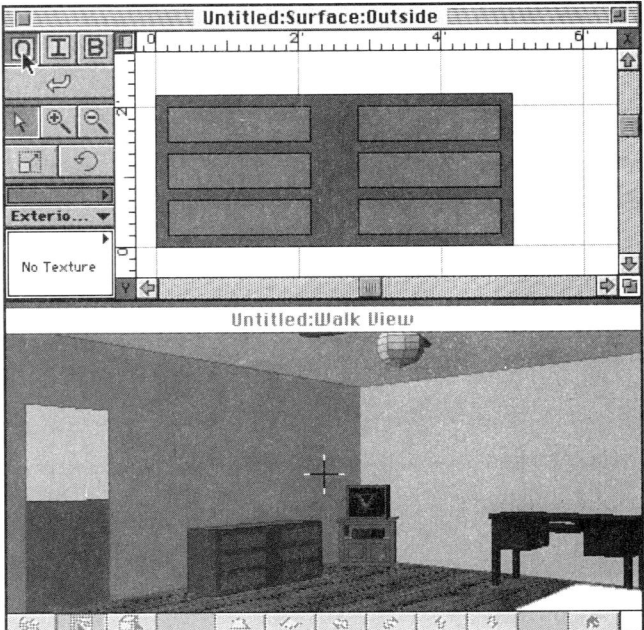

3. The drawers can be constructed from either 3-D gallery objects or 2-D surface features; you'll use 2-D surface features. In the Walk View, navigate until you're in front of the dresser. Click the Surface Editor button, and then click the dresser's front surface.

4. From the 2-D gallery items, drag and drop "Rectangle Opaque" onto the surface, and then size it as illustrated in Figure 11.21. With this rectangle (drawer) selected, choose an appropriate color for it. Duplicate the drawer and place it to the right of the original.

5. Now select both drawers and position them at the bottom of the surface. With both drawers still selected, duplicate them and place the duplicates above the originals. Duplicate again and arrange the drawers as shown.

6. Click the Return button to return to the Top View.

Framed Picture—To put a framed picture on the wall, you first need to create its frame:

1. From the 3-D Basic Shapes Gallery (Macintosh) or Basic 3-D Gallery (Windows), drag and drop a "Rectangle" into the Top View and place it outside of the rooms. Size the rectangle (picture frame) to

4 feet wide and 2 inches deep. (Zoom in on the rectangle so it is easier to make it thin.)

2. Switch to the Front View to make the rectangle 2 feet high. Next, move up the picture frame until the bottom of it is at a height of 4 feet. Switch back to the Top View to position the picture against the back wall of the bedroom, directly over the platform bed.

3. In the Walk View, select the picture frame by clicking the Select Object button and then clicking the frame. The picture frame is selected and centered in the Design View, which is now active.

4. Change its color to a deep gold. While still in the Design View, click the Surface Editor button and select the bottom edge (front surface) of the picture frame. See Figure 11.21.

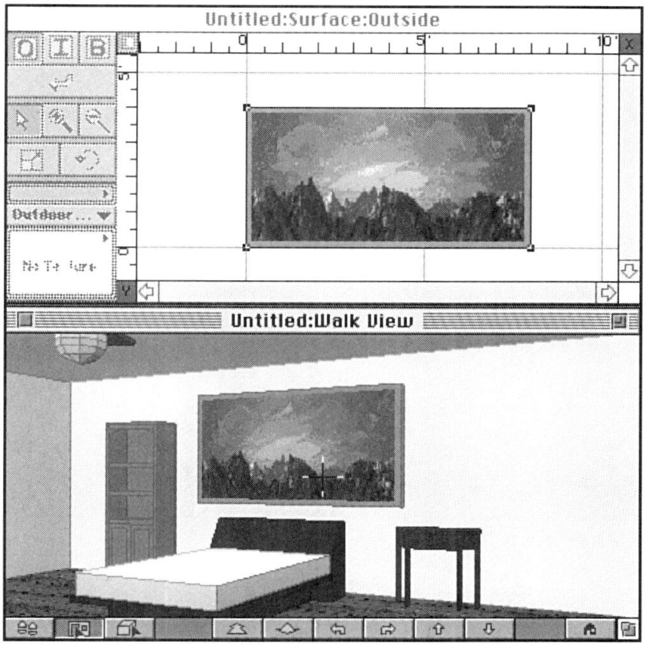

Figure 11.21:

Editing the picture.

5. Drag and drop a "Rectangle Opaque" from the 2-D galleries onto the frame's surface. Size this rectangle so it is one inch smaller (on all sides) than the frame, and then center it as shown in Figure 11.22. With the rectangle still selected, choose the texture palette named Outdoors Shaded (Macintosh) or Outdoor@ (Windows), and then choose "Mountains Shaded."

6. Click the Return button to return to the Top View.

Using the F and R Galleries

Adding a Roof—To add a roof to the bedroom and to the bathroom, you'll work with a triangle:

1. Switch to the Basic Shapes R Gallery and select "Triangle." Drop it into the Top View, somewhere outside the rooms (it will land at 0 feet).

2. Switch to the Front View and drag the triangle (roof) up until its base sits on top of the bedroom.

3. Now go back to the Top View and move the roof so its upper-right corner is at the 15,40 coordinate.

4. Drag the left side of the triangle to the –10 coordinate so that the roof covers the entire bedroom.

5. Switch to the Right View and drag the lower-left handle to the 20,10 coordinate. Drag the top of the triangle to the 30,20 coordinate. See Figure 11.22.

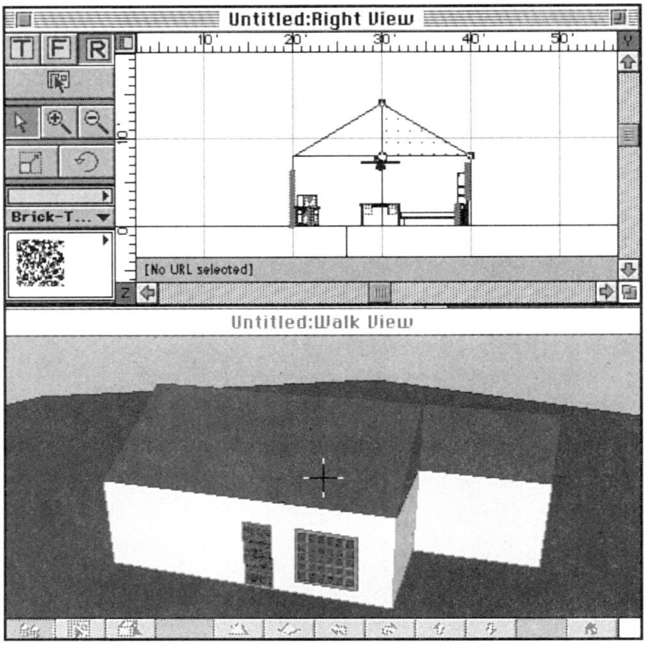

Figure 11.22:

Adding the right side of the roof.

Virtus VRML Toolkit

Set Design-Assassins   Mark Reaney

Viewing theater sets with Virtus Voyager.
http://ukanaix.cc.ukans.edu:80/~mreaney/

Dinosaurs viewed through Virtus Voyager.

Virtus VRML Toolkit

Using textures with the Alphabet Gallery.

The Temple of Neptune.

Virtus VRML Toolkit

Rendering art.

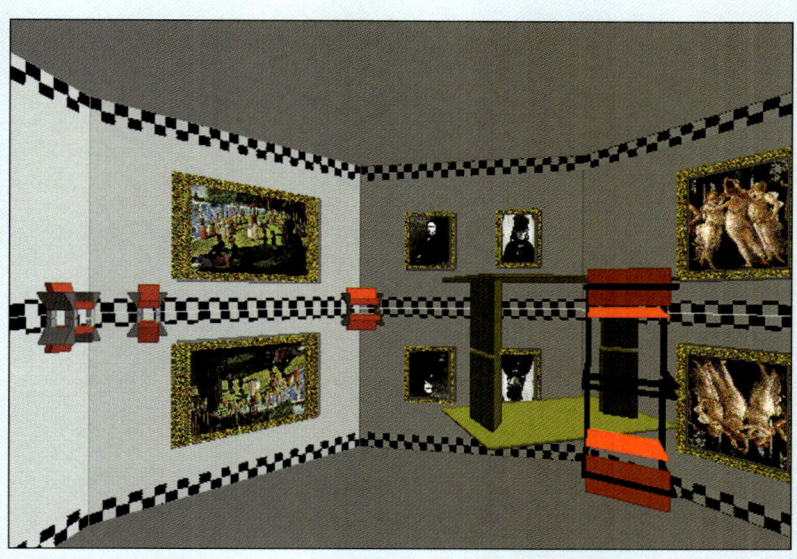

A mirror effect.

Virtus VRML Toolkit

The shrine of St. Sebastian.

Adding textures to a Meiji.

Virtus VRML Toolkit

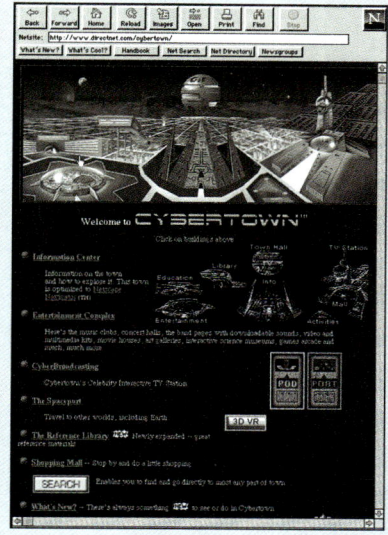

Cybertown, created in part by Pascal Baudar, the creative director at MultiMedia Magic. Cybertown as you can imagine, is this really neat world created using Virtus WalkThrough Pro (http://www.directnet.com/cybertown/)

Creating your own bedroom in Virtus VRML.

Virtus VRML Toolkit

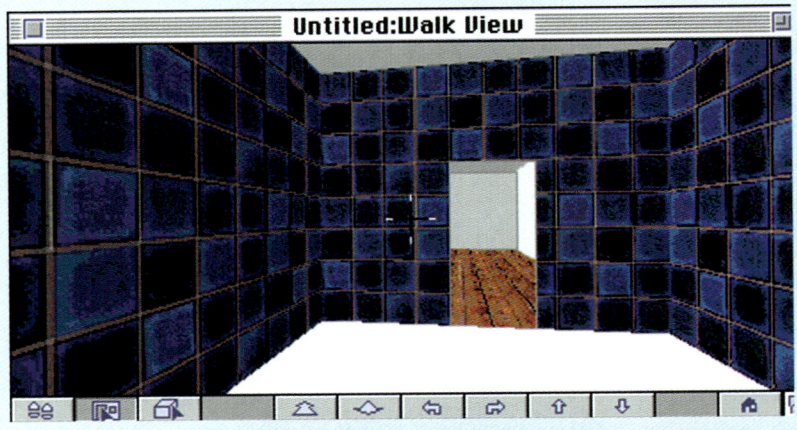

Adding textures to a wall in Virtus VRML.

Flat Shading   Gouraud shading

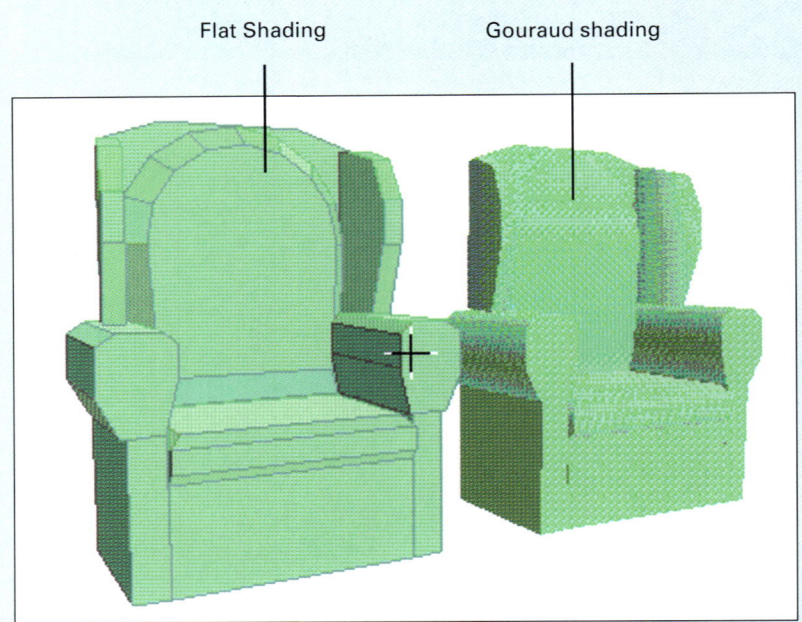

Flat shading versus Gouraud shading.

Virtus VRML Toolkit

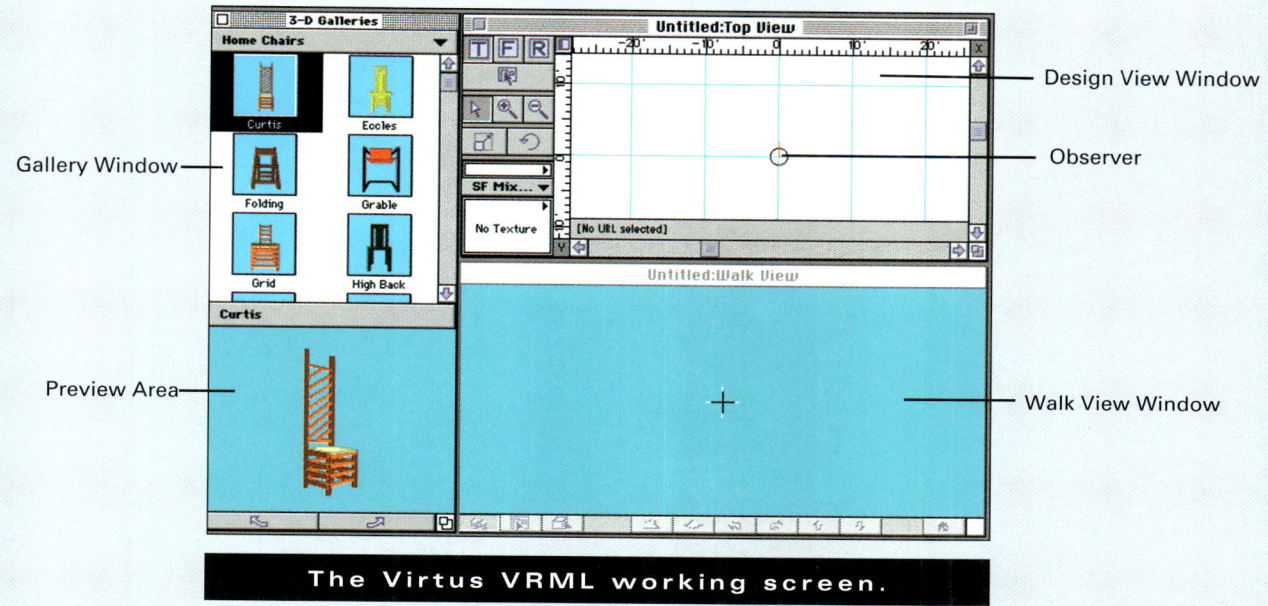

Gallery Window

Preview Area

Design View Window

Observer

Walk View Window

The Virtus VRML working screen.

A ray-traced image of a scene from the upcoming computer game,
Tom Clancy's First Contact: Derelict.

Virtus VRML Toolkit

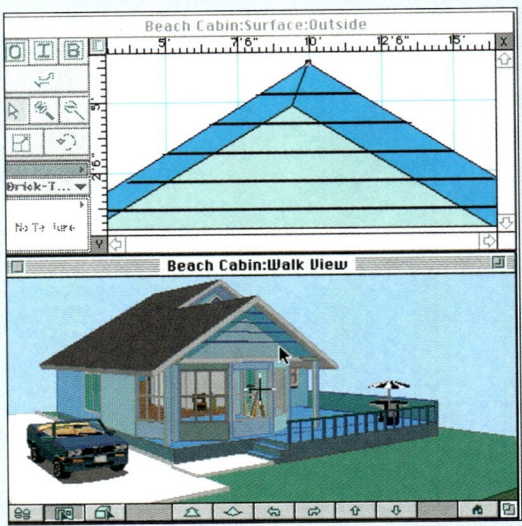

Beach cabin in Walk View.

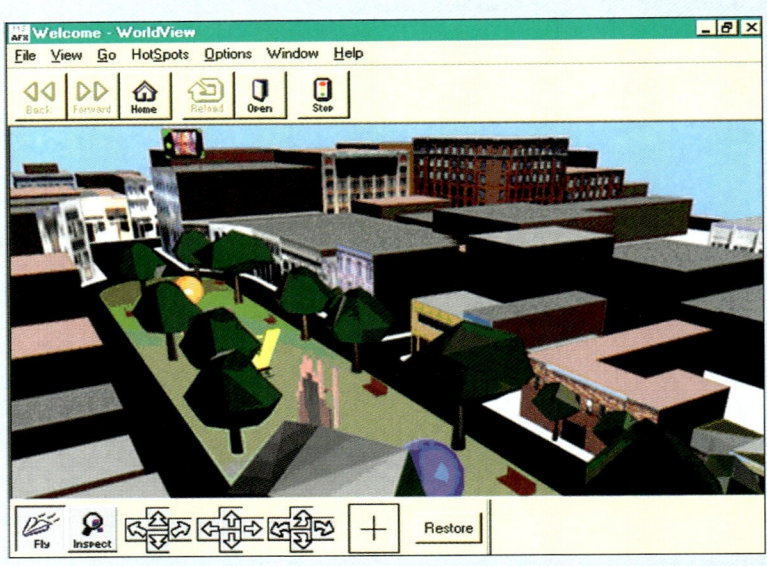

The WorldView VRML browser.
(See http://www.webmaster.com/vrml/.)

6. Click the Home button at the bottom right of the Walk View and take a look at your new roof. Using what you just learned, add a roof to the bathroom.

Adding a Mailbox—Finally, let's model a mailbox. First, switch to the 3-D Galleries Basic Shapes (Macintosh) or Basic 3-D Gallery (Windows) and we'll make a post:

1. Drag and drop "Rectangle" into the Top View, and then size it to 4 inches high by 4 inches wide. Now go to the Front View and make the post 3 feet tall. Color the post brown.

2. To make the mailbox, first switch to the Basic Shapes F Gallery and select "Pentagon." Drag and drop it into the Top View.

3. Size this object so that it's 2 feet from top to bottom. To do this: Select the object, click the Resize button, press the Shift key and click any handle of the pentagon (mailbox). With the Shift key still pressed, move the mouse to resize the pentagon as desired.

4. Switch to the Front View and size the mailbox to 9 inches in diameter. (Zoom in and scroll as necessary.) Color it a dark gray. Working in the Front and Top Views, place the mailbox on top of the post. (As illustrated in Figure 11.23, the Top View shows the mailbox centered over the post.)

Figure 11.23:

Top View shows the mail-box centered over the post.

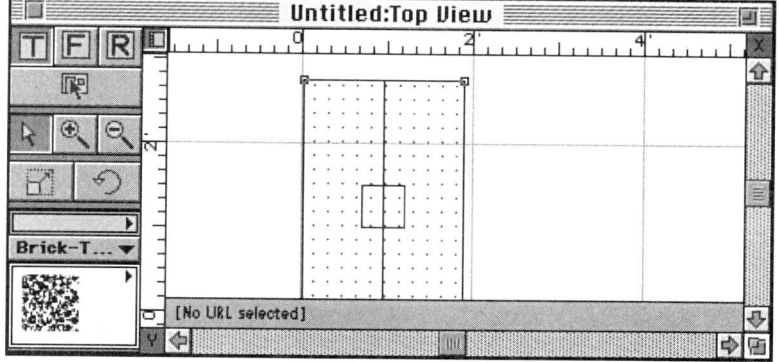

Saving Your File

You might think that saving your file should be as easy as selecting Save from the File menu. Well, you'd be partially right, but there are certain issues that I need to address so that your file can be viewed properly by others.

Because you just want to know how to save your file here, I'll just do that instead of giving you the Gettysburg Address version. In the next chapter, I'll give you the lowdown on working with textures and problems that you need to look out for.

To save your working file:

1. From the File menu, select Save or Save As... The Save As... dialog box appears as shown in Figure 11.24.

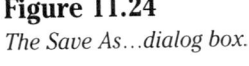

Figure 11.24

The Save As...dialog box.

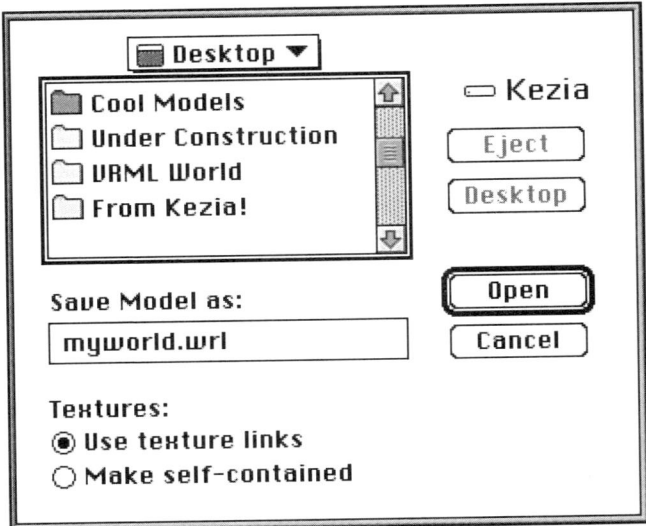

2. In the highlighted area, type the name of the model.

Because of the different computer platforms that connect the Internet, I advise you to use care when naming your files. Don't use symbols (@ # $ % / ~, and so on) or spaces in your file names and preferably use all lowercase letters. This will keep conflicts to a minimum as you work across platforms. As well, you must add the file extension **.wrl** to the end of the file name.

3. From Textures, select "Use texture links."

4. Now select the directory where you want to save your work and choose Save.

Pretty easy, but one of the real glitches with HTML/VRML is that the textures you use must be saved as texture links and must also use the extensions .gif or .jpg (which they won't already have).

If you have already (accidentally) saved your file using the 'Make self-contained' texture option, you can still rescue your file.

To correct a file that has been previously saved using the 'Make self-contained' texture:

1. Duplicate the file that you want to convert.

2. Select all of the textures on the model and delete them, one by one.

3. Save the file with the **.wrl** extension and select "Use texture links."

4. Now replace the textures one at a time in the model.

5. Resave the file and select "Use texture links" again.

Make sure you know where each of the textures is located that you have used and place each one in a separate folder.

Later, you will put each one in the same folder (directory) to use with your VRML (*.wrl) file, but this will keep you organized.

Summary

You have now learned how to create a simple 3-D world in Virtus VRML and have furnished it modestly. As well, you learned how to utilize 3-D galleries to cut your design time, how to apply a simple texture, and even how to create your own objects from scratch.

The next chapter is really short, but important. It explains the cold hard facts of how you must deal with textures in a VRML file. Even if you're a little sleepy, just read on and then you can sleep on it and it will imprint better....

12

Using Textures with VRML Files

An important issue to understand is how to use textures and how to handle them when your model is exported as a VRML file. If you worked through the tutorial in the last chapter, you may have understood part of it, but the whole process does need a little more clarification.

In this chapter, you:

- Learn how to add a texture to the Virtus program.

- Learn how to apply a texture to a surface or object.

- Learn how to export VRML files with and without textures.

- Learn how to convert your textures for viewing on the Web.

Adding a Texture

Lots of textures are included with the program and you can add to them with third-party textures or a desktop scanner. Suppose you want to place a photo of your family onto the TV set inside of your cyberworld (and I promise you that if you do this, they will get off your back for a while about staying in front of the computer so long…. First, you take the photo and scan it using your color desktop scanner. You can scan your photo at a relatively low resolution (72 dpi to 150 dpi) and at a depth of eight bits. If you are using a Macintosh, save the file as a PICT. If you are using Windows, save the file as a BMP.

To add your texture, follow these steps:

1. From the Edit menu, select Add Textures.

2. When the Find File dialog box appears, select the new PICT or BMP that you created and select Add… to load an entire folder of textures.

3. You can load individual textures by selecting the Add button on the right side of the dialog box.

The new textures are now available by selecting the Textures bar and choosing the desired textures.

After you launch the program again, the textures should be available by selecting the Textures bar and choosing the desired texture.

Applying Textures

Textures can be applied to an entire object, or to individual surfaces, or as surface features. Textures can be applied while you're in any Design View (Top, Front, or Right) or the Surface Editor. Once a texture is applied, it can be easily changed by selecting it and then choosing another texture from the Texture Palette.

When applying textures, you must pay close attention to the Placement Buttons (shown in the margin). Textures, like colors and surface features, can be applied on the inside, the outside, or on both sides of an object, depending on the choice of the Placement Buttons. As well, you may place a texture on one side of an object (Outside) and flip the surface and then place another texture on the other side (Inside).

Exporting Your VRML File

If your model does not contain textures, the steps for exporting are relatively easy. In fact, here again, a very important issue is knowing your audience and knowing what they will use to view your model.

Several of the VRML browsers available now do not read textures and actually crash when they encounter a model that contains them. You might opt to create only models without textures for a couple of reasons:

- They're less trouble to create.

- You can walk faster in models without lots of textures. Of course, the beauty of being able to create a virtual reality environment is to make it as realistic as possible.

Exporting a File without Textures

Follow these quick steps to export your file without textures:

1. From the File menu, select Export and drag over to VRML.

2. When the Export Options VRML dialog box comes up, you can ignore the Texture File Extension, but make sure that the "Include Texture Links" is unchecked.

If you would like to export a model that has textures, but don't want to use them with your VRML file, you can uncheck the "Include Texture Links" box and the resulting file will not have textures.

3. Select OK. That's all there is to it!

Exporting a File with Textures

Follow these steps to export a file with textures:

1. From the File menu, select Export and drag over to VRML.

2. When the Export Options VRML dialog box appears (as shown in Figure 12.1), type either **.jpg** (default) or **.gif** in the active cell. This sets the internal resources to look for those file formats in the textures that you have used in your model. It doesn't change or affect the texture files.

3. Make sure the "Include Texture Links" box is checked.

Figure 12.1:
The Export Options VRML dialog box.

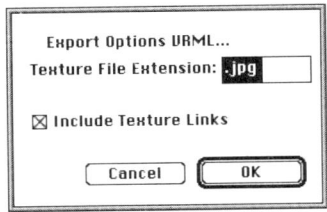

4. Select OK.

Converting Your Textures

Now that you have exported this model as a VRML file, it is ready for a VRML browser to see it on the WWW. But remember that I said Virtus VRML and other programs that are used to create 3-D worlds use the PICT and BMP graphic formats when they are displaying textures. But the WWW only understands GIF (.gif) or JPEG (.jpg) graphic files.

In the Export Options VRML dialog box (refer to Figure 12.1), we told the internal file that it should look for .jpg files whenever it loads that particular model. Now, all we have to do is convert those textures that we used in that model into JPEG format.

Using a graphic converter (freeware/shareware products are listed in the ReadMe file for both Macintosh and Windows) or a paint program (like Adobe Photoshop), convert the files from PICT (Macintosh) or BMP (Windows) to a JPEG or GIF format. Make sure that you do one or the other and that it agrees with the file extension that you selected in the Export Options dialog box.

The best way to do this is to know exactly which texture files you have used, duplicate them and place them into a separate folder, and convert the files from the duplicate folder. This way you don't run the risk of converting your only copy of these texture files into JPEGs or GIFs.

Converting a Texture for Use in a VRML File

To convert a texture for use in a model that will be exported as a VRML file, follow these steps:

1. Locate the textures that are used in the model and keep them in the same location or folder where they were originally.

2. Open the textures files in a paint program (like Adobe Photoshop) or a graphics converter and save a copy with the same name, but add the extension .jpg or .gif to each file.

This is a case-sensitive extension. Make sure the file names match the internal resource extension of those files.

Converting Self-Contained Textures

If you are using a previously created model that has been saved with the option "self-contained textures," you must create a copy of the model with textures that are linked, not embedded. To do this, you must:

1. Create a duplicate of the model or rename it using the Save As feature.

2. Locate the textures that are used in the model and keep them in a folder near the model.

3. Delete the textures from the model's surfaces and reapply them.

4. Select Save As from the File menu and select the texture option, "Use texture links" in the dialog box.

Saving Your File

In case you didn't understand this, when and if you worked through the tutorial, it's worth repeating.

To save your working file:

1. From the File menu, select Save or Save As.... The Save As... dialog box appears, as shown in Figure 12.2.

Figure 12.2:
The Save As dialog box.

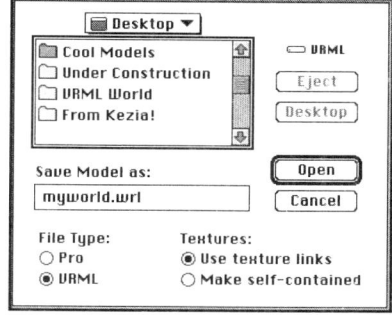

2. In the highlighted area, type the name of the model (in Figure 12.2, it is called **myworld.wrl**). Because of the different computer platforms that connect the Internet, I advise you to use care when naming your files. Don't use symbols (@ # $ % / ~, etc.) or spaces in your file names and preferably use all lowercase letters. This will keep conflicts to a minimum as you work across platforms. As well, you must add the file extension **.wrl** to the end of the file name.

3. From "Textures:" select "Use texture links."

4. Now select the directory where you want to save your work and choose Save.

Pretty easy, but one of the real glitches with HTML/VRML is that the textures you use must be saved as texture links and must also use the extensions .gif or .jpg (which they won't already have).

If you have already (accidentally) saved your file using the "Make self-contained" texture option, you can still rescue your file. To correct a file that has been previously saved using the "Make self-contained" texture:

1. Duplicate the file that you would like to convert.

2. Select all of the textures on the model and delete them, one by one.

3. Save the file with the **.wrl** extension and select "Use texture links."

4. Now replace the textures one at a time in the model.

5. Resave the file and select "Use texture links" again.

Make sure you know where each of the textures are located that you have used and place them in a separate folder.

Summary

I know what you're thinking. Couldn't someone please create a software that converted all of these textures into GIFs, made little files with copies of all the linked textures placed inside of it, and flagged internal file extension formats for me with a push of a button? Trust me, you don't want it any more than I do! And, of course, Virtus will certainly work towards that goal—but you must understand it's not something that can happen overnight. And remember you are a cutting-edge type person and you must have this right now even if in one month the technology is ancient. That's our price. I'd love to think it would only take a month for all of that to happen, but I think we'd be dreaming. Just deal with it for now. The future looks bright.

Now the fun begins! In the next chapter, you learn how to link files together and to create hotspots. It's a real hands-on chapter, so if you're in bed now, just go to sleep.

13

Adding URLs and Linking Worlds

Gosh, you've had to read 12 chapters just to get to this point. Whew! But you have learned a lot and you know that if I had started with all this Uniform Resource Locator (URL) stuff you might have not been ready for it. But now you are, so let's get started.

I'm going to give you a short example of how to add anchors to an object or a surface and then let you go crazy building stuff. A more complex model will not only be challenging (which is good…), but it may also end up being too slow for the average Internet connection.

Keep in mind that everyone doesn't have an ISDN or a T-1 connection like you do, so their walk speeds may not be blazing fast. But then, there are already sites with live video and live audio feed that are difficult for me to see/hear at home.... So the good part about this is that you are once again on the cutting edge. Just a little ahead of your time. These connections have got to come down one day.

In this chapter, I give you examples of how you use Virtus VRML to:

- Create links from one VRML file to another.

- Create a link from another Net browser like Netscape or Mosaic and then back to another VRML model.

- Learn what a hotspot is and how to create one.

All of this viewing on the Internet is accomplished through the use of a VRML browser, called Virtus Voyager, which you have on the CD-ROM that comes with this book. The Virtus Voyager 1.0 browser is located inside a folder that is appropiately called "Virtus Voyager." If you want to get started using the browser first, turn to Chapter 14 for instructions. Any updated instructions for the use of the browser can be found on the Virtus Web Page at http://www.virtus.com.

The version of the browser that ships with this book is in a *beta* stage of development at press time, but by the time you are reading these words, an updated version will be ready at the Virtus site (http://www.virtus.com) and you can download it fast and have the best and brightest that we offer—for free. Virtus Voyager is available for Macintosh, Windows 3.1, and Windows 95. In Chapter 15, we discuss several other browsers and their pros and cons. Again, remember that you are cutting edge and this is brand new technology; it changes rapidly as the language improves. What we have today, we'll all laugh about in three months as being archaic. You gotta keep up....

Adding a VRML Anchor

For the sake of simplicity, let's go back to that model that you were working on in Chapter 11. You know, that very neat peasant house you made and dazzled your spouse with. You may have saved it as **myhouse.wrl** if you exported it or some other name like that.

Windows users: If you have saved it only once with the extension .wrl, you need to make a duplicate of the file and change the extension to .vvr to reopen a file using Virtus VRML.

Adding a Basic Anchor

After you open the file, you should realize that it is very similar to the way you left it. In fact it's exactly the way you left it. That's called persistent data. That was a geek joke, sorry. Anyway, walk into the front door of your house and into the first room that we'll probably call a bedroom. Remember that we added lots of furniture, and I hope you added the pieces that I suggested.

If you didn't follow along with the tutorial, I guess that means that you don't have a model to use now. Out of the goodness of my heart (and those folks at Hayden), I have included it on the CD for you. In a folder called Tutorial, there are two folders, one for the Macintosh and one for Windows, that contain the file **myhouse.vvr**. Go there now and start that program.

Now follow this:

1. Walk to the left, and in the corner there should be a television set with a very cool Virtus logo on it.

2. Stay in the Walk View and select the television set with the 3-D Object Selector button (shown in the margin).

3. Look up in the Design View in Figure 13.1 and notice that the television set is now selected. We selected the object this way because if we tried to use the Select Object Tool, the roof or even the actual room that the television set was contained in would be selected first.

4. From the Edit menu, select VRML Anchor... (you must be in Design View for this menu option to be active).

5. When the dialog box appears, type **http://www.cbs.com**

6. Now click anywhere on the Design View and move the cursor over to the television set. As you move it over the TV, the URL for CBS should be displayed in the URL panel.

Figure 13.1:
The television set is selected.

URL panel

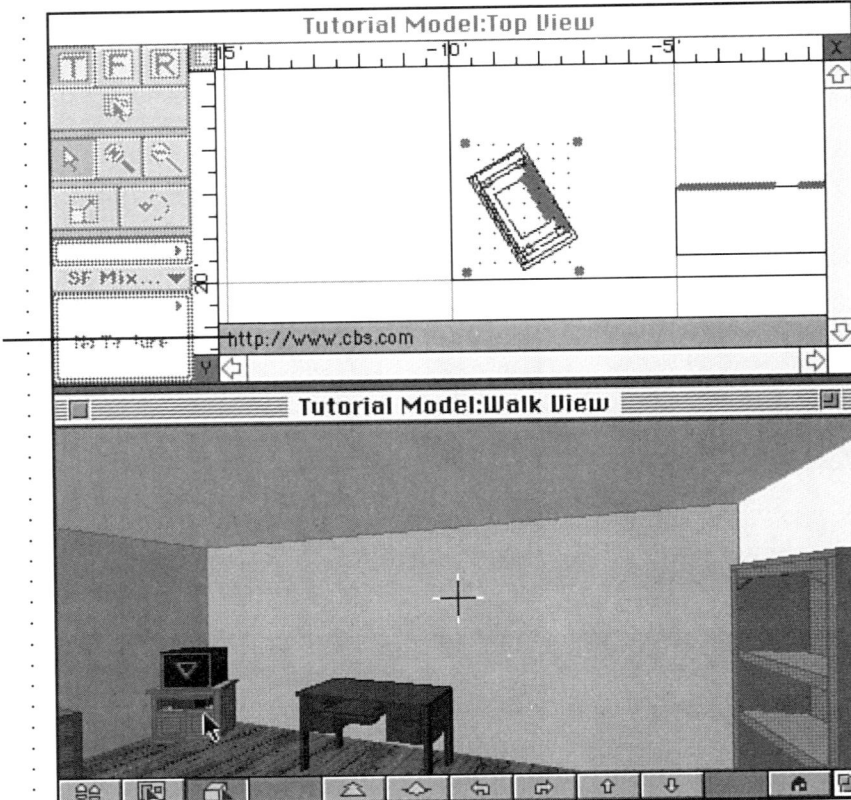

You have just set your first VRML anchors and whenever you or someone else walks into that television set, they will be sent to the CBS Home Page to find out what's on tonight.

Let's continue and add a few more anchors:

1. Select the bed (across from the TV) in the Walk View with the 3-D Object Selector button, as shown in Figure 13.2.

2. From the Edit menu, select VRML Anchor... and type:
   http://www.achilles.net/~bb
   (Remember that you must be in Design View to use this option.)

3. Now click anywhere on the Design View and move the cursor over the bed. As you move it over the bed, the URL for the Canadian Bed & Breakfast Online should show up. (OK, so I think some people from Canada are neat. Okay, I think one person is really neat. But there really are tons of places to go and stay there. You'll thank me one day....)

Figure 13.2:
Selecting the bed.

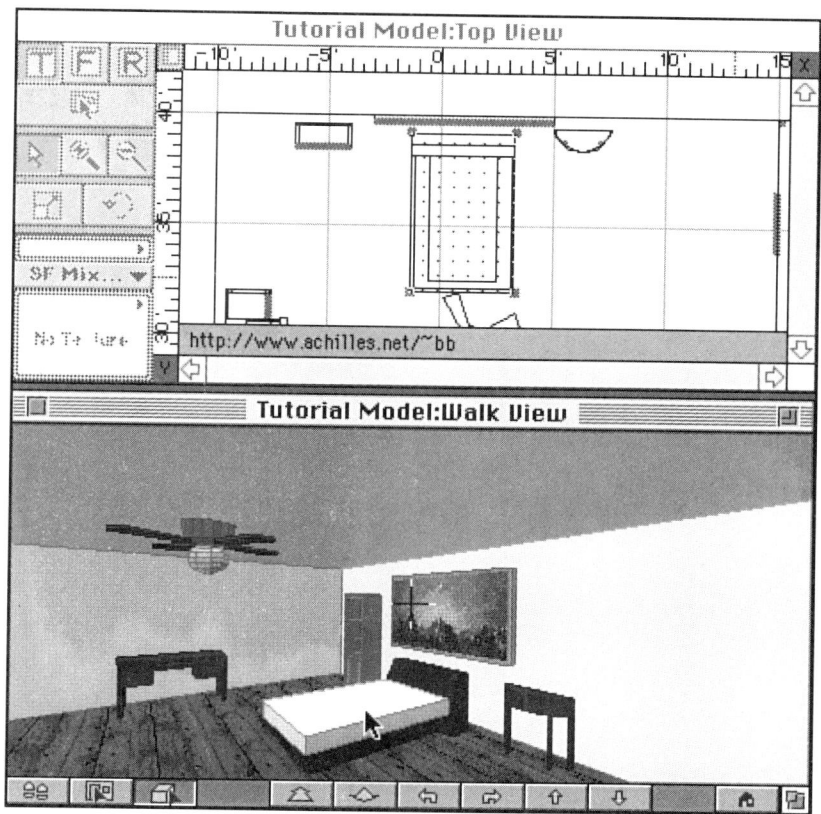

Adding an Anchor to a Surface (a Hotspot)

We have now added two different URLs to two different objects in our bedroom. Now walk into the bathroom (on the right of the bed) and look out into the bedroom. Boy, there's not much in mine. I forgot to put in a shower and a sink and a toilet. Before we go and furnish it, let's add a URL to a surface or better yet, let's add it to an *invisible* surface, like a doorway to the bathroom. To do that:

1. In the Walk View, select the 3-D Select Surface Tool and touch on the wall where the doorway is located, as illustrated in Figure 13.3. (If you tried to select the clear doorway you would actually be selecting something inside of the bedroom. This is a very smart program....)

Figure 13.3:

Selecting a wall with the 3-D Select Surface Tool.

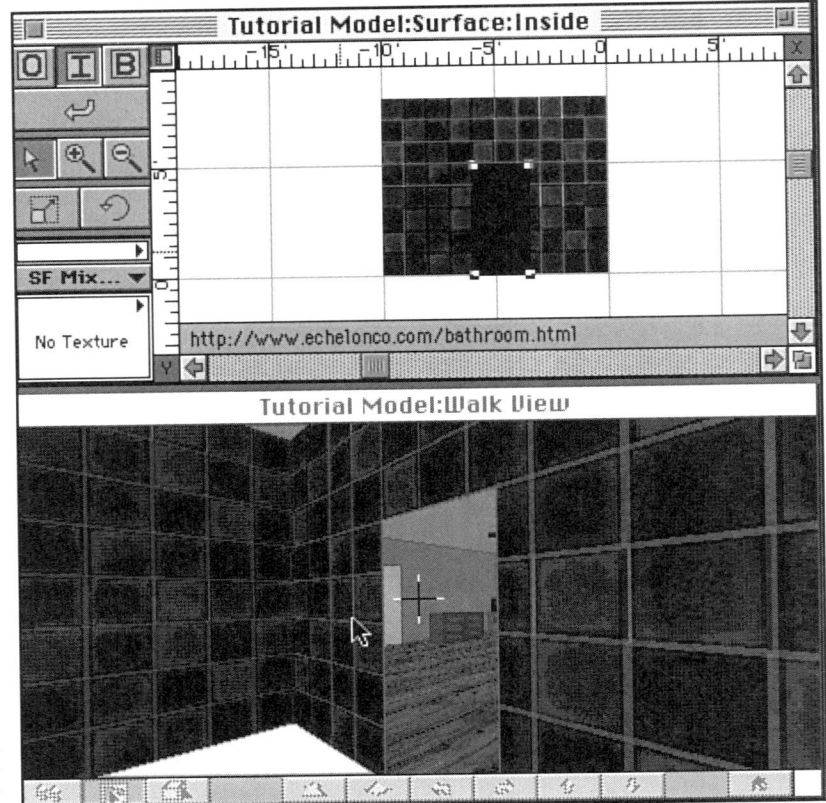

A **hotspot** is when you link a URL anchor to a 3-D object. When users move into the 3-D object, they are transported to the Web page indicated by the URL.

2. Now you're back in the Surface Editor and using the Select Tool, touch on the 'black' doorway to select it. (Remember that it is shown as black because it is clear and there's no way for us to actually show clear.)

3. From the Edit menu, select VRML Anchor... and type:
   http://www.echelonco.com/bathroom.html

This is the Web Page for Echelon's Bathroom Wall. You may not think this is as funny as I do, but it is a collection of hundreds, maybe thousands of things written on bathroom walls. (The best one I read the other day was from someone in New Zealand who wrote, "Who is O.J. Simpson?" Like we need to hear more...)

4. Test the connection by placing your cursor over the doorway and seeing whether the URL address is displayed.

5. Return to the Design View by closing the Surface Editor with the Return Button.

What you have just done here is learned how to add a URL anchor to a 3-D object that links us to a 2-D Web page (called a **hotspot**). We attached the link to both 3-D items as well as to a 2-D surface (the doorway of the bathroom).

Another link you might want to do is select the window on the front of the building using the 3-D Select Surface Tool and type in this URL for the Home Page of Pella® Windows: **http://www.pella.com/**.

Note

An important consideration here is that when you create a URL anchor for an opening on a wall's surface, you can't ever go through that door or window without getting zapped away somewhere in Cyberspace. That might be fine sometimes, but it also means that any links made for objects inside that room may never be used.

The Implications to Learning Visually

Now think of the possibilities of how you associate visual images with information. Maybe we can finally escape flatland. By creating a storehouse of 3-D "props," you can remember information for the Net differently.

Educators have long known that students learn in different ways. Books are great for some, but everyone relates to visual images more readily. Those old filmstrip projectors and yes, those poor overheads, made a stab at conveying information in a different way to us (if you didn't fall asleep in the process...). But now, using your computer, you are able to associate a TV set in your virtual world with the entire programming schedule for CBS. If you want to be more general, you could have just associated it with a search service like Yahoo with everything on the Web that contains the word "television."

Linking VRML Files to VRML Files

Creating a complex world with many different rooms and lots of textures and lots of objects can be taxing to your local computer and to your modem. One way to speed that up is to break the model into pieces after you complete it. Simply copy and paste the pieces of the model and place them into new files.

Depending on the type of model that you have built, I recommend that, for now, you have three or four rooms together in any one model and that you create separate files for other rooms and link to them.

As an example, I have created a kitchen that I would like for you to provide a link to from your original model. First, open the myhouse2.wr model (on the CD, it is located in the Tutorial folder), if it isn't already open, and walk over to the left side of the room.

1. Select the left wall of the bedroom (the one with the desk against it) using the 3-D Select Surface Tool. (See Figure 13.4.)

Figure 13.4:
Selecting the left wall of the bedroom.

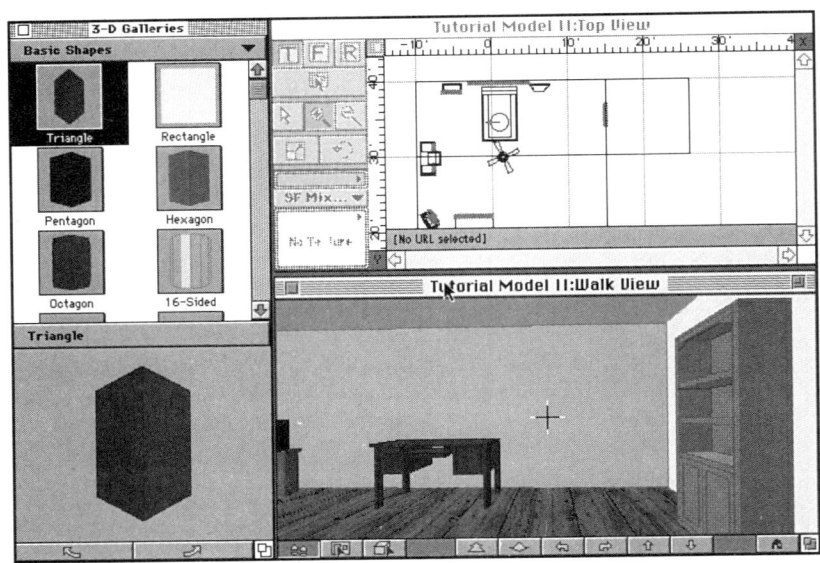

2. When you are in the Surface Editor, look in the Gallery window and choose the "Rectangle Opaque" and drag it over to the wall's surface. The object is too big so you need to resize the object and make it the size of a doorway.

3. The object is also very bright blue and it doesn't match this room's interior, so you need to change the color to something that I can live with; anything but that blue.... You do this by selecting the Color Bar and dragging across to select your desired color. (See Figure 13.5.)

Figure 13.5:

Selecting the Color Bar and dragging across to select a desired color.

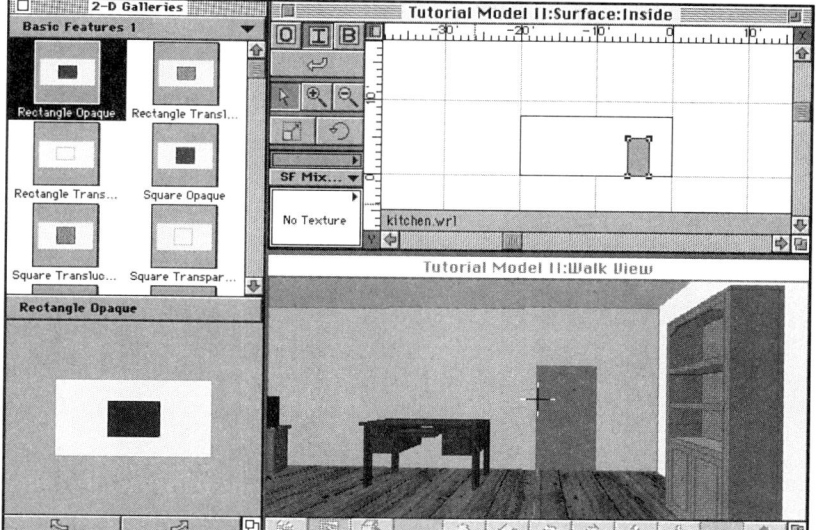

4. Still in the Surface Editor with the rectangle selected, place your cursor over the URL Panel and type: **kitchen.wrl** because that is the file that I want you to jump to. Figure 13.6 shows the new doorway.

5. Close the Surface Editor, save your model, and export it as a VRML file (explained in the next section).

Figure 13.6:
Placement of the new doorway added as a surface feature on the left wall.

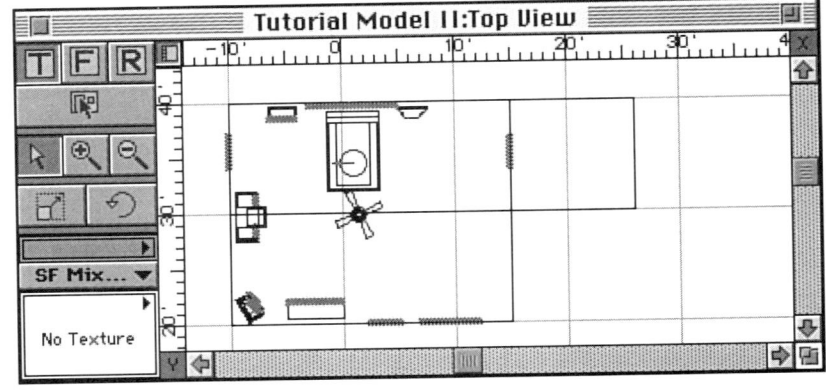

You'll see the kitchen model later, but Figure 13.7 shows a preview. I left it pretty bare so you can go in and drop a refrigerator and stove in someplace....

Figure 13.7:
The kitchen model.

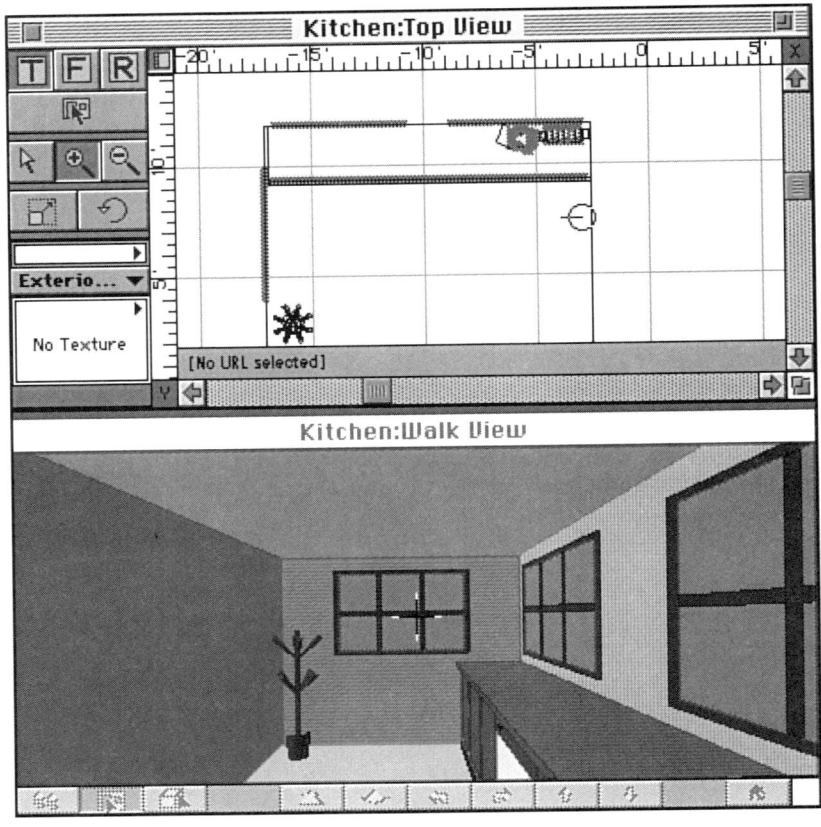

Exporting a File into VRML

Again, to export the model as a VRML:

1. From the File menu, select Export and then VRML.

2. Pick a texture file extension (.jpg is the standard) and click OK.

3. Navigate the file selection dialog to export the model to a selected location.

4. Type the name of the model using only eight lowercase letters and no symbols or spaces. Add the file extension **.wrl** to the end of the file. Example: **cyberwld.wrl**.

Summary

Now you have successfully created a simple model and assigned anchors to it. As well, I hope you understand the difference in linking a 3-D VRML model to a 2-D Web Page and linking two VRML files to each other. If you don't, skim back over that part. You also know that if you don't complete something (like a model), that I will give in and hand it to you on a silver platter, er, a silver disk....

Let's get browsing! Proceed to the next chapter and let's get up on that Net!

Browsing with Virtus Voyager

Now you're going to take advantage of your new-found knowledge and finally put it to work. You may have already installed your Virtus Voyager application from the CD-ROM. But if you haven't, and you have access to the Internet, I suggest that you rush to the Virtus home page and download the latest and greatest Virtus Voyager. Check the version number and if it is more recent than the one you have, download it. The Virtus home page URL is http://www.virtus.com.

In an effort to save your eyesight and facilitate your access to lots of stuff on the Internet, I have included a file on the CD (in the Tutorial folder) called **sites.txt** (just **Sites** on the Macintosh), which is an ASCII file that you should be able to open with any Simple Text reader or word processor. It includes lots of HTML sites that I think are great, but also some more sites that have VRML models. Just keep it running in the background while you're running Netscape/Voyager, and you can copy and paste the URLs without all that typing....

The Voyager Interface

After you have successfully installed Virtus Voyager from your CD (or downloaded the latest version from the Virtus home page), you should be able to double-click the application icon (shown in the margin) to start the browser.

Virtus Voyager will load and you should see a similar screen to Figure 14.1. (Some features may be disabled on your version at testing, but if you download the latest version, you will have the best.)

Take a moment to notice the elements of the Voyager interface so that you will be familiar with its functions. The buttons along the top of the browser are similar to other HTML browsers. And because Virtus VRML shared the same novice mode navigational tools along the bottom, they should be familiar to you. Of course, being able to utilize the Standard Virtus Navigation mode by using the center crosshair is by far the more convenient way to navigate.

One of the most important parts of the Voyager browser is the Online Information Panel located along the bottom frame. This panel gives you updated modem status, tool button information, and help with all buttons and functions whenever you need it.

Figure 14.1:
Virtus Voyager opening screen.

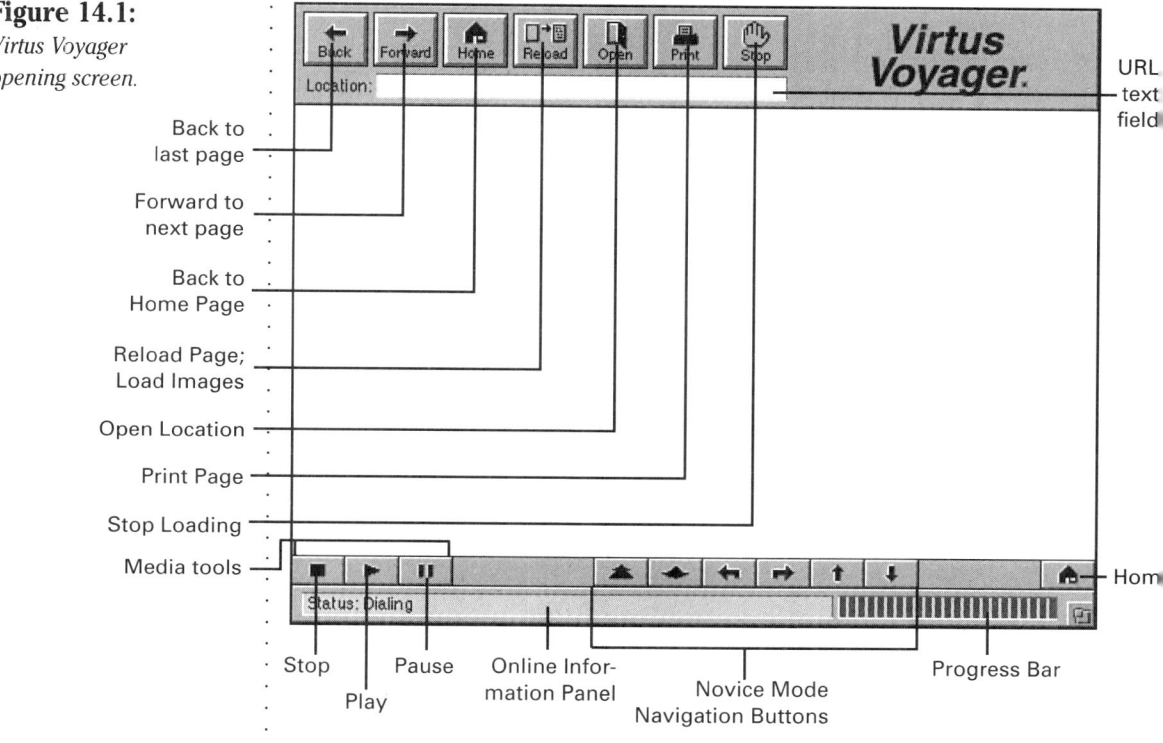

Back to last page

Forward to next page

Back to Home Page

Reload Page; Load Images

Open Location

Print Page

Stop Loading

Media tools

Stop

Play

Pause

Online Information Panel

Novice Mode Navigation Buttons

Progress Bar

URL text field

Home

Menus

Some of the Virtus Voyager menu options and commands are not standard for many of the programs that you have used on the Macintosh or Windows operating systems.

The File Menu

Figure 14.2 shows you the File menu and Table 14.1 explains the commands you find there.

Figure 14.2:
The File menu.

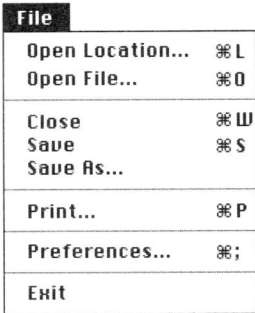

Command	Purpose
Open Location	Displays a dialog box in which you can type or paste a Uniform Resource Locator (URL).
Open File	Displays the standard Macintosh and Windows Open dialog box from which you can select an existing file to open. These are files located on your hard disk and may be Virtus VRML files (.wrl) or other Virtus file formats (.wlk, .vvr, .vmd).
Close	Closes the current file. If you made any changes to the file since the last time you saved it, you are prompted to save the changes before the file is closed.
Save	Saves the current file with the currently used name.
Save As	Opens the Macintosh and Windows Save dialog box, which allows you to save the current file with a new name.
Print	Prints the active window centered on the page.
Preferences	Allows you to set preferences for the appearance of Virtus VRML.
Quit (Macintosh) Exit (Windows)	Exits Virtus VRML. If a model is open and changes were made since the last time it was saved, you are prompted to save any changes before exiting.

Table 14.1

The File Menu Commands

The View Menu

Figure 14.3 shows you the View menu and Table 14.2 explains the commands you find there.

Figure 14.3:

The View menu.

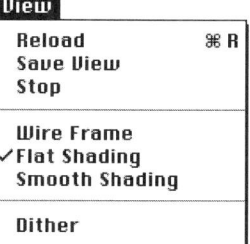

Table 14.2		
The View Menu Commands	Command	Purpose
	Reload	Reloads the current image model and refreshes the display.
	Save View	Saves the last view as a default.
	Stop	Ends the loading action of an URL.
	Wire Frame	Speeds up your navigation by displaying only wire frames of objects. No object color fill, surface features, or textures are displayed.
	Flat Shading	Displays all translucent and transparent object surfaces and surface features, and displays object color fill, wire frames, and textures as flat shaded polygons.
	Smooth Shading	Displays all opaque surfaces and surface features as Gouraud shaded polygons. This is more processor intensive, but gives a more realistic feeling to your model.
	Dither	Dithering allows more colors to display, thus more color-accurate renderings. The disadvantage of dithering is that the screen appears grainy.

Go Menu

Figure 14.4 shows you the Go menu and Table 14.3 explains the commands you find there.

Figure 14.4:
The Go menu.

```
Go
    Back
    Forward
    Home

    View History
```

Table 14.3

The Go Menu Commands

Remember from Chapter 13 that a **hotspot** is when you add a URL anchor to a 3-D object that links you to a 2-D Web page. You attach the link to 3-D items as well as to a 2-D surface. Your browser can then automatically jump to the URL anchor when you move into the surface.

Command	Purpose
Back	Takes you to the previous Web page or VRML file that you viewed.
Forward	Takes you forward to the next Web page or VRML file that you loaded.
Home	Takes you back to the default view of your model where it opened.
View History	Displays all of the URL sites that you have visited during the current session.

HotSpots Menu

Figure 14.5 shows you the HotSpots menu and Table 14.4 explains the commands you find there.

Figure 14.5:
The Hotspots menu.

```
HotSpots
    Add HotSpot
    View HotSpots
```

Table 14.4

The HotSpots Menu Commands

Command	Purpose
Add HotSpot	Selects the current file and adds the URL of the file into the HotSpots directory list.
View HotSpots	Lists all of the currently stored URLs for HotSpots.

Window Menu

Figure 14.6 shows you the Window menu and Table 14.5 explains the commands you find there.

Figure 14.6:

The Window menu.

Window
Cross Hair
✓Navigator
Mosaic

Table 14.5

The Window Menu Commands

Command	Purpose
Cross Hair	Toggles the center crosshair on and off. The crosshair is used as a reference point for navigation.
Navigator or Mosaic	(Parent Application Access) Allows you to select a parent application like Netscape or Mosaic when it is running with Virtus Voyager.

Opening a File

To open an existing model (from your hard disk):

1. Choose Open File... from the File menu and use the standard Macintosh or Windows Open dialog box to select the Virtus VRML file that you want to open.

Remember that you have an opportunity to open several different file formats with Voyager and many more are planned for later. Opening a VRML file as opposed to opening a regular Virtus file is a big difference. VRML files are approximately 10 times larger than regular Virtus files! That means they will load and walk slower. If you have the opportunity to open a standard Virtus file or a VRML file, choose the Virtus file for a more fluid experience. As well, when you build your sites for the Net, load *both* files to the site and give the user the choice of loading either the VRML file or the VMDL (Virtus) file.

2. For this example, navigate to the Scenes folder and open the file: **Industrial Room** (Macintosh) or **industr.vvr** (Windows). After the file opens, it should appear something like you see in Figure 14.7.

Figure 14.7:
*The **Industr.vvr** file.*

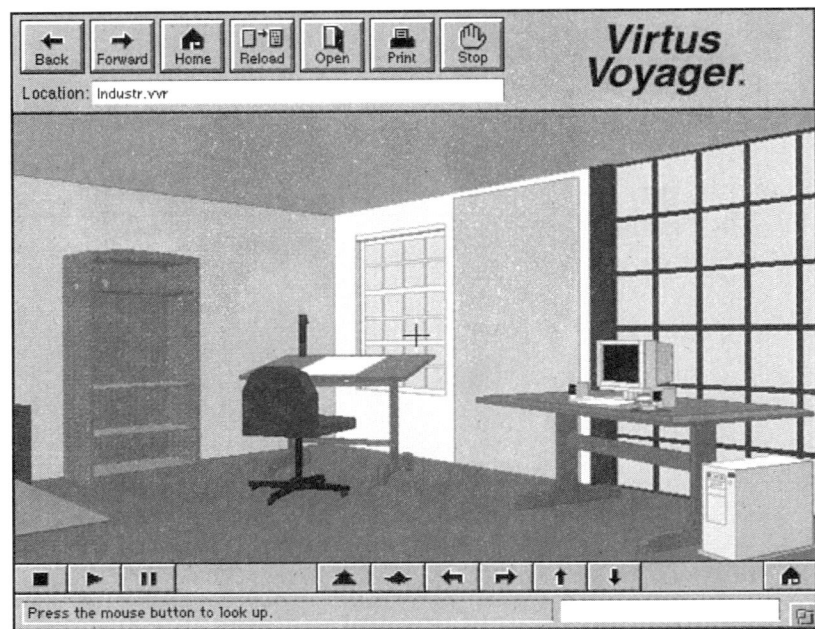

Walk around the room using the Standard Virtus Navigation technique by placing the cursor above the crosshair to move forward, under it to move backwards, and so on. If you get lost or confused, press the Home button—it returns you to the default view. See Chapters 7 and 8 for a detailed guide to navigating within a 3-D world.

3. Open another file in the Scenes or Model folders and practice walking around in it. It takes just a little practice to get the hang of this navigation thing, but after a while, it becomes easy.

Using Voyager as a Helper Application

I was going to assume that you have some general knowledge of using Internet browsers like Netscape or Mosaic before you delve into something as cutting edge as VRML. I'll just give you some general knowledge.

You can use almost any Internet Service Provider (ISP) to work with Virtus Voyager as long as they provide you with a SLIP (Serial Line Internet Protocol) or PPP (Point-to-Point) access account. Unlike other methods of Internet access, a SLIP or PPP connection turns your personal computer into an actual host on the Internet. As well, you may use Voyager as a *helper application* to Netscape, Mosaic, and Microsoft Explorer or you may use it as a standalone application.

For the sake of jumping into this quickly, it will be easier for you to be introduced to the VRML world if you use it as a helper application with Netscape or Mosaic. (All of the examples that I have here are using Netscape, but you may use any HTML browser that allows a configurable helper application.) If you don't have an HTML browser, skip on to the section entitled "Using Voyager as a Standalone Application."

When an HTML browser comes in contact with a file that it cannot read, like a VRML file, it looks for another application to launch that unrecognizable file. So Virtus Voyager will be launched as a **helper application** to Netscape or Mosaic.

Working with an HTML Browser

When the HTML browser application (like Netscape) retrieves a file with a format that it cannot read, the application attempts to use an external helper application capable of reading the file. Netscape and Mosaic have a Preferences dialog box (accessed from the Options menu) that allows you to examine and configure how a file's format maps to a helper application. The dialog box contains several fields and buttons to specify **MIME** (Multipurpose Internet Mail Extension) file types, helper applications, and associated actions.

MIME is a method of differentiating file formats using a suffix appended to a file name.

A scrolling text field lists the helper applications available to the HTML Browser. Each line of the text field contains information about one helper application. By clicking a line in the text field, you can see and modify preferences for the selected helper application in the area below the scrolling field.

Configuring Your HTML Browser

From the Finder or Main Window, launch Netscape or Mosaic or whatever is the biggest-selling browser at the time that you're reading this....

1. From the Options menu, select Preferences—Figure 14.8 shows the dialog box from Netscape. In the very center of the dialog box, click the pop-up menu and select Helper Application from it.

Figure 14.8:
Netscape Preferences dialog box.

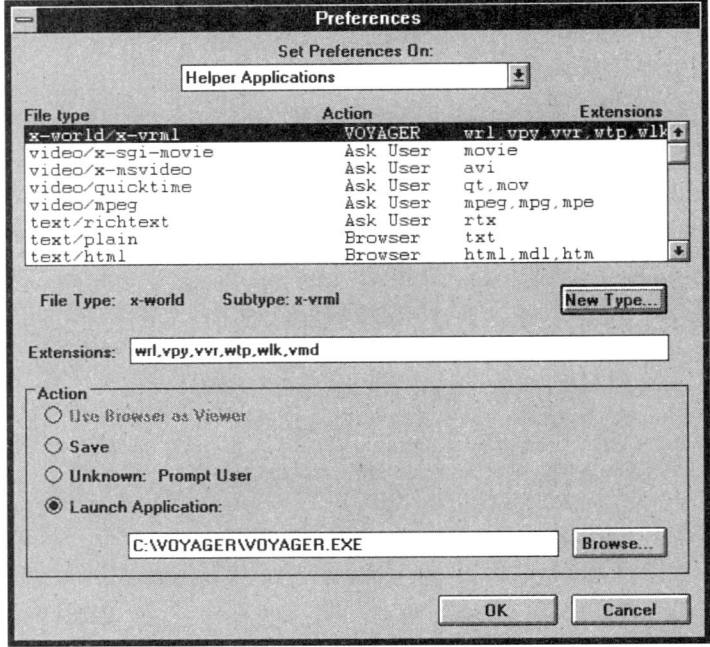

2. In the Extensions text field, enter **wrl, vpy, vvr, wtp, wlk, vmd**.

3. Now click the New Type button, which produces the New Type dialog box with two text fields for you to enter a MIME file type and MIME file subtype—see Figure 14.9.

Figure 14.9:
The Configure New Mime Type dialog box.

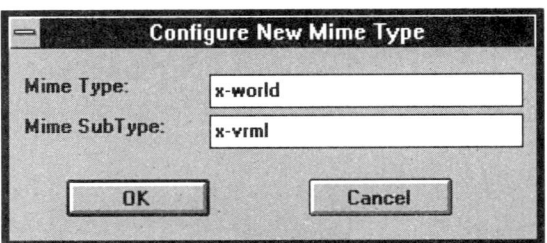

4. In the Mime Type text field, enter **x-world.**

5. In the Mime Subtype text field, enter **x-vrml.**

6. Click the OK button of the New Type dialog box to verify the data and, if valid, to add the file information to the list.

7. In the lower area of the dialog box is an Action area. Select the radio button that reads Launch Application. Click the Browse button to select Virtus Voyager as the new helper application.

8. (Macintosh only) Choose the application's default file type from the File Type pop-up menu.

9. Click the OK button.

Opening a Location

You've now configured your HTML Browser to be ready to understand what to do when it encounters a VRML file (.wrl). So let's go find one!

We're going to start easy and work from the CD first. Remember that really great model you made the other day? You knew that we would use it someday didn't you? Well for those of you who didn't, I have included the model on the CD in a folder called Tutorial.

There are actually two files, **MyHouse1.wrl** is just the bedroom and bathroom and **MyHouse2.wrl** has the kitchen attached. Use the first one (**MyHouse1.wrl**) so that you can see how great it is to work with these hotspots.

Hotspot Walking

1. From the File menu, select Open File... and select the file **My House.wrl** (Macintosh) or **myhouse.wrl** (Windows). It should open and look like Figure 14.10.

2. Now using either mode of navigation, walk toward the bed in the center of the room and then walk *into it.* Wham, you hit it! And Zap, your HTML browser takes you off to... you guessed it! Canadian Bed & Breakfast Online! Now after you peruse the offerings in Canadian hospitality (my Canadian experiences are good), you may either continue searching around this hotspot or go back to your VRML model.

Figure 14.10:

The My House file.

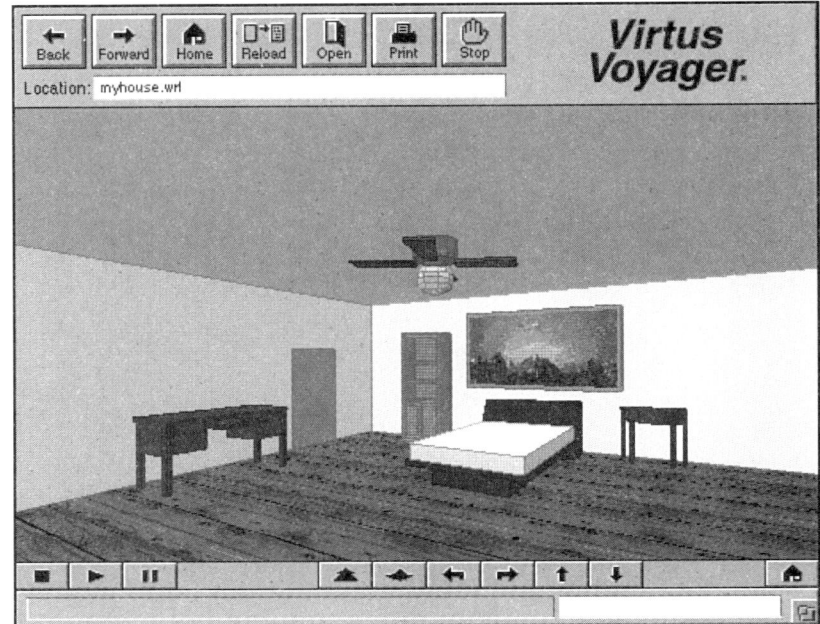

Let's go back to the VRML model because that's what I want to do. Someone has to be in control here.

3. Select the **Back** button at the top of your HTML browser and you'll return to the **MyHouse.wrl** file.

4. Now walk to your right and over to the *doorway* of the bathroom and walk into the bathroom. Remember, we set a hotspot on the doorway so that when you try to penetrate it, you get zapped somewhere... and you guessed it! You're at Echelon's Bathroom Wall Web Page! You have got to spend a second here looking at this very weird stuff, depending, of course, on your sense of humor.

5. When you've had enough, select the **Back** button at the top of your HTML browser and you'll return to the **MyHouse.wrl** file.

We have just experienced how it feels to be transported to an area of information via a visual arena. We did it once by actually walking "into" an object and once by walking "through" a surface (wall). Both are equally effective, but evoke different interaction "feelings." Ordinarily we don't walk *into* things to make something happen, nor do we walk *through* doorways and anticipate something magical will happen.

Visual Jumping

From a human interface standpoint, the way we make "jumps" with regard to visual cues is important for us to address. You can imagine someone who gets really cranked on this VRML/Internet stuff and literally spends hundreds of hours walking into things to get stuff to happen and then leaves the computer and goes out on the LA Freeway to "find" information. Scary thought... but I have actually worked 20 to 25 hours before in front of my computer on a really bad deadline and when I got up, dropped a book or something and thought to myself, "Command + Z!" (That's 'Undo' for those of you who don't know it...).

Because this technology is still in its infancy, lots of the interactivity issues will be addressed and will most likely be modified for the user's needs. You may conceivably use the Alt key or the Ctrl key and then click a hotspot with your mouse to make jumps to other areas. It's just something to think about....

Hotspot File Jumping

Now let's turn around from the bathroom and walk over toward that kitchen door. It's just beyond the bed. But don't make a mistake and walk *through* the bed. Because guess what would happen? You'd be sent back to bed in Canada (there are worse things, trust me...).

1. Walk over to that butterscotch-colored door (I was a design major, leave me alone...) and then walk *through* it. Zap! Voyager locates the file called **kitchen.wrl** and then jumps you into it. (And you thought you would end up somewhere in Canada didn't you?)

2. Walk around the kitchen and get to know it. Not much there, huh? You need to go back in your spare time and put some more appliances in it using Virtus VRML. I can't do everything for you or you'd never learn....

3. Now to get back to the main model, select the **Back** button at the top of your HTML browser and you'll return to the **MyHouse.wrl** file. You also may walk right back through the kitchen door toward the model and you will be zapped to the My House model via the hotspot that I set up for you.

When I made the kitchen, I added another URL on the kitchen's doorway to **MyHouse.wrl**. That way, I don't have to depend on the HTML browser to dictate my flow. You'll understand this better when you try to understand the linear and hierarchical structure that is used with 2-D HTML pages. The hierarchical structure gives you so many options that sometimes if you make the "wrong" decision to go down a "different" path, you might miss something that you would have really liked to see. Of course, life's that way too….

Figure 14.11:
You can set up a very complex linear and hierarchical structure using both HTML and VRML documents.

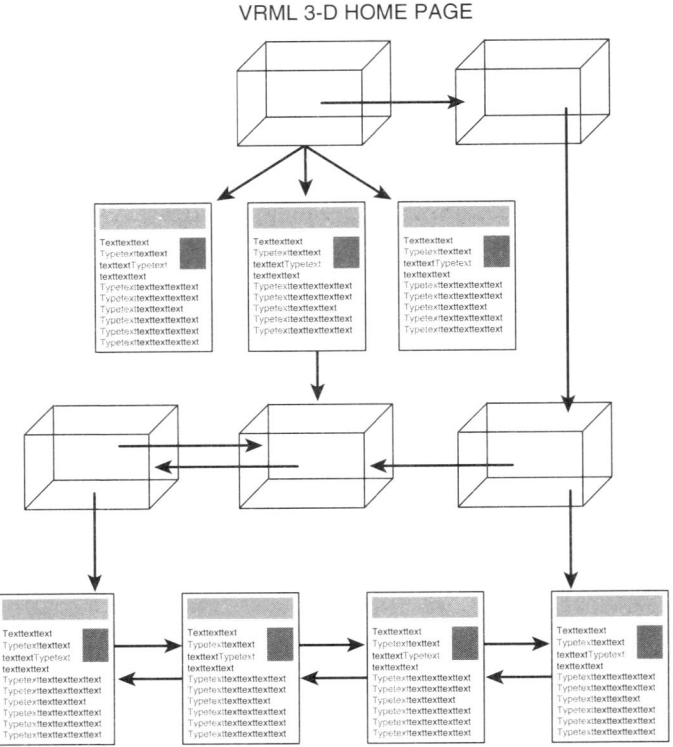

There is still one more hotspot that we set and that was on the television set in the corner. If you want to take a jump there, go ahead and do it on your own….

Tackling a Net Location

Now let's go directly to a VRML file at Virtus's site:

1. Go back to your Netscape browser and in the Netsite URL text field, type http://www.virtus.com/vrml/vstairs.wrl.

   Your browser will begin to look for the file. When it encounters the file, it will automatically launch Virtus Voyager as its helper application. Voyager will appear and, depending on your Internet/modem configuration, it will take a few moments for the file to load. After it loads, you should have a view that looks something like Figure 14.12.

Figure 14.12:
The WebMaster site opening screen.

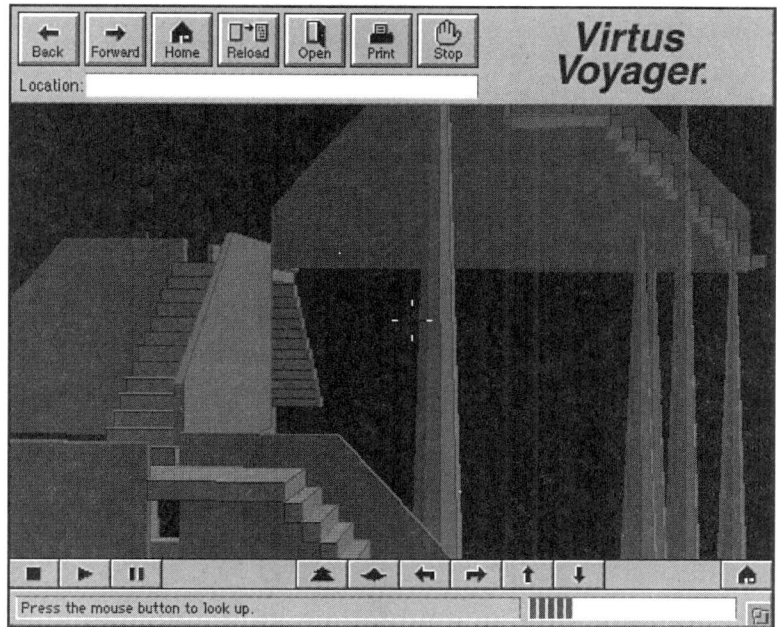

   There are lots of models here at Virtus Online to see, but this is an easy one to get you going.

2. To save the bookmark for this model so you can return here easily, select **Add HotSpots** from the HotSpots menu.

3. There are lots of sites emerging every day that have VRML models. But one of my favorites is called Cybertown, created in part by this really great guy, Pascal Baudar, the creative director at MultiMedia Magic. Cybertown, as you can imagine, is this really neat world created using Virtus WalkThrough Pro. Jump to it and go explore some the worlds that Pascal, et al have made for you (http://www.directnet.com/cybertown/). You'll really be quite amazed—see Figure 14.13.

Figure 14.13:
Cybertown.

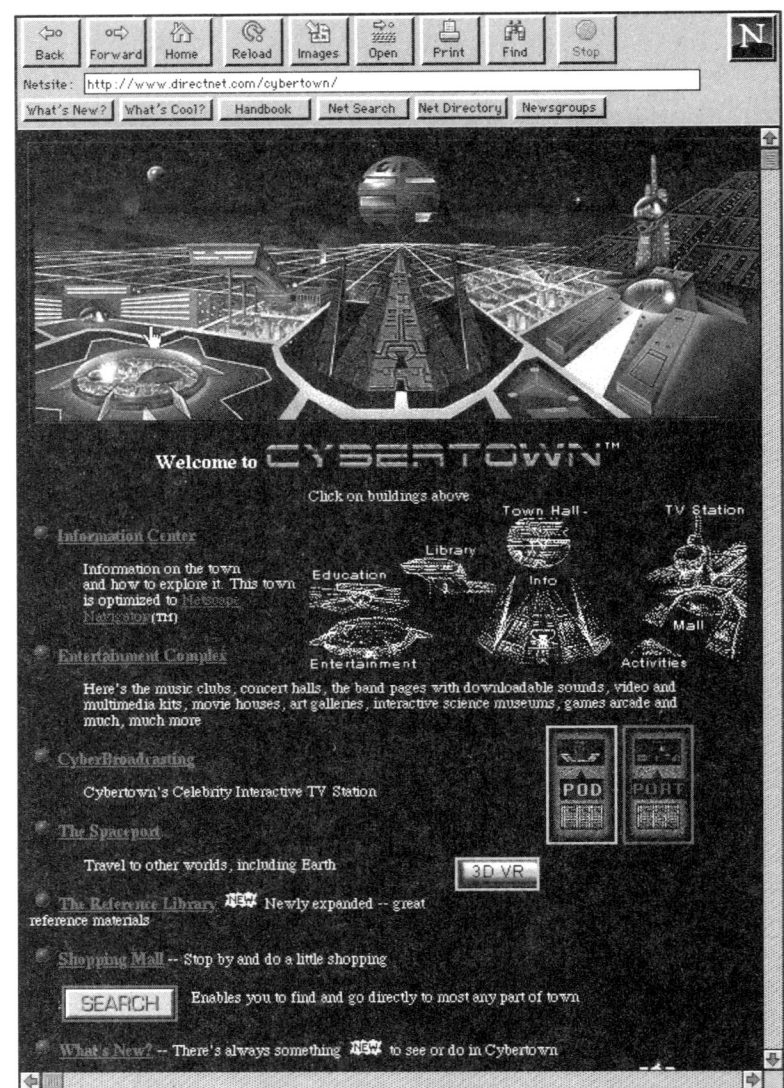

Using Voyager as a Standalone Application

After you have successfully installed Virtus Voyager from your CD, or downloaded the latest version from the Virtus home page, you should be able to double-click the Application icon (shown in the margin) to load the browser.

If your modem initializes correctly, Virtus Voyager will begin dialing your ISP. You will then see Connection Status information in the lower-left corner of the browser (the Online Information Panel), which indicates the different stages of your connection. Modem status information includes:

- On hook (modem has hung up)
- Initializing modem
- Dialing
- Negotiating
- Connected
- Disconnected

About Modems

Virtus Voyager supports most popular modems. If your modem is not listed during the modem configuration, you need to select a compatible modem type. *Hayes* is the default modem type; you should choose *Hayes* if you are unsure or cannot determine your modem type. (Consult your modem documentation if you are still having trouble getting connected.)

Your modem speed should be listed in your modem documentation; determine your modem's highest speed and set it there. This is one time that bigger is better....

It's also important that you know which communications port your computer is using. On Windows it will most likely be COM1, COM2, COM3, or COM4. On a Macintosh it will be the Phone, Printer, or Modem ports. If you have an internal modem, you shouldn't have any problems because it is set for you and for an external modem, it is the port that the modem is actually plugged into (yeah, you have to get behind your CPU to find that out...). You can check your modem connection status from the Online Information Panel—see Figure 14.14.

Figure 14.14:
Modem Connection Status is always available in the Online Information Panel.

Status: Dialing

Check the ReadMe file on your CD for any updated modem configuration information that may have been available after printing.

Okay, now let's go check a VMRL site and open some files. I have some easy files ready for you to load at the Virtus FTP (file transfer protocol) site.

1. From the HotSpots menu, select View HotSpots. I have saved several Virtus models for you to explore. Select one of them from the pop-up menu.

2. If none is available on your version of Voyager, in the URL Location panel (white panel below the buttons), type http://www.virtus.com/vrml/vstairs.wrl.

   It will take a moment for the files to load, depending, of course, on the size of the files.

VRML files are 10 times larger than standard Virtus files. If you have an opportunity on our site or any other site to load a file with the extensions: .vpy, .vvr, .wtp, .wlk, or .vmd, load them first. I know that's a long list to remember, at least commit to memory .vvr (for Virtus VR) and .wtp (for WalkThrough Pro).

Publishing Your VRML Files

Publishing your files as a host server is no different from working with HTML files. After you have created your files and exported them as VMDL files (Virtus format) or VRML files, your are ready to upload them to your server or Internet Service Provider (ISP) using any of many products, like Fetch, from the Trustees of Dartmouth College in New Hampshire.

Remember that you should give your users a choice of the files that they download; either a VRML file or a Virtus file. Export both from your application and they can select their choice.

Summary

Assuming you've been able to stay awake during this whole chapter, you've taken in a lot. You were able to use the model that you created in an early chapter and walk around in it using a 3-D VRML browser, Virtus Voyager. With that, you were able to understand and experience how powerful hotspots can be with hotspot walking and you found out all about Canadian Bed & Breakfast Online, not to mentioned Echelon's Bathroom Wall.

In Chapter 15, we cover other VRML browsers that are currently (or expected) to be out for both the Macintosh and Windows.

Cyber Dreams Realized

Part III

15

VRML Browsers

There may be many uncertainties about the final contribution of the VRML specification to the progress of 3-D on the Internet, but it certainly spawned a cottage industry in mid-1995 in the creation of VRML browsers. With the specifications published at the VRML Web site, anyone with some programming knowledge can create a VRML **browser**.

New Browser Specs

A **browser** is a viewer that loads files, VRML files for our discussion, and allows navigation in and interaction with a 3-D space. These browsers may run as standalone applications or within other 2-D browsers like Netscape and Mosaic as "helper" applications.

As this is being written, a number of companies are already straying from Pesce's original Chataqua movement VRML spec in their own direction to create their own brand of VRML. Almost all companies support VRML formats on the most basic level, but their browsers will tend to look for certain formats first to display their advantages and will load a vanilla VRML file only if the preferred format is not present.

> In the white paper, *The VRML of Babel*, Jan Hardenbergh said, "VRML 1.0 is a standard. While it is the ideal starting point; it lets people create static scenes and was 'easy' to get done, it is far from a REAL Virtual Reality Modeling Language. Already we are splintering: WebFX has collision detection, VRML+ has chat & interaction, IVRML is similar and SGI is using features from Inventor."

This is a workable model that ensures continuity among the formats while still providing customers with performance enhancements like increased speed or added interactivity where possible.

In Part II, you learned how to build VRML worlds with the Virtus VRML Toolkit. You also learned that it is prudent to save your models both as VMDL files and as VRML files.

What Virtus Voyager Gives You

When the Virtus Voyager browser finds 3-D information on a Website, it looks first for the VMDL file format. If this is present, the model loads faster because the file size is 1/10 the size of the same VRML file, and it also runs up to 10 times faster because of patented 3-D database handling inherent in all Virtus software. Virtus VMDL files also benefit from the extensible architecture built into it that allows other developers to plug in code to add physics and animation attributes to worlds created with Virtus VRML software.

Because Virtus Voyager is distributed freely and aggressively over the Internet and through software, hardware, and book bundles internationally, you can be assured that a high percentage of visitors to your 3-D information landscape will enjoy those performance enhancements.

In the following section, we investigate some of the browsers that were available prior to the printing of this book. Some of these were still in beta and are labeled as such.

The greatest difficulty we had was looking for Macintosh browsers. Virtus demonstrated VRML-creation software for the Macintosh at the MAC-WORLD Boston Expo show in August of 1995, but we had no Mac browsers for testing.

Macintosh Browsers

What follows are browsers we reviewed for the Macintosh.

Whurlwind

Company: Apple Computer, Inc.

Current Version: 1.0d3

Current File Types: 3DMF and VRML (.wrl)

Requires: QuickDraw 3D

Navigation: Consists of using the mouse with three buttons. Button one controls in and out movement; button two controls up, down, left, and right movement; button three controls look up, down, and turn left and right directions.

Pros:

- This was one of two available MAC VRML browsers at press time.

- Includes the capability to set background color.

- Can be used as a helper application in Netscape or Mosaic.

Cons: This product is still very much in the beta stage. It could read some VRML files, but had a lot of trouble reading larger VRML files.

Figure 15.1 shows the Whurlwind browser.

Figure 15.1:
Whurlwind in action.

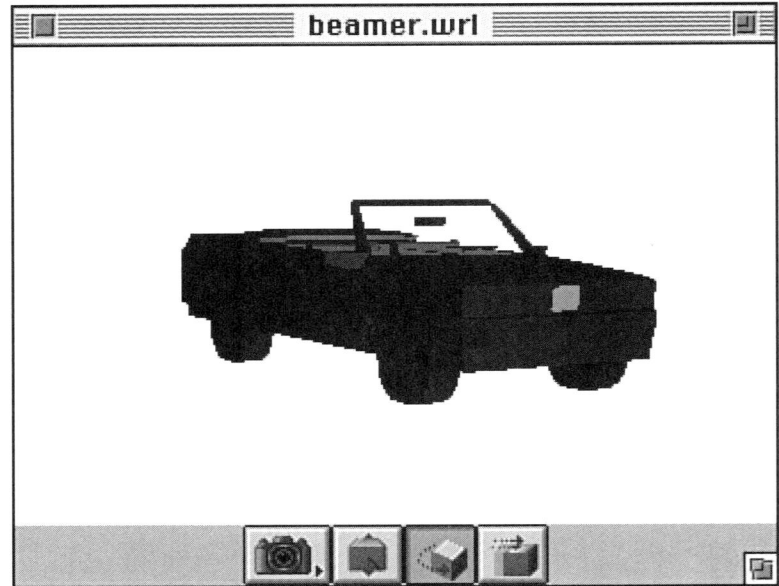

Virtus Voyager

Company: Virtus Corporation

Current version: 1.0

Current file types: VRML and VMDL

Platforms: Macintosh/Power Macintosh, Windows 3.1, Windows 95

Navigation: Navigation of six degrees of freedom using a one-, two-, or three-button mouse, navigation buttons, or keyboard.

Pros: The VMDL file format makes loading and navigation up to 10 times faster than regular VRML files; it is built upon Opendoc, so it is extensible. A beta version is included on the book's CD.

Cons: Still in beta. The final version can be downloaded for free at http://www.virtus.com.

Figure 15.2 shows the Virtus Voyager browser.

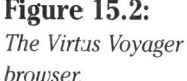

Figure 15.2:
The Virtus Voyager browser.

Windows Browsers

What follows are browsers we reviewed for Windows.

WorldView

Company: Intervista Software

Current Version: 0.9e

Current File Types: VRML

Platforms: Win 3.1, Win 95, Win NT

Navigation: WorldView navigation is good when using the buttons. It has three sets of four-way arrows, each of which tell you what direction it takes you (it uses the Microsoft Office Smart Icons for this). Mouse movement is more difficult especially because you have to begin in a box outside the viewing area to initiate mouse movement. The program also has Walk (walk around the model), Fly (moves you around the world), and Inspect (allows you to move and tilt the 3-D model) buttons.

Pros:

- WorldView can be run as a standalone browser or as a Netscape helper application.

- Models can be viewed with several shading choices including: wire frame, flat, Gouraud, and phong shading.

- Good button navigation; includes restore to original position button.

Cons:

- Cannot set background color.

- Mouse movement leaves much to be desired.

Figure 15.3 shows WorldView.

Figure 15.3:
The WorldView browser.

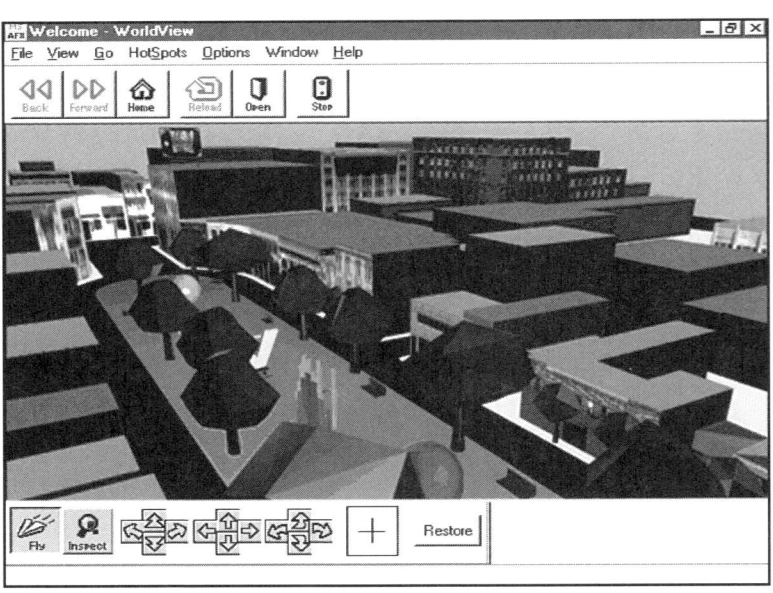

Web FX

Company: Paper Software

Current Version: Beta Release 1

Current File Types: WRL, WRZ, RWX

Platforms: Win 3.1, Win 95, Win NT

Requires: Netscape, Spyglass, or Q Mosaic.

Navigation: You can use the mouse in connection with the Ctrl and Alt keys. There is an extensive set of keyboard controls. The three types of movement are walking, flying, and authoring. The walking keys are the same as in Doom. The flying keys are the same as in Descent.

Pros: Right mouse activation; view solids, wire frames, and paint clouds; good mouse navigation; restore to original position button; heads up display (HUD).

Cons: Cannot set background color.

Figure 15.4 shows this browser in action.

Figure 15.4:
Web FX.

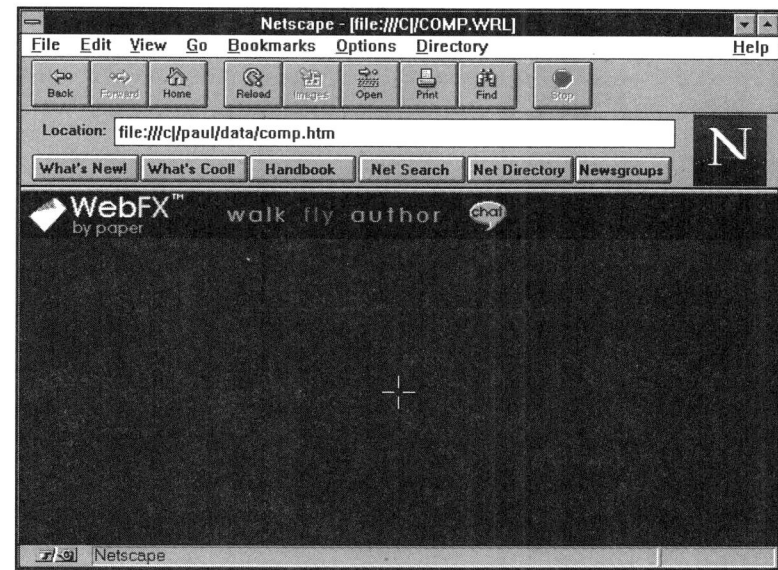

VRweb

Current Version: 0.53 Beta

Current File Types: WRL, SDF

Platforms: Win 3.1, Win 95

Navigation: Use both the left and right mouse buttons to navigate; a heads up display can also be used to navigate.

Pros: Can be used as a helper application; reset view feature.

Cons: Smooth shading very rough, flat shading just as bad with actual VRML files (not ones that came with program). Opened some VRML files, but displayed nothing except in wire frame view; very slow even in wire frame view.

Figure 15.5 shows VRweb.

Figure 15.5:
VRweb.

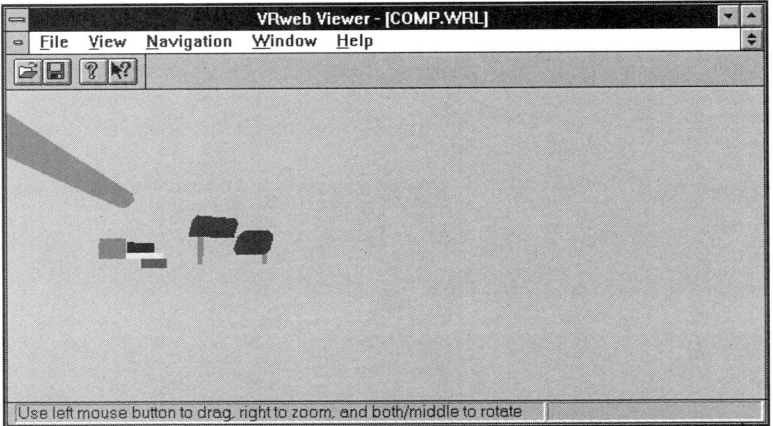

Webspace

Company: Template Graphics Software, Inc.

Web address: http://www.tgs.com

Current Version: beta

Current File Types: DXF, 3DS, NAV, WRL

Platforms: Win 3.1, Win 95, Win NT

Navigation: Sluggish

Pros: Future versions will be written to the 3-D Device Driver Interface.

Cons: Slow, poor navigation

VR Scout

Developer: Chaco Communications, Inc.

Web address: http://www.chaco.com

Current Version: 2.2b beta

Current File Types: DXF, 3DS, NAV, WRL

Platforms: Win 3.1, Win 95, Win NT

Navigation: Walk, examine, and fly modes

Pros: Supports a variety of textures including GIF, JPEG, and BMP. Free for non-commercial use. $49 for support or commercial use.

Cons: No Mac version.

Figure 15.6 shows VR Scout.

Figure 15.6:

The VR Scout browser.

For More Information

For more information on VRML specs and expected features, visit these sites:

- WaxWeb—`http://bug.village.virginia.edu/vrml`

- Java—`http://java.sun.com`

- Sony CSL Virtual Society—`http://www.csl.sony.co.jp/project/VS/VRML95.ps.Z`

- DIVE—`http://www.sics.se/dce/dive/dive.html`

- ALIVE—`www.media.mit.edu`—projects/autonomous agents

- MERL—`www.merl.com`—good info online

- `www.paperinc.com`—collision detection in WebFX—info online

- Chaco Peublo—`www.chaco.com`—IVRML specs?

- DIS (SIMNET, now NPSNET?)—`http://dis.pica.army.mil/index.html`

- Division—`www.division.com`—good specs online

- `www.besoft.com`—Behavior Engine specs online

- TBAG—SIGGRAPH94

Summary

Because the barriers to entry in this business are so low, it is surprising that some companies are attempting to sell basic browsers for as much as $99. The standard software industry practice established by companies like Macromedia (with Director) and Adobe (with Acrobat) is to distribute viewers free of charge.

Most companies distribute an unsupported viewer free of charge and distribute a supported version with extra features for a small fee designed to cover registration and technical support fees. The money to be made in software is in the VRML creation and editing tools. This makes sense because the people using these tools are, generally speaking, the ones who will be making money from VRML, not those using browsers. By the time this book is published, most companies will probably have adopted this model.

Chapter 16 covers component-based architectures like OLE, OpenDoc, Java, and Taligent, and how they are affecting VRML products.

16

The Component Era

One of the technological movements that will shape the way we develop, buy, and use software in the future is the advent of component based architectures like OLE, OpenDoc, Java, and Taligent. These architectures will greatly increase the ease with which we will build information landscapes in the future because we will be able to quickly develop and reuse both static and animated 3-D objects and mini-applications. These objects are often referred to as applets, parts, or components.

All about Java

HotJava is a World Wide Web browser that can execute applets, programs written in the Java programming language and included (like images) in HTML pages. **Java** is the programming language that makes HotJava possible. It is an object-oriented programming language optimized for the creation of distributed, executable applications. Because Java is compiled into machine-independent bytecodes, applications written in Java can migrate transparently over the Internet accessible by anyone using the HotJava browser.

Mark Pesce, in one of his more colorful emails to the VRML list said: "We are all about to participate in a complete revolution in computing; the two essential elements of cyberspace—space and time—will come together for once and all. VRML, which describes perfectly how things look but is utterly mute about what they do, is to marry a partner who is all action, and no talk. This partner—Java—has precisely complementary characteristics; it commands all, articulating nothing. Object and behavior begin a dance which creates the virtual world."

—From: mpesce@netcom.com (Mark Pesce)

—Subject: ADMIN: VRML + JAVA—A Wedding

—Date: October 13, 1995

Components are small applications that can be embedded as a part of another application. An example of this is the QuickTime extension that allows the user to embed a movie into an existing document. A component architecture is simply a generalization of this idea where the embedded object can be of any data type.

This is the subject of this chapter: component architecture and how it relates to VRML. In this chapter, you learn:

- What are component architectures?

- How OpenDoc can help users.

- How OpenDoc can help developers.

- What OpenDoc means for Virtus VRML.

Component Architecture

One of the main goals behind component architecture is to move from an application-centered focus to a document or task-centered focus. When a quarterly report is due for the boss on Monday, we will be able to use components to create a single document that contains a spreadsheet, text, charts, and perhaps a multimedia presentation on the marketing campaign for the quarter.

This is a step in the right direction for usability. Component architectures essentially create a common language that programmers can use to create mini-applications that work with any other applications that speak that language, regardless of who develops it.

There was a time when a few programmers could get together in someone's garage and write a word-processing program or a game. That time is gone. The increasing complexity of software means that garage programmers can't compete with companies like Microsoft who can throw 50 programmers at a spellchecker. This reduced competition means less diversity for end users. Component architectures, combined with electronic distribution via the Internet, promise to resuscitate this cottage industry.

Monolithic applications like Microsoft Word 6.0 can be created by end users who choose components from different developers as they need them. For instance, users can purchase Microsoft's text editor, someone else's spellchecker, thesaurus, fonts, and then write a graphics editor of their own for placing pictures in it or to add desktop publishing features.

This is a notable milestone in the computer software industry and the Internet in particular because it means that individual programmers will be able to write small applications or components that will improve on existing applications. It may also loosen the constricting grip of Microsoft on the software industry. Bonus!

Separating Creativity from Code-Creation

What this component architecture means to the artists who are intent upon creating virtual worlds is that they should be able to buy pre-constructed 2-D and 3-D media that they can put together to build worlds with little or no programming. This essentially frees the artist from having to be a programmer.

As we mentioned in Chapter 4, the technicians creating the technology aren't necessarily the best artists. Just as the camera had to be freed from the grasp of the people who built the first movie cameras before interesting cinema was created, so will we need to empower virtual world artists of the future by freeing them from having to code every piece of a world. The more time they have to contemplate the content, the more compelling cyberspace will become.

Of the component architectures mentioned, OpenDoc seems the most promising. It is a very robust system that is also compatible with Microsoft's OLE (object linking and embedding) technology. A description follows in the next section. For those of you who would like to know more about how this technology relates to the software on the CD-ROM with this book, please feel free to skip the following nuts and bolts description and go to the section entitled "What OpenDoc means for VRML."

OpenDoc

OpenDoc is designed to facilitate the easy construction of compound, customizable, collaborative, and cross-platform documents. To do this, OpenDoc provides a document-centric user model instead of today's application-centric one. That is, the user focuses on a document rather than the application that manipulates that document.

Another extremely important property of the OpenDoc architecture is that it is defined in a completely recursive fashion. That is, every programmer-defined part that makes up the system can have all of the properties that the base system has. It can be thought of almost as a **recursive** operating system.

> **OpenDoc** can be thought of as being a recursive operating system in the sense that just as a windows application is contained inside of windows itself, an OpenDoc part can be contained inside yet another OpenDoc part, which can in turn be contained inside yet another OpenDoc part, and so on.

OpenDoc documents allow much more flexibility to both the user and the programmer of the system. The user has the ability to mix all kinds of media types within the same document. The programmers have the ability to add new media types and be assured that they will still be able to integrate the new type into existing documents.

OpenDoc User Benefits

The OpenDoc benefits to the user include:

- Easy creation of compound documents
- Editing "in place"
- Powerful document management
- Cross-platform support
- Portable software
- Consistency of operation

Each of these concepts is explained in the following sections.

Easy Creation of Compound Documents

OpenDoc is designed to handle current *and* future types of media. Users can place any kind of media into an OpenDoc document using cut and paste or drag-and-drop manipulation. A component-aware application will allow the user to both embed this part into an OpenDoc document and embed other documents (of other types) into it.

Editing "In Place"

With OpenDoc, users can edit any type of content within a single document without having to cut and paste between different applications. This is particularly useful for manipulating 3-D worlds and performing any transaction processing.

Powerful Document Management

Rather than manually assembling the various pieces of the document, users can let an OpenDoc document hold all of them. This reduces the task of managing files and facilitates document exchange and updating. As documents are edited, changes are tracked through drafts, ensuring greater data integrity and allowing users to work on shared documents without content loss from version to version.

Cross-Platform Support

Because OpenDoc is designed to offer full interoperability between platforms, OpenDoc users will be able to share and interact with complex documents, regardless of differences in software and hardware, or which platforms the documents reside on. This ensures that component aware documents will go anywhere that OpenDoc can be moved, and because you can obtain the rights to move OpenDoc to additional platforms on your own if necessary, there seem to be absolutely no restrictions to any platforms.

Portable Software

Software must be designed to be portable. The rate at which hardware changes implies that the real value of this technology is in the software. The only real guarantee you have in hardware is that it will probably be obsolete in about a year. It certainly will no longer have a competitive edge. This means that in order for software to be successful, it must be designed to be portable from the start. This will allow it to always take advantage of the next generation of hardware at a minimal cost.

Consistency of Operation

Because users can specify preferred part editors, they need learn only one way to edit each type of data—for example, using the same text editor for word processing, entering spreadsheet data, or labeling diagrams.

OpenDoc Developer Benefits

The OpenDoc benefits to the developer include:

- Faster, more efficient development

- Reduction of application complexity

- Diminished cost of software development

Each of these concepts is explained in the following sections.

Faster, More Efficient Development

Software developers can reuse already developed parts, eliminating the need to start from scratch with each development effort. This ability to reuse existing parts also means that developers can spend less time on parts that are peripheral to their main area of expertise. Pre-made parts will allow any developer to create complex interactive 2-D and 3-D multimedia documents extremely quickly.

Reduction of Application Complexity

Because OpenDoc parts are independent of one another, a collection of parts that is less complex than the large monolithic applications of today can offer equivalent functionality.

Diminished Cost of Software Development

The fact that parts are smaller than applications makes them both quicker and cheaper to write, which reduces the penalties for failure.

OpenDoc Communications Kernel

The communications kernel allows the virtual universe to communicate with the rest of the environment. This communication is between any of the following objects:

- Ourselves

- Our colleagues and others

- Our agents
- Tools
- The virtual universe and its contents

OpenDoc Rendering/Graphics Kernel

OpenDoc presumes a rendering kernel that can either be software- or hardware-based. Virtus has developed a high-quality, high-performance portable software rendering kernel for platforms that do not provide the appropriate capabilities. The rendering kernel has the following capabilities:

- **Flat shading**—a shading technique in which the lighting is calculated once per facet and a single shade of color is used for the entire facet.

- **Gouraud shading**—a shading technique that interpolates colors between vertices of a facet. Henri Gouraud invented this process in 1971. See Figure 16.1 for a visual difference between flat and Gouraud shading.

- **Perspective correct texture mapping**—using any canvas as the texture. A canvas can be any 2-D data type.

Figure 16.1:
Flat-shaded versus Gouraud-shaded polygons.

Flat shading

Gouraud shading

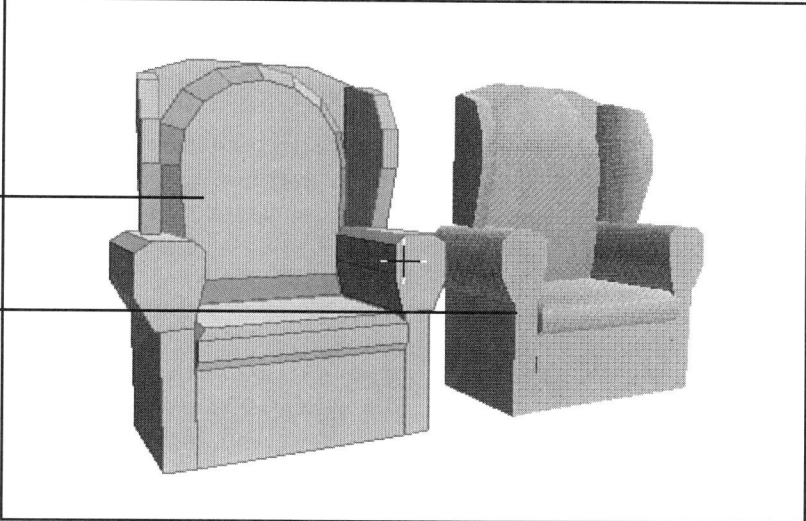

The last is a critical component because of the requirement of embedding a variety of 2-D information into the 3-D environment.

OpenDoc Micro Kernel

Most of the functionality that the Micro Kernel provides is hidden from the higher levels via the communications kernel. Its basic use is data I/O to fixed media devices (ROM, CD,...), I/O from network-based devices, and I/O from user-control systems. This means that the Micro Kernel can be any already existing operating system, such as Macintosh or Windows, or it can be a basic low-level system such as that which exists on set-top devices.

Hardware

OpenDoc will make no assumptions about hardware capabilities. The system is designed to be cross-platform. Given that, the requirements for adequate performance are minimal.

What OpenDoc Means for VRML

What this all means for our budding 3-D world creators is that pre-made 2-D and 3-D components can be added to virtual worlds and possibly edited without creating them from scratch. Non-programmers won't have to write code, they will only combine components to create new applications. This was the attraction of HTML for the web. By combining word processing and style editing non-programmers could author Web pages.

In MUDs—multi-user dungeons—one can create objects that can be sold or traded to other MUDders. These objects are entirely text-based. This same paradigm can be applied to virtual worlds as well as mainstream software applications. But in the 3-D MUDs of the future, these objects will be 3-D and have attributes.

VirtusCube is a 3-D desktop application on which you can place 2-D components such as calendars, movies, clocks, and crossword puzzles. There is no limit to the number and type of 2-D components that can be added to this application.

Today we are able to embed fully operational 2-D components such as a word processor or paint package into a 3-D environment by mapping it onto a surface the same way you place textures on surfaces in Virtus VRML. For a good example of this, check out the **VirtusCube** published by Simon and Schuster Interactive (but created by those ever-industrious Virtus programmers). 2-D components can be applied to the surface of the VirtusCube as a fully functional resource. On the six sides of the cube one can place a clock, an appointment calendar, a picture of one's family, a movie, a crossword puzzle and...why not another VirtusCube! On that VirtusCube we can place a chess game, another picture, and so on. Escher would be proud.

Web Implications

This also has some implications immediately for the Web. A student reading up on Stonehenge may find, in addition to text, pictures, and video clips, a small window embedded in the text with a 3-D model of Stonehenge. A Microsoft Word document could look like Figure 16.2. The reader can click right in the window to the right to walk around in the 3-D world.

Figure 16.2:
Embedded 3-D worlds.

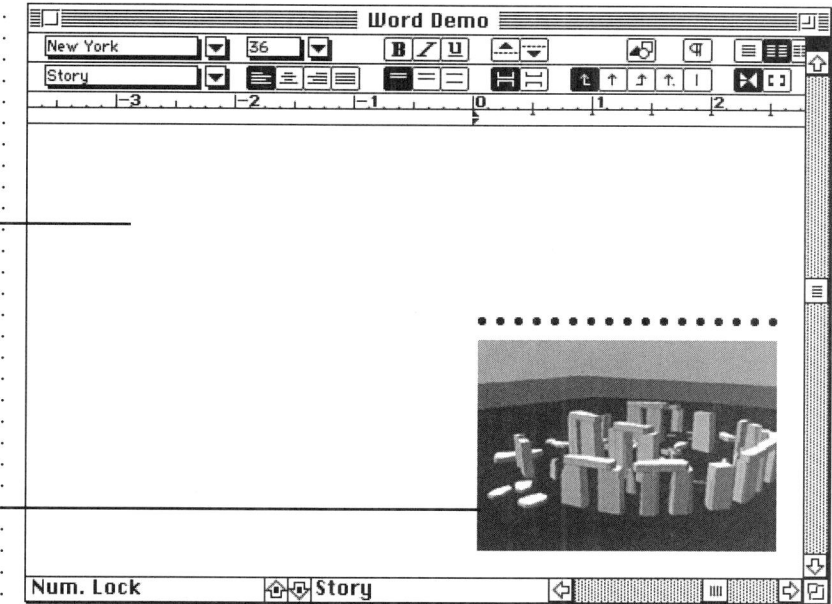

Text would go here, as usual

Storybook land could look something like this

By clicking the mouse in that window, our insatiably curious student can wander around Stonehenge, perhaps walking to different vantage points to witness how the sun lines up with certain rock formations during the Winter solstice. Again, a word-processing document containing a description of the Winter solstice and how the rocks were believed to be used might be mapped to one of the stones. This is a completely recursive architecture. Is this a great time to be alive or what?

In the near future we will also be able to embed 3-D components into 3-D worlds. That's when the virtual sparks will really begin to fly.

Dinosaur Terrarium

In February of 1995, I had the distinct pleasure of dining at the Oxford flat of Richard Dawkins, the pre-eminent scholar on Darwinian evolution and author of *The Selfish Gene*, *The Blind Watchmaker*, and *River Out of Eden*, among other works. An amateur programmer himself, Dawkins explained to me and my fellow dinner guests that he once created a program that simulated evolution. He was able to watch entities grow and mutate into new entities in succeeding generations. He confided that his dream was to see the same drama played out in a 3-D cyberspace environment. During the dinner, artfully and graciously prepared and served by his lovely wife, Lalla Ward (of *Dr. Who* and Shakespeare theatre fame), we set about hashing out the details of such a world. In the process, we determined that it would be infinitely more convenient if some of the simpler tasks were already created so we could just assemble them and perhaps modify a behavior here and there. It went something like this:

Take Virtus WalkThrough Pro and create a cubic mile space. Take Company A's terrain building engine and create a terrain that can be merged into the Virtus world. We now have a ground plane. It's time for shrubbery. Take some OpenDoc-compatible flora applets from a popular landscape design company's package and sprinkle liberally over the landscape. Ideally, we decided, the landscape company would have had enough foresight to have plant libraries that actually have characteristics like growth rates and tolerances for different atmospheric conditions. Each of these of course is easily editable so that we can create our own interesting variations for our virtual world just by editing a dialog box. Conveniently enough, someone in Mombassa, Kenya has written an OpenDoc part that creates atmospheric simulations in a 3-D environment. We'll just download that from the Internet after she exacts her *eCash fee* of course, and plug that into our world.

Now we have a world with topography, atmosphere, and plants. Next we'll need some critters (deep south slang for animals). We will start with some of the most basic autonomous agents like insects and rodents and personal injury lawyers (hey, its a virtual world, we can add what we want!) and then we will move up to the more interesting fauna. Each of these "agents" are 3-D **sprites** that have editable behaviors assigned to them. Because OpenDoc is a seamlessly recursive architecture, all of these parts will work together, despite the fact that each individual dinosaur may be created by a separate programmer.

I like the Tyrannosaurus Rex designed by a High School student in Skokie, Illinois and the Pterodactyl designed by a retired RAF colonel in London. We continue to browse the Web getting demos and purchasing the exact pieces we want for our little simulation.

When we are done we can get a cold drink, press the start button, and sit back and watch some real emergent behavior. Our T-Rex begins devouring everything that moves while the other creatures try to avoid it and eat as much of the flora as they can hold. When the T-Rex is full it slumbers for a while and the rest of our fauna busy themselves gorging on plants and each other. Alas, our personal injury lawyer seems ill-equipped for our little terrarium and perishes rather abruptly. The next round we may have to give him some extra capability (but not too much) and see how he fares.

We can fast forward a couple of centuries to see who are the winners and losers in the game of life. No...still no personal injury lawyers. But some of the flora and fauna have begun to evolve nicely. It seems in this run the amphibians are getting the larger brains. Maybe lawyers will evolve after all.

A **sprite** is an animated 2-D or 3-D object that has been assigned special behaviors such as animation and prescribed reactions to certain conditions or other sprites.

What we have created is a rather nice tool for learning about the processes of evolution firsthand. After some tweaking of the behaviors we may decide to put our creation out on the market as an educational tool. Of course, we will want to make sure that the proper royalties are paid to all of the various contributors, and we may decide to add some interface pieces we like from various companies to direct the student of life and add multimedia explanations for some of the phenomena she will witness. This is our added value as an artist or teacher. But we accomplish everything without getting involved with the 1s and 0s and arcane programming languages. We channel our energies toward the artistic fulfillment of our vision. We are artists (pronounced arteeeests).

Summary

Now for the good news. The hypothetical model we just described is very near to becoming a reality. In fact, the Virtus Voyager VRML browser included with this book on the CD-ROM will evolve as an OpenDoc-compliant kernel awaiting some enterprising programmers to take up the gauntlet and create the parts we described. The Stonehenge document is possible today just using OLE or OpenDoc compliant applications. A new age of empowerment (can we still use that word?) is dawning with the Internet and the publishing power it embodies at its center.

That's enough of the future. Let's look at what we can do now. See the next chapter for some ways that you can use your new-found real-time 3-D talents both on and off the net.

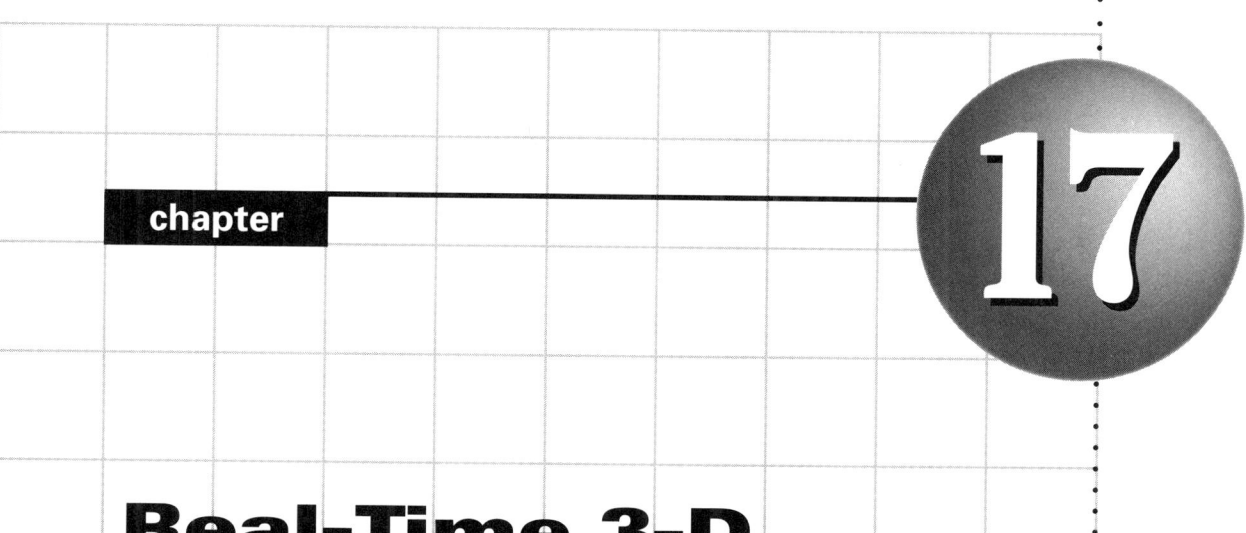

Real-Time 3-D User Stories

Now that you have the tools and technical skills to create 3-D worlds from scratch, we would like to provide a bit of inspiration to show you how others have used real-time 3-D in real-world applications. Where possible, email or Web addresses have been provided.

ImageWorks

Contact: Gilbert B. Hammer, Bedford, NY

Address: imagewks@aol.com

ImageWorks is a visualization design company that specializes in generating 3-D models and storyboards on computers for use in the production of feature films and commercials. The company's main focus is visualizing sets in 3-D and assisting directors in troubleshooting and problem-solving in relation to specific scenes.

ImageWorks uses Virtus WalkThrough Pro because the software enables it to storyboard in 3-D and "fly around" to explore all the possible options afforded by the set. The software offers a variety of tools that are specific to the film industry and enable the production crew to experiment with "what-if" scenarios quickly and easily .

"WalkThrough Pro is an excellent tool for helping a director communicate ideas to the rest of the people involved in the production," says Gilbert Hammer, president of ImageWorks. "You can tell a gaffer where to put the lights, but if you can show him [or her], you are communicating much more effectively. Having these explorable 3-D models also encourages more collaboration on the set because the crew can easily try out their ideas in virtual reality and quickly tell if they will work or not."

A specific problem that Gilbert used WalkThrough Pro to solve involved some thorny coverage problems in advance of principle photography for a public service announcement. This PSA was an informative piece on the perils of gang membership and was shot in a hallway-wide jail cell in Elizabeth, New Jersey. The Director, Michael Finan, and the Director of Photography, Donald Schwartz, wanted to create a feeling of apprehension to get their point across to the audience.

Gilbert offered a wide range of options as to how to position and move the camera as well as advice on which camera lens would work the best to achieve the effect the director wanted. Gilbert felt that at least a 95mm wide angle lens would probably do the job, particularly with that lens' capability to distort around the edges of the shot. They experimented with several of the choices available in WalkThrough Pro and eventually settled on a 85mm. It was also important to pre-visualize the camera movement because the director wanted to try a number of different mood enhanced "looks" for the piece. Moving through a Virtus model prior to filming afforded time to experiment without the cost of numerous camera setups. See Figure 17.1.

ImageWorks' Gilbert Hammer is committed to making visualization tools a integral part of the production process by demonstrating how programs such as WalkThrough Pro can be used to solve real-world problems. ImageWorks can either work in their studios or go on site with a laptop computer or full-blown computer setup including desktop computer, monitor, VCR, and printer.

Gilbert welcomes the opportunity to explore with visionary producers, directors, and directors of photography the creative options offered by using visualization software. The leading East Coast film cinematographers local, I.A.T.S.E 644 has taken the plunge.

Figure 17.1 represents how directors can use Virtus' products to explore camera angles in the preproduction stage of filming. This screen was used in the planning of a public service announcement about gangs; it shows the view from inside a jail cell looking out.

Figure 17.1:
ImageWorks design from inside a jail cell looking out.

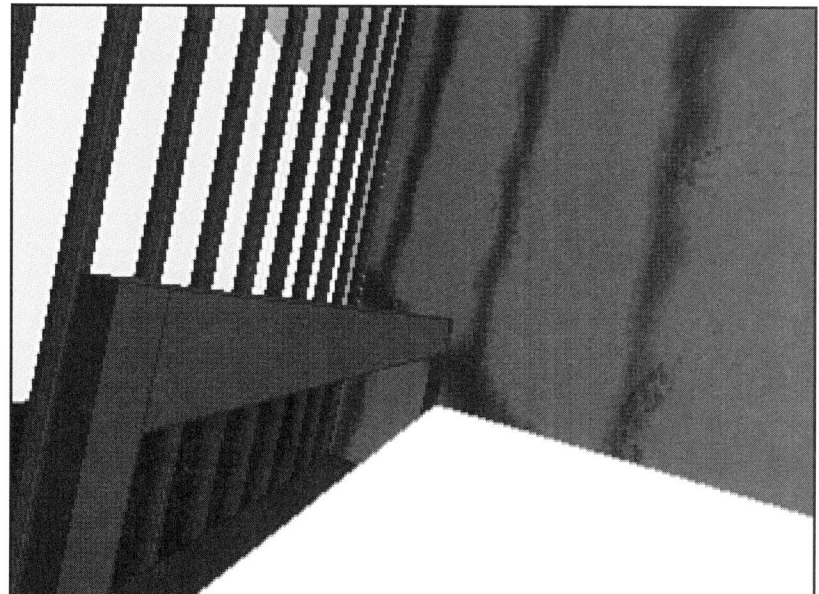

Virtual Theater

University of Kansas
317 Murphy Hall
Lawrence, KS 66045

Contact: Mark Reaney, Associate Professor of Theater & Film

Address: mreaney@kuhub.cc.ukans.edu

As an associate professor of theater and a virtual reality hobbyist, Mark Reaney has often used Virtus WalkThrough Pro in its traditional role as a pre-production tool. Designing sets and storyboarding in virtual reality prompted Mark to envision other uses for the software as they applied to the theater. One of his more intriguing ideas was the use of WalkThrough Pro as an actual performance medium.

The play Mark chose to showcase his vision of virtual theater was Elmer Rice's "The Adding Machine." The 1923 expressionist play traces the life, death, and afterlife of Mr. Zero, an accounting clerk who loses his job of 25 years to an adding machine and, in rebellion, murders his boss. The original intent of the play was to examine the dehumanizing impact of technology on early 20th-century society; to present the play in virtual reality creates an even more ironic production.

Mark rendered the sets on his desktop computer using WalkThrough Pro. A customized version of the software enabled the audience to watch through polarized glasses while the actors performed in front of a large screen on which the three-dimensional sets were projected.

According to Mark, "WalkThrough Pro's real-time, at-will navigational capabilities makes it my software of choice. With WalkThrough Pro, you can build a structure, or as in this case, a theater set and move freely throughout the model. Although it is possible to prerecord a navigation path with Virtus software, this was a live theater production and the scenery needed to be reactive to the actors."

The offstage computer operator of the virtual scenery had to watch the play on a monitor to see where the actors were and how they lined up with the virtual scenery. As the actors moved, the computer operator panned the scenery right or left to make sure that the actors didn't walk through the images.

"The Adding Machine" opened April 18, 1995, and ran through April 30. Mark is currently producing a documentary video about the making of "The Adding Machine."

For more information about "The Adding Machine" visit Mark's home page on the World Wide Web. The address is `http://ukanaix.cc.ukans.edu:80/~mreaney/`. From there you can download Virtus Player files of actual sets used in the production of "A Streetcar Named Desire" (see Figure 17.2), as well as screen shots of other Virtus models he has created.

Fuel for Thought

Summit Design, Inc.
Paoli, PA

Contact: Jeffory Beckers

Jeffory Beckers has an unusual specialty: he designs gas stations for major companies like Sunoco and Mobil. WalkThrough Pro has substantially enhanced the marketability and effectiveness of his designs by permitting him to provide models of proposed sites that people could explore before any construction began. He recently took a WalkThrough Pro model of a proposed gas station to a local town meeting where citizens were speaking out against the station's construction.

"Once they saw how attractive the place was, and could assure themselves that it wouldn't mar the view, they were much more comfortable with the idea," he says. "The texture-mapping feature was key to the success of the venture. The realistic signs helped people feel that they were seeing the real thing, which reduced their fears and allowed them to pinpoint their concerns."

Beckers adds, "I was stunned by how easy it was to build models and add textures. With WalkThrough Pro, I can create realistic logos and put natural-looking text and signs where they belong, which helps dramatically. The program is incredibly easy to use—you can create and place textures in a very intuitive way. You can even create your own texture libraries, which is great for me, since I'm developing logos and signage that can be used over and over again."

Figure 17.2:
Theatre sets at `http:/`
`ukanaix.cc.ukans.`
`edu:80/~mreaney/.`

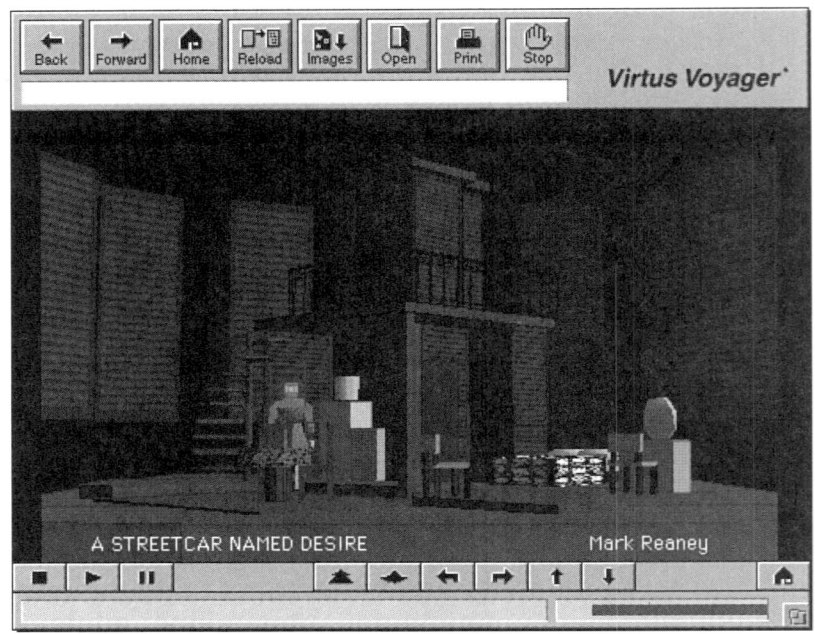

Poetry in Motion

St. Petersburg Junior College
Instructional Technology
Pinellas Park, FL

Contact: Tim Brock

Phone: (813) 341-3343

Imagine a computerized display of images that pass through your mind while reading a poem—the sights, sounds, words, colors, shapes, and forms. That's exactly what the Instructional Technology department at St. Petersburg Junior College has been doing with Virtus WalkThrough Pro.

In a special project produced for inclusion in the *McGraw-Hill Multimedia Handbook*, published in 1994, computer graphics specialist Tim Brock and communications instructor Dave Hartman created a 3-D WalkThrough Pro model of environments invoked by poetry. Brock and Hartman envision the model as an educational tool that can enhance the power of written language for computer-generation students, providing clues to the hidden meanings and implications of literary imagery.

Brock applauds WalkThrough Pro for its speed, responsiveness, and ease of use. "It allowed us to combine storyboarding and on-screen trial walk-throughs in a single step, giving us an immediacy that is rare in creative environments," he says. Brock used WalkThrough Pro's texture mapping feature extensively, utilizing QuickTime movies to create multiple layers of animation. "During the development process, we could easily and quickly apply QuickTime movies to specific poetic visuals; then immediately switch to WalkThrough mode to view the effect. The process is extremely intuitive."

And the results? "The people who have seen the model have been intrigued by the whole apparatus. They understand the poetry better and are stimulated by the new instructional process," Brock said.

Textured Architecture

William T. Medlow, Architects
Jericho, N.Y.

Contact: Bill Medlow

Say you're a building manager and one of your corporate tenants wants to remodel. What's the best way to ensure that the renovations meet your high standards? Architect Bill Medlow says that WalkThrough Pro provides an ideal solution. "Clients with offices in large commercial buildings often ask for a computerized preview of remodeled entrances, lobbies, or entire floors to demonstrate how the area will look, and they want to walk through the site on their computer screens," says Medlow.

He adds that WalkThrough Pro's texturing capability makes the models more impressive and more realistic, adding a sense of scale as well as surface detail and background. "With WalkThrough Pro, objects aren't just anonymous shapes. You can surround buildings with trees, put pictures on the wall, or show scenery through a window. WalkThrough Pro gives a special vitality and personality to each individual environment."

Medlow spends 95 percent of his design time on a computer, using Walk-Through Pro with 2-D CAD programs for projects ranging from mall interiors to entire commercial structures. His WalkThrough models—which frequently include QuickTime movies that have been applied as textures—also serve as sales and marketing tools.

"Often, I'll present my ideas in WalkThrough Pro; then return to my 2-D software for the day-to-day development phase," says Medlow. "Walk-Through Pro works quickly, is easy to use, and helps clients make better design decisions."

Model Museums

University of Central Oklahoma
Presentation Technology Lab
Edmond, OK

When officials decided to expand the National Cowboy Hall of Fame and Western Heritage Center in Oklahoma City, they faced the challenge of finding new places for a number of massive sculptures and large-scale murals costing nearly $1 million.

The problem: how to visualize the best positions for the displays without hauling them from spot to spot. The Presentations Technology Lab at the University of Central Oklahoma came to the rescue by designing a model of the museum in WalkThrough Pro, and then experimenting with exhibits on-screen.

"With WalkThrough Pro, we can easily see how the statues will look from various angles, and pinpoint when they will come into view as visitors move down the halls," says Dave Hesse, production supervisor. "You can show how the murals will look in the display room and even see what will be visible outside the windows. When you move an item to a new position, you know right away how the change will affect a viewer's experience."

Hesse also utilizes WalkThrough Pro for campus planning. Well-known architectural firms such as HTB Inc. frequently consult with the Presentation Technologies Lab to preview building designs and ensure that proposed plans work into the university's master site plan. Hesse's diverse WalkThrough Pro projects have included a model of underground campus phone lines.

He points out that WalkThrough Pro's texture-mapping feature allows him to create more realistic models. For example, it enables him create and expand landscaping to show the changes that would occur over time. "Texture mapping really enhances the effectiveness of architectural presentations," he says. "It knocks people out when they see the results."

Look for the entire story of the creation of this multimedia virtual poem in the 1994 *Multimedia Handbook* published by McGraw Hill.

Sydney Pollack

Film Director

On the set of *The Firm*

Virtus WalkThrough played a key, behind-the-scenes, technical role in the filming of the movie *The Firm*. Assisted by computer technology consultant Frank Dutro, director Sydney Pollack used Virtus WalkThrough to plan each day's shots, develop sets, and pre-visualize individual scenes to make decisions about lighting, camera angles, movement, space design, and other production and creative issues.

WalkThrough gave Pollack new ways to think about and influence the process of making movies, including practical ways to contain high production costs.

Pollack was very enthusiastic about WalkThrough's capability to present 3-D floor plans and capture the feeling of the movie's Memphis law firm on his notebook-size computer.

"It gives me an enormous advantage to get a feeling of movement and a visual perspective before going onto a set to shoot," Pollack said. "With WalkThrough, I can use my computer to easily assign any focal length I want for the camera. I can put people where I want them to be. I can preview and record angles and shots. By trying the mechanics of the set before it's built, I can go back to the production designer and say, 'I need an L-shape in there.' Obviously, if I can do that before the set is built, I save money."

Frank Dutro, who introduced Pollack to Virtus WalkThrough and handled the technical end of creating the online floor plans and sets during filming, agrees that WalkThrough saved a tremendous amount of energy, time, headaches, and money.

"With WalkThrough, you get the opportunity to work out scenes ahead of time instead of making your decisions while the meter is running, with cast and crew standing around for each shot," said Dutro. "And if you make a mistake or don't like what you've done, changing the shot on the computer is a lot less expensive than re-shooting."

Further emphasizing the cost issue, Pollack pointed out, "As everyone knows, our time is big money. A movie company spends anywhere from $90,000 to $200,000 a day, depending on how heavy the production crew is. So it's very, very costly when the director's standing around scratching his head figuring out these things with the cast and crew waiting."

Before WalkThrough, Pollack often mapped out shots by hand. "If you look at my working scripts for *Out of Africa*, *Tootsie*, or any of the films I've directed, they're filled with little badly drawn stick figures and crisscrosses of shots," Pollack said. "But now, with WalkThrough, I can actually get a sense of looking at the scene. It's a way to effortlessly visualize whatever I can imagine. This is a much desired thing."

Pollack also highlighted the convenience and control offered by Walk-Through. "Hollywood has been making use of really high-tech graphic software, but those of us who direct films don't do special effects ourselves. Rather, we conceive them. I like WalkThrough because I can operate it myself, from my portable computer. I can carry it around with me and have creative control."

Figure 17.3 shows Sydney Pollack and Frank Dutro using Virtus software.

Figure 17.3:

Sydney Pollack and Frank Dutro using Virtus software.

File Makers Paradise

Virtus WalkThrough is being used by other Hollywood directors as well, including John Badham (*Saturday Night Fever, Blue Thunder, Whose Life Is It, Anyway?*) and Brian De Palma (*Bonfire of the Vanities, Scarface, The Untouchables*), who used the product to storyboard the movie *Raising Cain* and is currently using it on the set of *Mission Impossible*. In addition, independent film makers such as Jonathan Wade of New York-based Elixir Films are adopting technologies like Virtus WalkThrough to maximize limited budgets and experiment with new approaches to the creative film process.

The program is ideal for filmmakers or other creative professionals who want to create and view spatial ideas quickly and inexpensively. By developing 3-D spaces on computer, users can avoid the time and costs involved in building to-scale models or creating detailed artists' renderings. A Virtus WalkThrough 3-D model lets users see their ideas from every conceivable angle permitting them to detect flaws in set design, camera angles, lighting, or the movement of actors in a particular scene.

Capturing Concepts

Dwight Morejohn
Davis, CA

Dwight Morejohn of Davis, California has incorporated Virtus Walk-Through Pro into several projects, from home to airport renovations. He consistently pushes the limits of Virtus WalkThrough Pro by creating very large models, a few over 800K in size. (800K is about 15 times the average Virtus WalkThrough Pro model size.)

Computer drawings and animation are now the main product of Dwight's company, Capturing Concepts, but it wasn't always that way. For 17 years, Dwight did hand-drawn conceptual work for engineering firms.

"I had always shied away from computers," he says, "but when I saw that I could add motion to my drawing I became interested. And when I realized the computer wasn't taking the place of my work but becoming an addition to it, I really got interested. I still do drawings by hand, but they are more of a supplement to the services I offer."

Dwight says Virtus WalkThrough Pro and Stratavision 3-D are the backbone of his operation. He uses both software packages in conjunction with each other to model just about anything his clients ask for. Then he presents his models as QuickTime movies after editing them with Adobe Premier. He often transfers these QuickTime movies to videotape using a SuperMac VideoSpigot.

But it's more than fast drawing the Virtus WalkThrough Pro offers Dwight's clients.

"On the airport project I just finished there was a big, beautiful, golden, dome-shaped building proposed, but the architects weren't sure it could be seen from the road as people drove into the airport. I positioned the Observer at the level of a car, and I used the Euro Widescreen aspect ratio to give the effect of looking out of a car window. Then I drove down the entrance to the airport and over a bridge that is actually the highest point of the airport area. I showed that from car level the dome was not, in fact, visible."

Dwight has been using Virtus WalkThrough Pro enough to develop some new tricks: "The airport was an interesting project, and I used some unusual techniques to add to the realism. For example, I modeled airplanes and scattered them on the tarmac, which in itself added a lot of realism, but then I used the surface editor to simulate shadows beneath the airplanes. The simulated shadows really made the airplanes stand out."

"I used another trick when doing a flyby from high above the airport looking down, I positioned an airplane about 700 feet up, which was just below the position of the Observer. Then as I was moving the Observer, I passed over the airplane close enough to look like it was actually flying underneath me. When the sequence was played back as a QuickTime movie it looked like I just missed a collision with a 707."

Most of Dwight's projects have involved exterior spaces. He has worked on three different airport projects, constructed sawmills, heavy equipment, skyscrapers, churches, houses, and city scapes using Virtus WalkThrough. But some of his projects have involved interiors of private residences.

But his next project involves yet another exterior space. "A client wants to build an exotic farm in the vein of French-Mediterranean vegetable garden. It will have several buildings and he already has an idea of what he wants the layout to be. And it is important to him to be able to see certain things from certain spots. Eventually, he wants a photo-realistic flyby done in Stratavision, but in the interim Virtus WalkThrough is helping with the decisions of where to place the buildings and roads because they can be so easily moved around."

Cybertown

Pascal Baudar, Creative Director, MultiMedia Magic

"I have been working in the graphic industry for several years in animation, creating images in 3-D and creating Web sites on the Internet. I recently bought Virtus WalkThrough Pro 2.5 with the intention of using that program for the World Wide Web. We have created several Web sites for some businesses and we are also creating a town called Cybertown in which we want to use cutting-edge technology—see Figure 17.5.

Figure 17.4:
Deinonicus.

Figure 17.5:
*Cybertown broke
ground October
25,1995.*

I was amazed at the program when I got it, I actually had no idea that the
program was so elaborate! After a day, I was able to create a house and

when someone was entering the house there was actually music and video on the screen of a TV I placed in one of the rooms!

My next surprise was how small the file sizes of the models I was creating were. You can actually place most of your models on a floppy disk, which makes it easy to share with others either by mail or by sending it through the Internet or other online services.

I've been working with several other 3-D programs, but Virtus Walk-Through Pro is a brand new category. For the first, time I can create something as an artist and have other people actually walk through my creation. It has offered me a new dimension and will offer the same thing for many artists in the future.

I was also amazed by the fact that it was very easy to learn; most programs take days to study before you can actually do something that you would consider good enough. With this program, I was able to do it in a matter of hours. One of the best features was the fact that I was able to build something and actually see it in 3-D as I was building it. That has saved me a lot of time, as I could see what was good and what needed correction right away.

My next step is VRML (Virtual Reality for the World Wide Web) and I have complete confidence that Virtus will play a major role in making the World Wide Web exciting and entertaining and a place where artists, designers, architects, people in the movie industry, and others can share their imagination with millions of others."

Lamuz

A.J. Peralta, Director
Lamuz, Tokyo, Japan
Web Address: `http://www.lamuz.co.jp/~lamuz`
Spatial Acquisition

A.J. Peralta is a native Californian who now makes his residence in the bustling city of Tokyo, Japan. A.J.'s background is in still photography, video, and film. His company, Lamuz, named after an island off of the east coast of Africa where the principals met, has successfully translated those capabilities into a thriving service and distribution business in Asia.

Lamuz creates 3-D multimedia content for major corporations like Toyota and Pioneer. In the last year, Lamuz has been honing its Internet skills creating Web sites for companies and events like the Cannes Film Festival. For Lamuz, adding 3-D to the Internet was a natural progression and one that it conquered quickly. See Figure 17.6.

"It's probably a bit philosophical for our customers, but our business is not about technology. We're content producers, and creating communities—the look, feel, design, and allure—around the content is the key. This is true whether that's bringing powerful and easy-to-use software to the retail user or creating custom projects that go beyond the digital brochure mentality. 3-D is quickly proving itself as the natural metaphor for the interface that appeals, entices, and services the average user."

Figure 17.6:
Lamuz Netropolis.

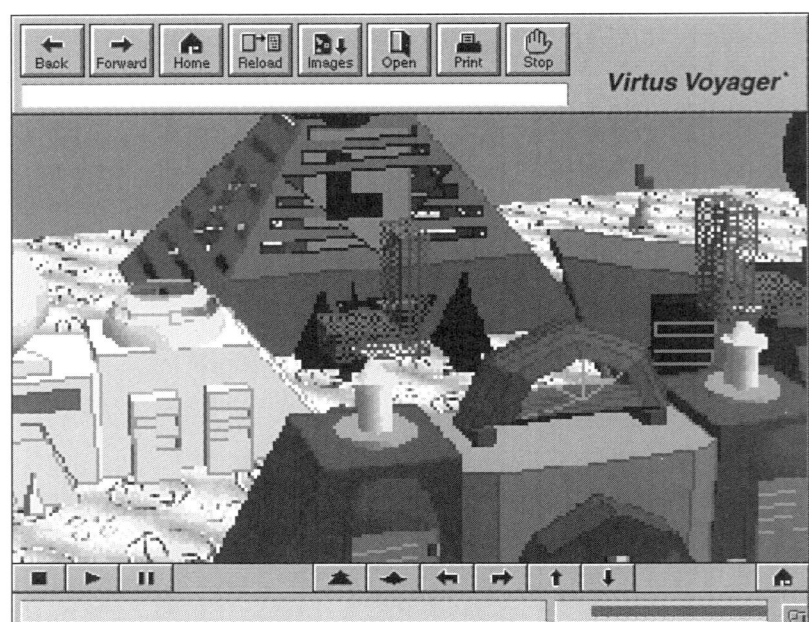

Summary

So, now you see all the incredible things that you can do with Virtus VRML—is limited only by your imagination. From this point, you can begin working from the CD, turn to Chapter 7 for hands-on specifics in using Virtus, if you haven't already done so, or close the book and get a good night's sleep! Welcome to the world of 3-D reality!

Appendixes

Part IV

A

Virtus VRML Installation and CD Information

What's Here

CD-ROM

Your VRML Toolkit CD-ROM is a *hybrid CD*, that is, it is formatted for use on both the Macintosh and Windows 3.1 computers. Here's what you'll find on the CD:

- The Virtus VRML application.

- Numerous files and models with the package including a VRML folder that contains models that have already been exported as VRML files.

- Virtus Voyager, the premier 3-D VRML browser, is also included in beta format at first printing. Updated versions of Virtus Voyager may be downloaded free of charge from Virtus' home page: http://www.virtus.com/. Virtus Voyager is available for Macintosh, Windows 3.1 and Windows 95. If your version doesn't appear on the CD, please download it from Virtus.

- Bonus Virtus Galleries, *Home Remodeling* and *Archaeology,* are also included with your CD, which total 57 separate collections of sample and specific 2-D and 3-D items. As well, each specific collection includes numerous coordinating scenes and models.

Installation

Two separate directories are on the CD, one for Macintosh and one for Windows, as well as separate installation directories. You have the choice of either running the application off the CD or installing it directly onto your hard drive. Running it off of your hard drive will be quicker, so I recommend going through the installation.

After inserting the *Virtus VRML Toolbox* CD into your CD-ROM drive, open the proper directory for your particular computer to find the installer.

Macintosh Recommended Configuration

Minimum: Apple Macintosh LC, Mac II, PowerBook, Centris, Quadra, or Power Macintosh with 13 inch or larger monitor; 8MB RAM, System 6.05 or later.

Recommended: Quadra, Centris, 68040-based PowerBook, Power Macintosh; 8MB+ RAM, System 7.1 or later.

Macintosh Installation

Locate the Macintosh Virtus VRML Install Directory. If you are familiar with basic Macintosh operating procedures, you are ready to install Virtus VRML by following these steps:

1. Locate and open the Macintosh Virtus VRML Install folder.

2. Double-click the Installer icon.

3. Select the installation options in the dialog box. The default installation is the Virtus VRML application, and all Galleries and Models (Scenes).

4. The Put File dialog box asks you to select a folder or place in which the Virtus VRML application will be extracted. (Be sure to install Virtus VR in the same place as your old version of WalkThrough Pro, if you have one.)

5. The progress meter displays the progress of the installation.

6. After the program has installed, double-click the Virtus VRML icon.

7. When the personalization panel appears, type your name and organization in the text box, the serial number should already be entered for you. Should you require online support or updates, refer to this number: 29766Hayden

8. Restart Virtus VR by double-clicking the icon.

To begin using Virtus VRML right away, jump to Chapter 7 to begin understanding the basics.

PC/Windows Recommended Configuration

80386-based or better PC; 8MB RAM Microsoft Windows 3.1; VGA or Super VGA display adapter.

PC/Windows Installation

If Windows is successfully installed on your computer and you are familiar with basic Windows functions and features, your Virtus VRML application is ready to install by following these steps:

1. From the File menu, select Run. When the dialog box appears, locate the Windows Virtus VRML setup program and click OK.

2. Select the installation options that you want to include in the dialog box. The default installation is the Virtus VRML application, and all Galleries and Models (Scenes).

3. Type the path directory.

4. The program will begin the installation.

5. After the program has installed, double-click the Virtus VRML icon.

6. When the personalization panel appears, type your name and organization in the text box; the serial number should already be entered for you. Should you require online support or updates, you will refer to this number: 29766Hayden.

To begin using Virtus VRML right away, jump to Chapter 7 to begin learning the basics.

If you have questions or problems with your product, please call Macmillan Technical Support Services at 913-661-0808 or Virtus Corporation Technical Support at 919-467-9700 from 9 a.m.–6p.m. Eastern, Monday–Friday.

Glossary

A

Applets: Software-independent mini-applications that provide flexibility to both users and developers because of their interoperability.

Archie: A network service that searches FTP sites for files.

Auto Connection: A feature that makes the adjacent parallel surfaces of two objects share the same surface attributes.

B

Browser: A viewer that loads files (VRML files for our discussion) and allows navigation in and interaction with a 3-D space. These browsers may run as stand-alone applications, or within other 2-D browsers like Netscape and Mosaic as "helper" applications. (Provides an interface to the World Wide Web.)

C

CableComm: Motorola Multimedia's strategy to use its expertise in radio frequency (RF) technology to create a two-way, interactive network out of the existing fiber/coax infrastructure, which enables network operators to overcome the interactive bottleneck of coax and to offer next-generation interactive services to subscribers.

CERN: The European collective of high-energy physics researchers (European Organization for Nuclear Research).

Client: A computer or program that requests a service of another computer or program obtaining software.

Client/Server Architecture: A structure in which programs use and provide distributed services.

Components: Small applications that can be embedded as part of another application. An example of this is the QuickTime extension that allows the user to embed a movie into an existing document. A component architecture is simply a generalization of this idea where the embedded object can be of any data type.

Containment: A property that objects must occupy only *one space* at a time (as opposed to an object overlapping another) or all objects that are contained in one space must be wholly contained. A contained object is one that is entirely contained inside of another object.

Crosshair: A crosshair is the thin cross that appears in the middle of the Walk View to indicate relative movement. If you click the mouse to the right of the crosshair, for example, you move to the right. The closer to the crosshair you click, the slower you move. Clicking above the crosshair causes you to move forward and clicking below the crosshair causes you to move backward.

CSO: Central Services Organization. A service that facilitates user and address look-up in databases.

Cyberspace: An environment of both correct and incorrect electronic information that is connected to the physical world via one way (televisions) and two way (computers and phones) portals and umbilical cords of copper, coaxial and fiber optic cable, and magnetic waves.

D-E

Design View: The Virtus window on the left side of the screen that shows the two-dimensional items that you placed there. This is where you add objects, add surfaces to them, and otherwise edit your scene. Includes Top, Right, and Front views of your objects.

Digital Bandwidth: The transmission capacity per unit time of a given medium that is usually expressed in bits per second (bps).

Digital Compression: Involves limiting the number of bits required to represent a signal based on the idea that many of the bits are redundant.

Dithering: A technique that allows for more colors in an object, which in turn results in more color-accurate renderings.

Doug Engelbart: The inventor of many common devices and ideas used in computing today, including the mouse.

F

Finger: A service that responds to queries and retrieves user information remotely.

Flat Shading: Shading where each polygon can be only one color. If a room has one light source pointing down from the ceiling, the floor will be lighter than the walls, which are in turn lighter than the ceiling. Flat shading is fast, but less realistic than Gouraud shading.

Frequency: Number of times a cycle is repeated per second; is measured in Hertz.

(FTP) File Transfer Protocol: A common method of transferring files across networks.

G

(GIF) Graphics Interchange Format: A commonly used graphics format that compresses the image and stores color information within the file.

Gopher: A versatile menu-driven information service.

Gouraud shading: Shading for polygons that is characterized by smooth gradations of color from lighter to darker. More realistic than flat shading, but renders slower.

H

HTML Browser: A 2-D viewer that provides a graphical user interface for Internet Hypertext language. Netscape, Mosaic, and Microsoft Explorer are all examples of popular browsers.

HTML+: The latest version of HTML (also called HTML 3.0).

Handles: When you click (select) an object in Virtus VR, you'll see that small square boxes appear around it. These are called handles and in Virtus VRML, these can be black, white, or gray. See Chapter 9 for a detailed discussion of the differences among these handles.

Helper Application: An application that provides assistance to a parent application when its features become limited.

Home Page: The default document World Wide Web users see when connecting to a Web server for the first time; also called an Index Page.

HotJava: A World Wide Web browser that can execute applets, programs written in the Java programming language and included (like images) in HTML pages.

Hotspot: Created when you link an URL anchor to a 3-D object. When users move into the 3-D object, they are transported to the Web page indicated by the URL. (See also Hyperlink.)

(HTML) HyperText Markup Language: The standard language used for creating hypermedia documents within the World Wide Web.

(HTTP) HyperText Transmission Protocol: The standard language that World Wide Web clients and servers use to communicate.

HyperCard: A personal hypermedia/multimedia creation system used on Apple computers.

Hyper-g: A distributed hypertext system mostly popular in Europe.

Hyperlink: A connection between hypermedia or hypertext documents and other media. Also called a hotspot or hotlink.

Hypermedia: Hypertext that includes or links to other forms of media reports.

Hypertext: Text that, when selected, has the capability to present connected documents.

Hytelnet: A hypertext interface to Telnet.

I-K

Information Landscape: A three-dimensional environment where information is represented by 3-D and 2-D multimedia and through which we explore in whatever direction our quest for information, education, and entertainment takes us.

In-Line Image: A graphic within a hypermedia document that is displayed on the same page as text.

Internet: The global collective of computer networks.

ISO 8859: A character set defined by international standards that includes accented letters and symbols.

(ISP) Internet Service Provider: A vendor that provides access to the Internet for a monthly fee.

(JPEG) Joint Photographic Experts Group: A file compression format used for graphics that is supported on the Internet.

L-M

Latency: The time it takes to send a packet and receive a response based on the contents of the sent packet.

Man Page: Manual page. Online documentation that commonly comes bundled with computers running the Unix operating system.

Mark Pesce: The co-creator of VRML and an Internet visionary.

MEMEX: A conceptual machine that could show the trails of information that its users viewed.

Menu Bar: A common element in graphic computer interfaces that allows users to select options from pull-down menus.

(MIME) Multipurpose Internet Mail Extension: A method of differentiating file formats using a suffix appended to a file name.

Mosaic: A mouse-driven interface to the World Wide Web developed by the NCSA.

Motion Parallax: The sensation of changing perspectives as one moves through a space.

(MPEG) Motion Pictures Entertainment Group: A consortium of experts in the entertainment industry who developed the MPEG standard format for digital video and audio.

N

Navigate: This means to walk through a 3-D world. You can walk around in your Virtus VRML model by either of these methods:

- Clicking the navigation buttons at the bottom of your Walk View.

- Clicking in the Walk View at any location around, or distance from, the crosshair.

Navigational Buttons: Elements within a graphic computer World Wide Web interface that allow users to review the information they have previously seen in a number of ways.

(NCSA) National Center for Supercomputing Applications: A federally funded organization whose mission is to develop and research high-technology resources for the scientific community.

NCSA Collage: Collaborative (shared white board) software developed by the NCSA.

Netscape: A popular HTML browser for the Internet.

(NNTP) Network News Transfer Protocol: A common method by which articles over UseNet are transferred.

(NSF) National Science Foundation: A federally funded organization that manages the NSFnet, which connects every major research institution and campus in the United States.

O-P

Observer: In the Design View, it's the circle with a line extending from its center. The tip of the line (outside of the circle) points in the direction in which you're looking while in your model's Walk View.

Online Information Panel: A text panel at the bottom of Virtus Voyager that gives modem status, navigation information, and online help.

Page: A hypermedia document as viewed through a World Wide Web browser.

Phong Shading: Each polygon or surface can be multiple colors when rendering it. This method also allows for specular reflections.

Placement Depth: The concept that every object that you drop into your world will go automatically to ground zero (0). That is, everything goes to the lowest point and you must move up the object manually (in the Front or Right Views) to elevate it.

(PPP) Point-to-Point: An Internet account that gives you direct access.

Q-R

QuickTime: A digital video format developed by Apple Computer that integrates synchronized video and audio with compression techniques.

Radiosity: Multiple light sources used to render an object, including ambient light and reflections and diffusions.

Ray-Traced Rendering: The process of calculating the path of every ray of light through a 3-D scene—tracing the paths—and generating from this a realistic view of the 3-D scene.

Recursive Program: A program that calls itself.

Rendering: See Three-Dimensional Rendering.

(RTF) Rich Text Format: A common interchange format for the exchange of electronic documents among computers.

S

Scroll Bar: A graphical computer interface element that allows the user to scroll electronic documents on the computer screen.

Server: A program that provides a service to other client programs.

(SLIP) Serial Line Internet Protocol: An Internet account that gives you direct access. (See also PPP.)

Smoothing: The process of calculating the difference between pairs of frames and inserting additional frames if necessary to make the recorded path smoother.

Sprite: An animated 2-D or 3-D object that has been assigned special behaviors such as animation and prescribed reactions to certain conditions or other sprites.

Surface: A single side or face of an object.

Surface Editor: Allows you to create and edit surface features while in Design View.

Surface Feature: A two-dimensional feature (window, door, and so on) on an object's surface.

T

Ted Nelson: The inventor of many common ideas related to hypertext, including the word "hypertext" itself.

Telnet: A program that allows users to use computers remotely across networks.

Texinfo: A common campus-wide information system.

Three-Dimensional Rendering: The process of turning 3-D defined objects into images that give the illusion of depth.

Tim Berners-Lee: The inventor of the World Wide Web.

Tools Pad: Located on the left side of the Design View, it displays the program's tools.

Topbox: A computer resembling a channel converter that connects to television.

U-V

(URL) Uniform Resource Locator: A standardized way of representing different documents, media, and network services on the World Wide Web.

UseNet: The global news-reading network.

Vannevar Bush: Originator of the concept of hypertext.

(VMDL) Virtus Modeling: An efficient 3-D vector-based file that can be read by VRML browsers such as Virtus Voyager.

Vertex: Where two object surfaces, or faces, meet.

Veronica: A network service that allows users to search Gopher systems for documents.

Virtual Reality: A computer system that can immerse the user in the illusion of a computer-generated world and permit the user to navigate through this world at will.

VirtusCube: A 3-D desktop application on which you can place 2-D components such as calendars, movies, clocks, and crossword puzzles. There is no limit to the number and type of 2-D components that can be added to this application.

(VRML) Virtual Reality Modeling Language: 3-D vector-based language developed to extend the information on the WWW to 3-D graphics.

W

(WAIS) Wide-Area Information Servers: A service that allows users to search intelligently for information among databases distributed throughout the Internet.

Walk View: Displays a three-dimensional rendering of the two-dimensional items that you place in the Design View. In this window, you can navigate through (walk through) your model. The crosshair appears in Walk View to aid your navigation.

Wavelength: The distance traveled from a zero value of a signal, to the highest positive value, back to 0, to the lowest negative value, and then back to 0.

Webmaster: The administrator responsible for the management and often design of a World Wide Web site.

Whois: A name look-up service.

World Wide Web (World Wide Web Project): The initiative to create a universal, hypermedia-based method of access to information. Also used to refer to the Internet.

X-Z

(XBM) X bitmap: A standard two-color bitmap image format supported by the X Windows system.

X500: A standard that defines electronic mail directory services. Mostly used in Europe.

Xanadu: A client/server system based on networked hypertext that emphasizes electronic publishing and commerce.

XCMD: A program module that extends HyperCard by giving it new functionality.

Index

C

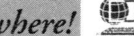

PLUG YOURSELF INTO...

THE MACMILLAN INFORMATION SUPERLIBRARY™

Free information and vast computer resources from the world's leading computer book publisher—online!

FIND THE BOOKS THAT ARE RIGHT FOR YOU!
A complete online catalog, plus sample chapters and tables of contents!

- **STAY INFORMED** with the latest computer industry news through our online newsletter, press releases, and customized Information SuperLibrary Reports.

- **GET FAST ANSWERS** to your questions about Macmillan Computer Publishing books.

- **VISIT** our online bookstore for the latest information and editions!

- **COMMUNICATE** with our expert authors through e-mail and conferences.

- **DOWNLOAD SOFTWARE** from the immense Macmillan Computer Publishing library:
    - Source code, shareware, freeware, and demos

- **DISCOVER HOT SPOTS** on other parts of the Internet.

- **WIN BOOKS** in ongoing contests and giveaways!

TO PLUG INTO MCP:

WORLD WIDE WEB: http://www.mcp.com

FTP: ftp.mcp.com

WANT MORE INFORMATION?

CHECK OUT THESE RELATED TOPICS OR SEE YOUR LOCAL BOOKSTORE

CAD and 3D Studio

As the number one CAD publisher in the world, and as a Registered Publisher of Autodesk, New Riders Publishing provides unequaled content on this complex topic. Industry-leading products include AutoCAD and 3D Studio.

Networking

As the leading Novell NetWare publisher, New Riders Publishing delivers cutting-edge products for network professionals. We publish books for all levels of users, from those wanting to gain NetWare Certification, to those administering or installing a network. Leading books in this category include *Inside NetWare 3.12*, *CNE Training Guide: Managing NetWare Systems*, *Inside TCP/IP*, and *NetWare: The Professional Reference*.

Graphics

New Riders provides readers with the most comprehensive product tutorials and references available for the graphics market. Best-sellers include *Inside CorelDRAW! 5*, *Inside Photoshop 3*, and *Adobe Photoshop NOW!*

Internet and Communications

As one of the fastest growing publishers in the communications market, New Riders provides unparalleled information and detail on this ever-changing topic area. We publish international best-sellers such as *New Riders' Official Internet Yellow Pages, 2nd Edition*, a directory of over 10,000 listings of Internet sites and resources from around the world, and *Riding the Internet Highway, Deluxe Edition*.

Operating Systems

Expanding off our expertise in technical markets, and driven by the needs of the computing and business professional, New Riders offers comprehensive references for experienced and advanced users of today's most popular operating systems, including *Understanding Windows 95*, *Inside Unix*, *Inside Windows 3.11 Platinum Edition*, *Inside OS/2 Warp Version 3*, and *Inside MS-DOS 6.22*.

Other Markets

Professionals looking to increase productivity and maximize the potential of their software and hardware should spend time discovering our line of products for Word, Excel, and Lotus 1-2-3. These titles include *Inside Word 6 for Windows*, *Inside Excel 5 for Windows*, *Inside 1-2-3 Release 5*, and *Inside WordPerfect for Windows*.

Orders/Customer Service **1-800-653-6156** Source Code **NRP95**

New Riders Publishing 201 West 103rd Street ◆ Indianapolis, Indiana 46290 USA

REGISTRATION CARD

Virtus VRML Toolkit

Hayden
Books

Name _____ Title _____

Company_____Type of business _____

Address _____

City/State/ZIP _____

Have you used these types of books before? ☐ yes ☐ no

If yes, which ones? _____
_____

How many computer books do you purchase each year? ☐ 1–5 ☐ 6 or more

How did you learn about this book? _____

☐ recommended by friend   ☐ received ad in mail
☐ recommended by store personnel   ☐ read book review
☐ saw in catalog   ☐ saw on bookshelf

Where did you purchase this book? _____

Which applications do you currently use? _____

Which computer magazines do you subscribe to? _____

What trade shows do you attend? _____

Please number the top three factors that most influenced your decision for this book purchase.

☐ cover   ☐ price
☐ approach to content   ☐ author's reputation
☐ logo   ☐ publisher's reputation
☐ layout/design   ☐ other _____

Would you like to be placed on our preferred mailing list? ☐ yes ☐ no e-mail address _____

☐ **I would like to see my name in print!** You may use my name and quote me in future Hayden
products and promotions. My daytime phone number is: _____

Comments _____
_____
_____

Hayden Books Attn: Product Marketing ◆ 201 West 103rd Street ◆ Indianapolis, Indiana 46290 USA

Fax to **317-581-3576**   Visit our Web Page   **http://www.mcp.com/hayden/**

Fold Here

BUSINESS REPLY MAIL
FIRST-CLASS MAIL PERMIT NO. 9918 INDIANAPOLIS IN

POSTAGE WILL BE PAID BY THE ADDRESSEE

HAYDEN BOOKS
Attn: Product Marketing
201 W 103RD ST
INDIANAPOLIS IN 46290-9058

Software License Agreement

Important—Read This Carefully Before Breaking Seal

By opening the sealed CD package, you agree to be bound by the terms of this Virtus license agreement. If you do not agree to the terms of this license agreement, promptly return the unopened CD package and the accompanying items (including written materials and binders or other containers) to the place where you obtained them for a full refund.

The enclosed computer program(s) ("Software") is licensed, not sold, to you, under the serial number affixed to the disk on which the software is recorded, by Virtus Corporation, ("Virtus") for use under the following terms. Virtus reserves any rights not expressly granted to you by this license agreement. You own the CD on which any Software is recorded, but Virtus retains ownership of all copies of the Software itself.

Virtus Software License

1. Grant of license. Virtus grants to you the nontransferable, non-exclusive right to use one copy of the enclosed Virtus Software on one single-user computer.

2. Copyright. The Software is owned by Virtus or its suppliers and is protected by United States copyright laws and international treaty provisions. You may make one copy of the Software in machine readable form, provided that such copy or the original is used solely for backup purposes. You may not copy the written materials accompanying the Software. You agree *not* to remove any product identification, copyright notice, patents or trademarks, or notice of any proprietary restrictions from the Software or accompanying materials or to place thereon any mark or notice.

3. Restrictions. You may *not* distribute copies of the Software to others or electronically transfer the Software from one computer to another over a network. The Software contains trade secrets and to protect them, you may *not* uncompile, reverse engineer, disassemble or otherwise reduce the Software to a human perceivable form. *You may not modify, adapt, translate, rent, lease, loan, resale for profit, distribute, network, or create derivative works based upon the software or any part thereof.*

4. Termination. This license is effective until terminated. This License will terminate immediately without notice from Virtus if you fail to comply with any of its provisions. Upon termination, you must destroy the Software and all copies thereof, and you may terminate this License at any time by doing so.

Limited Warranty

Virtus warrants that the Software will perform substantially in accordance with the accompanying written materials for a period of 30 days from the date of receipt. Any implied warranties on the Software are limited to 30 days. Virtus' entire liability and your exclusive remedy shall be, either (a) return of the price paid or (b) repair or replacement of the Software that does not meet Virtus' Limited Warranty and which is returned to the place where you obtained it, along with a copy of your purchase receipt. Any replacement Software will be warranted for the remainder of the original warranty period or 30 days, whichever is longer. *These remedies are not available outside the United States of America.*

No other warranties. *Virtus disclaims all other warranties, either expressed or implied, including but not limited to implied warranties of merchantability and fitness for a particular purpose, with respect to the software and the accompanying written materials.*

No liabilities for consequential damages. In no event will Virtus, or its developers, directors, officers, employees, affiliates, or its suppliers be liable to you for any consequential, incidental, or indirect damages (including damages for loss of business profits, business interruption, loss of business information, or other pecuniary loss) arising out of the use of or inability to use the software or accompanying written materials, even if Virtus or an authorized Virtus representative has been advised of the possibility of such damages.

Because some states do not allow the exclusion or limitation of liability for consequential or incidental damages, the above limitations may not apply to you.

Virtus' liability to you for actual damages for any cause whatsoever, and regardless of the form of the action, will be limited to the greater of $500 or the money paid for the Software that caused the damages.

U.S. GOVERNMENT RESTRICTED RIGHTS

The Software and documentation are provided with *restricted* RIGHTS. Use, duplication, or disclosure by the Government is subject to Federal Acquisition Regulations as set forth in subparagraph (c)(1)(ii) of The Rights in Technical Data and Computer Software Clause at 52.227-7013. Contractor/manufacturer is

Virtus Corporation
118 MacKenan Dr., Suite 250
Cary, North Carolina 27511

General

This Agreement is governed by the laws of the State of North Carolina. If any provision of this License is held by a court of competent jurisdiction to be contrary to law, that provision will be enforced to maximum extent permissible, and the remaining provisions of this License will remain in full force and effect. Should you have any questions concerning this Agreement, or if you wish to contact Virtus for any reason, please write Virtus Corporation at the above address.

Contact Macmillan Technical Support at (913) 661-0808 or Virtus Technical Support at (919) 467-9700 for questions or problems with your CD.